Bookkeeping Workbook

FOR

DUMMIES®

Bookkeeping Workbook
FOR
DUMMIES®

by Jane Kelly, ACMA and Lita Epstein, MBA

A John Wiley and Sons, Ltd, Publication

Bookkeeping Workbook For Dummies®

Published by
John Wiley & Sons, Ltd
The Atrium
Southern Gate
Chichester
West Sussex
PO19 8SQ
England

E-mail (for orders and customer service enquires): cs-books@wiley.co.uk

Visit our Home Page on www.wiley.com

For general information on our other products and services, please contact our Customer Care Department within the U.S. at 877-762-2974, outside the U.S. at 317-572-3993, or fax 317-572-4002.

For technical support, please visit www.wiley.com/techsupport.

Wiley also publishes its books in a variety of electronic formats. Some content that appears in print may not be available in electronic books.

British Library Cataloguing in Publication Data: A catalogue record for this book is available from the British Library

ISBN: 978-0-470-74420-8

Printed and bound in Great Britain by TJ International, Padstow, Cornwall.

10 9 8 7 6 5 4 3 2

About the Authors

Jane Kelly trained as a Chartered Management Accountant whilst working in industry. Her roles ranged from Company Accountant in a small advertising business to Financial Controller for a national house-builder. For the last few years Jane has specialised in Sage software, both as a user and as a Director of a training company. She has taught a wide variety of small business owners and employees the benefits of using Sage. Jane has written and delivered a range of Sage training courses, conducted on both a one-to-one basis and in group training sessions.

Lita Epstein, who earned her MBA from Emory University's Goizueta Business School, enjoys helping people develop good financial, investing, and tax planning skills.

While getting her MBS, Lita worked as a teaching assistant for the financial accounting department and ran the accounting lab. After completing her MBA, she managed finances for a small nonprofit organization and for the facilities management section of a large medical clinic.

She designs and teaches online courses on topics such as investing for retirement, getting ready for tax time, and finance and investing for women. She's written more than ten books, including *Streetwise Retirement Planning* and *Trading For Dummies*.

Lita was the content director for a financial services Web site, MostChoice.com, and managed the website Investing for Women. As a Congressional press secretary, Lita gained firsthand knowledge about how to work within and around the Federal bureaucracy, which gives her great insight into how government programmes work. In the past, Lita has been a daily newspaper reporter, magazine editor and fundraiser for the international activities of former US President Jimmy Carter through The Carter Center.

Dedication

From Jane: I would like to dedicate this book to my daughter, Megan. I hope that she will be proud of her mum and maybe even write a book of her own one day – even if it is about Disney princesses and fairies!

From Lita: To my father, Jerome Kirschbrown, who taught me the importance of accounting, bookkeeping, and watching every detail.

Authors' Acknowledgements

From Jane: I hope that this book will help the many small businesses out there who are struggling with their accounting systems. I want people to understand that if a system is properly set up it should be very easy to use, and the business will gain maximum benefit from it. In the past, I've only been able to reach small local audiences, but this book gives me the opportunity to reach the masses.

I want to thank everyone at Wiley, who have been incredibly kind and supportive through my first experience of becoming an author. I would like to extend special thanks to Samantha Spickernell who gave me the opportunity to work with Wiley and also to Simon Bell and his development team who made the book what it is today.

Finally, I would like to thank my husband, Malcolm, and daughter, Megan, who have put up for long periods with an 'absentee wife and mother'.

From Lita: Many people were involved in making this book a reality. First, a special thank you to Stacy Kennedy, my acquisitions editor at Wiley, who successfully championed this book through the editorial board process. Also at Wiley, a special thanks to Jennifer Connolly, my project editor, whose helpful and insightful comments, as well as her expert editing, helped make this book the best it could be. In addition, I want to thank my agent, Jessica Faust, who helps me regularly with all my book projects. And finally, last but not least, my husband, H.G. Wolpin, who puts up with all my craziness as I try to meet deadlines.

Publisher's Acknowledgments

We're proud of this book; please send us your comments through our Dummies online registration form located at www.dummies.com/register/.

Some of the people who helped bring this book to market include the following:

Acquisitions, Editorial, and Media Development

Project Editor: Simon Bell
  (Previous Edition: Jennifer Connolly)

Commissioning Editor: Samantha Spickernell

Publishing Assistant: Jennifer Prytherch

Technical Editor: Ken Morrow

Assistant Production Manager: Daniel Mersey

Copy Editor: Sally Osborn

Cover Photos: ©Yo/Getty Images

Cartoons: Ed McLachlan

Composition Services

Project Coordinator: Lynsey Stanford

Layout and Graphics: Christin Swinford

Proofreaders: Melissa Cossell, John Greenough

Indexer: Claudia Bourbeau

Contents at a Glance

Introduction 1

Part I: Exploring Bookkeeping Basics 5

Chapter 1: Deciphering the Basics 7

Chapter 2: Designing Your Bookkeeping System 17

Chapter 3: Sorting Out Your Chart of accounts 27

Part II: Putting It All on Paper 39

Chapter 4: Looking at the Ledgers 41

Chapter 5: Journaling – The Devil's in the Details 53

Chapter 6: Designing Controls for Your Books, Your Records, and Your Money 67

Part III: Tracking Day-to-Day Business Operations with Your Books 79

Chapter 7: Purchasing Goods and Tracking Your Purchases 81

Chapter 8: Calculating and Monitoring Sales 93

Chapter 9: Paying Your Employees 117

Part IV: Getting Ready for Year's (Or Month's) End 133

Chapter 10: Depreciating Your Assets 135

Chapter 11: Paying and Collecting Interest 145

Chapter 12: Checking Your Books 157

Chapter 13: Correcting Your Books 173

Part V: Putting on Your Best Financial Face 189

Chapter 14: Showing Everything's in Balance 191

Chapter 15: Producing a Profit and Loss Statement 203

Chapter 16: Reporting for Not-for-profit Organisations 215

Chapter 17: Doing Your Business Taxes 229

Chapter 18: Completing Year End Payroll and Reports 237

Chapter 19: Getting Ready for a New Bookkeeping Year 243

Part VI: The Part of Tens 249

Chapter 20: Ten Top Ways to Manage Your Cash 251

Chapter 20: Ten Top Accounts You Should Monitor 255

Chapter 22: Ten Top Problems You Should Practise 259

Index 261

Table of Contents

Introduction 1

About This Book 1
Foolish Assumptions 2
How This Book Is Organised 2
    Part I: Exploring Bookkeeping Basics 2
    Part II: Putting It All on Paper 2
    Part III: Tracking Day-to-Day Business Operations with Your Books ... 2
    Part IV: Getting Ready for Year's
       (Or Month's) End 3
    Part V: Putting on Your Best Financial Face 3
    Part VI: The Part of Tens 3
Icons Used in This Book 3
Where to Go from Here 4

Part 1: Exploring Bookkeeping Basics 5

Chapter 1: Deciphering the Basics 7

Sorting Out Assets, Liabilities, and Capital 7
Tracking the Daily Finances 9
Keeping a Paper Trail 9
Testing Your Work 11
Naming the Financial Statements 11
Types of Business Organisations 11
    Sole Trader 11
    Partnership 12
    Limited Company 12
Basic Accounting Methods 12
Answers to Exercises on Deciphering the Basics 16

Chapter 2: Designing Your Bookkeeping System 17

Introducing the Accounts 17
    Balance sheet basics 18
    Profit and loss accounts 18
Learning the Lingo 19
Cycling Through the Bookkeeping Process 20
Seeing Double with Double-Entry Bookkeeping 20
    Bookkeeping Rules 21
Answers to Problems on Designing Your Bookkeeping System 25
Answers to the Quick Quiz 26

Chapter 3: Sorting Out Your Chart of Accounts 27

Charting Your Accounts 27
Detailing Your Balance Sheet Accounts 29
    Casting an eye over current assets 29
    Finding out about Fixed Assets 30
    Calculating Current Liabilities 31
    Looking at Long Term Liabilities 32
    Contemplating Capital 33

Discovering Your Profit and Loss Accounts 33
        Reviewing your Revenue...34
        Considering Cost of Goods Sold 34
        Evaluating Expenses 35
    Setting Up Your Chart of Accounts 37
    Answers to Exercises on Sorting Out Your Chart of Accounts 38

Part II: Putting It All on Paper 39

Chapter 4: Looking at the Ledgers............................41
    Preparing the Core of Your Financial Details...............................41
    Developing Entries for the Ledger..43
    Posting Your Entries 46
    Adjusting for Errors...50
    Answers to Exercises on Looking at the Ledgers.......................51

Chapter 5: Journaling – The Devil's in the Details............53
    Defining Your Journals...53
    Tracking Cash 54
        Tracking the Receipts...54
        Keeping an eye on outgoing cash 56
    Managing Sales...58
    Watching Purchases...60
    Dealing with Miscellaneous Transactions 61
    Answers to Exercises on Journaling – The Devil's in the Details 63

Chapter 6: Designing Controls for Your Books, Your Records and Your Money . . .67
    Getting a Handle on Cash 67
        Current accounts 67
        Savings accounts...70
        Petty cash accounts 70
        Cash registers..73
    Organising Your Record Keeping 74
    Protecting Your Business
        from Theft and Fraud 75
    Answers to Exercises on Designing Controls for Your Books,
        Your Records and Your Money..77

Part III: Tracking Day-to-Day Business Operations with Your Books.............................79

Chapter 7: Purchasing Goods and Tracking Your Purchases.............................81
    Detailing and Managing Your Stock 81
    Determining Stock Value 82
    Buying and Monitoring Office Supplies 87
    Paying Your Invoices..87
    Answers to Exercises on Purchasing Goods and Tracking Your Purchases 90
    Answers to Quick Quiz...91

Chapter 8: Calculating and Monitoring Sales **93**

    Taking in Cash 93

    Selling on Credit 98

    Checking Your Register 102

    Discounting Sales 104

    Recording Sales Returns and Allowances 107

        Sales returns 107

    Sales allowances 109

        Tracking sales returns and allowances 109

    Monitor Collections from Your Customers 110

    Writing Off Bad Accounts 112

    Answers to Problems on Calculating and Monitoring Sales 113

Chapter 9: Paying Your Employees **117**

    Setting Up Payroll 117

    New Starter Forms 118

        Requesting a P45 118

        Completing a P46 for employees without a P45 118

        Completing forms for foreign workers 119

    Determining Pay Periods 120

    Collecting Employee Payroll Taxes 121

        Calculating National Insurance Contributions (NICs) 121

        Working out PAYE tax 122

        Statutory Payments 124

    Figuring Out Net Pay 125

    Calculating Payroll 125

        Calculating pay for hourly employees 125

        Calculating pay for salaried employees 126

        Calculating pay for commissioned employees 127

        Calculating pay for employees who earn tips 127

    Settling up with Revenue and Customs 129

    Answers to Exercises on Paying Your Employees 130

Part IV: Getting Ready for Year's (Or Month's) End *133*

Chapter 10: Depreciating Your Assets **135**

    Understanding Depreciation 135

        Working out the useful life of an asset 137

        Determining the cost basis 137

    Depreciating Your Assets 139

        Straight-line method 139

        Reducing balance method 140

        Bookkeeping entries for depreciation 141

    Setting Schedules 141

    Tackling Taxes and Depreciation 142

    Answers to Problems on Depreciating Your Assets 143

    Answers to the Quick Quiz 144

Chapter 11: Paying and Collecting Interest **145**

Determining Interest Types 145
    Simple interest 145
    Compound interest 146
Determining Interest on Debt 147
    Credit cards 147
    Recording payments on a credit card 148
Recording Interest on Bank Loans 150
Booking Interest Income 152
Answers to Exercises on Paying and Collecting Interest 154

Chapter 12: Checking Your Books **157**

Checking Cash 157
Checking You've Accounted for All Your Cash Transactions 159
    Understanding credit card fees 159
    Reconciling your credit card statements 160
    Accruing your invoices 162
Reconciling Bank Accounts 163
Closing Journals and Posting to the Ledger 165
Answers to Exercises on Checking Your Books 169

Chapter 13: Correcting Your Books **173**

Doing a Trial Balance Worksheet 173
Making Adjustments 176
    Depreciation 177
    Prepaid expenses 178
    Stock 179
    Bad debts 180
    Unpaid salaries and wages 181
Reworking Your Chart of Accounts 183
Answers to Exercises on Checking and Correcting Your Books 185

Part V: Putting on Your Best Financial Face **189**

Chapter 14: Showing Everything's in Balance **191**

Exploring the Balance Sheet 191
Gathering the Numbers 191
Preparing the Balance Sheet 192
    Horizontal format 193
    Vertical format 194
    Working with Your Balance Sheet Numbers 195
    Current ratio 195
    Acid test (quick) ratio 196
    Debt-to-equity ratio 198
Answers to Exercises on Developing a Balance Sheet 200
Answers to Quick Quiz 202

Chapter 15: Producing a Profit and Loss Statement **203**

Exploring the Profit and Loss Statement 203
Formatting the Profit and Loss Statement 204
Preparing the Numbers 206
    Net Sales 206
    Cost of Goods Sold 207
    Administrative and sales expenses 208

Analysing Your Profit and Loss Results..208
    Return on Sales 209
    Return on Assets...209
    Return on Equity...210
Answers to Exercises on Producing a Profit and Loss Statement...........211
Answers to Quick Quiz..212

Chapter 16: Reporting for Not-For-Profit Organisations 215

Keeping Simple Receipts and Payments Records 215
Developing Income and Expenditure Accounts...216
    Preparing an Income and Expenditure account........................217
Answers to Exercises on Reporting for Not-For-Profit Organisations 225
Answers to Quick Quiz..227

Chapter 17: Doing Your Business Taxes 229

Exploring Business Types 229
Tax Reporting..230
    Sole traders..230
    Partnerships...232
    Limited companies 233
Vexing about VAT..234
    Having a look at VAT..234
    Calculating VAT..235
Answers to the Quick Quiz 236
Answers to Exercises on Doing Your Business Taxes 236

Chapter 18: Completing Year-End Payroll and Reports.......................237

Form P14..237
Detailing Benefits on Forms P9D, P11D and P11D (b)..............................238
    Types of benefit in kind...238
Forms P38, P38A and P38 (S) 239
P35 240
    Deadline dates..240
Sending Your Returns Online..241
Answer to Exercise on Completing Year End Payroll and Reports............242
Answers to Quick Quiz..242

Chapter 19: Getting Ready for a New Bookkeeping Year.....................243

Finalising the Ledger 243
    Closing Profit and Loss accounts..243
    Carrying over Balance Sheet accounts 244
Reviewing Customer Accounts...244
Assessing Supplier Accounts 245
Deleting Accounts..245
Preparing to Restart the Business Cycle 246
Answers to Exercises on Getting Ready for a New Bookkeeping Year.......248
Answers to Quick Quiz...248

Part VI: The Part of Tens 249

Chapter 20: Top Ten Ways to Manage Your Cash 251
Charting the Way...251
Balancing Your Entries 251
Posting Your Transactions..251
Keeping On Top Of Credit Control 252
Paying Bills Accurately and on Time 252
Planning Profits..252
Comparing Budget to Actual Expenses 252
Comparing Sales Goals to Actual Sales...253
Monitoring Cost Trends...253
Making Pricing Decisions...253

Chapter 21: Top Ten Accounts You Should Monitor 255
Cash..255
Debtors (Accounts Receivable)...255
Stock...255
Trade Creditors (Accounts Payable) 256
Loans Payable 256
Sales 256
Purchases 256
Payroll Expenses..256
Office Overheads 257
Capital 257
Retained Earnings..257

Chapter 22: Top Ten Problems You Should Practise 259
Identifying Accounts and Using Double-Entry Bookkeeping 259
Keeping Journals 259
Paying Bills and Managing Stock 259
Monitoring Sales 260
Testing Your Balance 260
Reporting Profits..260
Closing the Books and Starting Over 260

Index 261

Introduction

*B*ookkeepers are the keepers of the cash and the crucial caretakers of all information about the company's transactions. People both inside the business (managers, owners and employees) and people outside the business (investors, lenders and the tax authorities) all depend on the accurate recording of financial transactions by the bookkeeper.

- ✔ Financial institutions won't loan money to a company unless they trust the financial reports that have been prepared by that company when it applies for a loan.
- ✔ Investors won't invest in a company if they don't trust its financial reporting.
- ✔ Employees need to know their job will still be there tomorrow and many employees are dependent on accurate financial reports in order to do their jobs.

If you subscribe to the idea that information is power, which we do, you'll find that the bookkeeper has a tremendous amount of power in a company. Information tracked in the books helps business owners make key decisions involving sales planning, product offerings and how to manage many other financial aspects of their business.

Whether you are an owner keeping the books yourself or you are an employee keeping the books for a small business owner, your job is critical for the smooth financial operation of the company.

Bookkeepers must be detail oriented, must enjoy working with numbers, and must be meticulous about accurately entering those numbers in a company's books. They must be good about keeping a paper trail and filing all needed backup information about the financial transactions they enter into the books.

Bookkeeping has a language and method of operation all its own. Understanding that new language and operating under the rules of bookkeeping can be foreign to anyone who's never been exposed to it before; it takes practice. In this workbook, we introduce you to the world of bookkeeping and give you opportunities to practise the key concepts.

About This Book

In this book, we take you through the continuous cycle of bookkeeping, which begins with setting up your company's books, developing a list of your company's accounts (Chart of Accounts; see Chapter 3), developing your company's Nominal Ledger (which summarises all the activity in a company's accounts; see Chapter 4), and developing your company's journals (which give details about all of a company's financial transactions; see Chapter 5).

Then we take you through the process of recording all your transactions – sales, purchases and other financial activity. We also talk about how to manage payroll, governmental reporting and external financial reporting.

Finally, we show you how to start the yearly cycle all over again by closing out the necessary accounts for the current year and opening up any new ones for the next year.

However, although bookkeeping is a continuous cycle, a For Dummies book is not. You don't have to follow the entire cycle or go through it in order if you don't want to. The reference style of this book allows you to skip around to the chapters you need to know more about, or you can go through all of them to practise all the skills we outline in this book.

Foolish Assumptions

While writing this book, we made some key assumptions about who you are and why you want to learn more about bookkeeping. we assume that you are one of the following:

- **A business owner who wants to know how to do your own books:** You have a good understanding of business and its terminology, but have little or no knowledge of bookkeeping and accounting.

- **A person who does bookkeeping or plans to do bookkeeping for a small business and needs to know more about how to set up and keep the books:** Again, we assume you have some basic knowledge of business terminology, but don't know much about bookkeeping or accounting.

- **A staff person in a small business and have just been asked to take over the bookkeeping duties for the company:** You need to know more detail about how transactions are entered into the books accurately and how to prove out the transactions that have been entered into the books.

How This Book Is Organised

We organised this workbook into six parts, which we outline in the sections below.

Part I: Exploring Bookkeeping Basics

In Part I, we discuss the importance of bookkeeping, explain the basics about how it works, and help you get started with setting up of your books. You'll find questions and problems that will help you learn bookkeeping's unique terms and how to set up the roadmap for your books – the Chart of Accounts.

Part II: Putting It All on Paper

In Part II, we show you to how to enter your financial transactions in the books, how to post transactions to your Nominal Ledger (the granddaddy of your bookkeeping system), how to track all the transaction details in your journals, and how to develop a good internal control system for managing your books and your company's cash. Questions and problems will give you an opportunity to practise these tasks.

Part III: Tracking Day-to-Day Business Operations with Your Books

In Part III, we show you how to track your day-to-day business operations including recording sales and purchases, as well as recording any adjustments to those sales and purchases, such as discounts and returns. In addition, we talk about the basics of setting up and managing employee payroll, as well as all the government paperwork you'll need to complete as soon as you decide to hire employees. You'll also find problems that give you an opportunity to practice how to perform these key duties of a bookkeeper.

Part IV: Getting Ready for Year's (Or Month's) End

In Part IV, we introduce you to the process of preparing your books for closing out the accounting period, whether you're closing out the books at the end of a month or the end of a year. You'll learn about the key adjustments needed to record depreciation of your assets (a process which tracks the use of your tangible assets, such as cars and buildings), which must be done before you close the books. You'll also learn about how to calculate and record your interest payments and receipts in your books. Then we'll talk about various aspects of proving out your books – checking your cash, testing the balance of your books, and making any needed adjustments or corrections. In addition, you'll find problems that will give you time to practise these tasks for preparing the books for the end of the accounting period.

Part V: Putting on Your Best Financial Face

In Part V, you explore how to report all your hard work keeping the books to others inside and outside the company. We also explore the various structures of a business and what forms must be filed with the IRS. Finally we talk about how you close out the books at year-end and get ready for the next year.

Part VI: The Part of Tens

Part VI is the hallmark of the For Dummies series – the Part of Tens. In it, we highlight the top ten accounts you should monitor and a top ten checklist for managing cash.

Icons Used in This Book

To make spotting certain info even easier, we use the following icons:

When we give you specific tidbits of info that can help make your efforts run more smoothly or more quickly, we tag them with this icon.

We use this icon when we provide you some info that we definitely don't want you to forget.

Now, it wouldn't be any fun to work in a workbook without seeing some examples first, now would it? To make these examples easy to spot, we use this icon.

This icon is a prompt to note something down, think something over, or otherwise get your head round a key concept through doing something.

This icon indicates a quickfire burst of short, sharp but challenging questions which check you've been paying attention.

Where to Go from Here

You're now ready to enter the world of bookkeeping. You can start anywhere in the book you would like.

If you already know the bookkeeping basics, are familiar with the key terminology, and know how to set up a chart of accounts, you may want to start with Part II. If you need to learn all the basics or want to refresh your knowledge then start with Part I.

If you've got your books already set up and know the basics, you may want to start with how to enter various transactions in Part III. If your first priority is understanding how to use the financial information, then you may want to look at financial reporting options in Part V first.

Part I
Exploring Bookkeeping Basics

'So for all you eager investors, our latest
financial report will be read to you by our
new accountant, Mr Mesmero.'

In this part . . .

Bookkeeping can look like a foreign language to anyone who's never seen it before. In this part you'll explore the basics about how bookkeeping works. You'll also begin to relearn terms you may already think you know but have a unique meaning in the world of bookkeeping – like ledgers, journals, posting, debits and credits. Then you'll delve into how to set up the roadmap for your books – the Chart of Accounts.

Chapter 1

Deciphering the Basics

In This Chapter

▶ Understanding assets, liabilities, and capital

▶ Managing transactions daily

▶ Putting it all on paper

▶ Checking the books

▶ Introducing the financial statements

▶ Types of business organisation

▶ Cash based vs. accrual

*B*ookkeepers are the accountant's eyes and ears. Few accountants actually take the time to enter the numbers into the accounting books. That job instead goes to the bookkeepers. Bookkeeping, when done properly, gives a business owner an excellent gauge of how well his business is doing financially.

In this chapter, you will get an overview of a bookkeeper's work and introduction to some of the key accounting concepts.

Sorting Out Assets, Liabilities, and Capital

When you first start a business you need to have some money to get it going. This is known as *capital*. Capital is usually money lent to the business by the business owner, but you can also raise money to start a business by borrowing money, either from a bank (in the form of a loan) or perhaps from other people such as family members. Borrowed money is categorised as a *liability* because the business is liable to pay back that money. Once you are trading, liabilities become anything that the business owes.

There are two types of liability:

▶ **Short-term Liabilities:** These are items that are owed that will be repaid within 12 months. They include items such as:

 • **Trade creditors:** The name given to the bookkeeping account dealing with money owed to suppliers.

 • **Bank overdrafts:** Arrangements with a bank allowing the customer to take more money out of their accounts than is actually in them.

 • **Value Added Tax (VAT):** VAT registered companies have to calculate how much VAT they owe to the Inland Revenue at the end of each VAT quarter. The VAT is *accrued* (allowed to be accumulated) in the VAT account, which is considered a liability of the company until it is paid. (More details on VAT can be found in Chapter 17).

- **PAYE and NI:** When you pay your employees you collect taxes that the employee owes the Inland Revenue. This is known as the Pay As You Earn (PAYE) system. PAYE is paid monthly, although there is a quarterly payment option for small employers, provided that you estimate that your total PAYE and National Insurance (NI) will be less than £1500 per month. Both taxes are accrued in a liability account until the tax is due. (PAYE is discussed in Chapter 9 in more detail).

✔ **Long-term liabilities:** These are items that are due to be repaid later than 12 months. They include mortgages and long term loans.

Once you have got some money to invest in the business, you will need to purchase business **assets** for example, office equipment and maybe plant and machinery to make the products that you are going to sell. There are two types of assets; fixed assets and current assets.

✔ **Fixed assets:** Are items held in the business for a long period of time (certainly more than 12 months). They are used to operate the business, they include things like, Land and Buildings, Plant and Machinery, Motor Vehicles.

✔ **Current assets:** These are items that can be converted into cash relatively quickly, such as Stock, Debtors (those customers that have bought on credit), and cash at bank.

All the above assets are known as **tangible assets** (assets you can touch and feel). In addition to tangible assets there are **intangible assets** – assets that you can't touch and feel. Patents, and copyrights and start up costs are good examples of intangible assets.

In order to keep your books in balance, you need to carefully track all these different items in the right place. The key formula used in accounting for balancing the books is:

Assets = Liabilities + Capital

In other words everything your business owns is balanced against claims against those items owned. Suppliers and lenders, who account for most of your liabilities, have claims against the assets for the money you owe them. Owners of the business have claims against the remaining assets.

Exercise 1

List the following assets as either fixed assets or current assets:

Stock

Plant and Machinery

Cash at Bank

Land and Buildings

Office Equipment

Debtors

Exercise 2

Explain a current liability and give three examples.

Tracking the Daily Finances

Bookkeepers need to keep accurate day-to day records of business activities. They must record sales made to customers, purchases made from suppliers, and be able to manage all the payments and receipts transactions in the bank account. They must also learn how to maintain stock and handle payroll.

Every business owner enjoys finding out how much he took in from sales of his products or services. You need to keep that data up-to-date, so the owner of the business can quickly see how well the business is doing and find trends that may indicate either an upswing or downswing in sales. If there is an upswing, the owner may need to bring in more products to sell. If there is a downswing, the owner may need to slow down his ordering to avoid having too much stock on hand. We talk more about the bookkeeper's responsibility for tracking sales in Chapter 8.

It's critically important for any business to know what stock it has on hand and how much that stock costs. The tracking of those details falls to the bookkeeper. I talk more about the bookkeeper's responsibilities for tracking purchases and buying stock in Chapter 7.

Bookkeepers must also be aware that cash is very important and is the lifeblood of a business. They must therefore be able to keep track of cash movements within the bank account and reconcile all transactions flowing through all accounts. Accurate recording of all banking transactions make this job a lot easier. Have a look at Chapter 12 for more information about bank reconciliations.

Finally, you must make sure the employees are paid accurately. You also have to be sure the Inland Revenue gets any taxes due related to the payroll. I talk more about managing payroll in Chapter 9.

Keeping a Paper Trail

In addition to recording all your company's transactions in the books, you also need to keep an accurate paper trail about those transactions so that if a question comes up later you have all the detail you need to provide an answer about a particular expense or revenue. It's the only way that you can track both the company's financial successes and its failures.

A company owner needs to know what succeeded, so he can repeat that success in the future and also needs to know what failed, so you can avoid repeating those errors in the future. Your books and the supporting paper trail help the business owner to do that.

You will hear the phrase *books of prime entry*. These are where the original entries are made for each transaction. They include:

- ✔ The Sales journal for credit sales
- ✔ The Purchase journal for credit purchases
- ✔ The Returns Inwards journal for returns from customers
- ✔ The Returns Outwards journal for returns to suppliers
- ✔ The Cash book for receipts and payments for both cash and cheques
- ✔ The General journal for other items

These journals may just as easily be described as books (just to try and confuse you further!) So the cash payment journal can be described as the cash book, or the sales journal as the sales book.

As a bookkeeper you will use the 'double entry bookkeeping system' which is described in Chapter 2. You will keep a series of ledgers (again sometimes known as books). The word *ledger* means 'book' but it is commonly used in both manual and computerised systems.

There are three main ledgers:

- ✔ **Sales Ledger:** This is the individual accounts of each customer who has bought goods on credit. These customers are known as 'debtors' as they owe the business money. This ledger is also sometimes known as the *debtors ledger*.
- ✔ **Purchase Ledger:** These are the individual supplier accounts. They have sold the business goods on credit and the business is therefore liable to pay these debts. They are known as 'creditors'. The ledger is also sometimes known as the *creditors ledger*.
- ✔ **Nominal (general) Ledger:** This contains all the other accounts in the accounts system. This summarises all your accounts during the year. You record transactions in the nominal ledger by way of journals. We talk more about how Nominal ledgers are used in Chapter 4 and how journals are used in Chapter 5.

To understand how journals and ledgers tie together, consider an example of recording a sales transaction. The original sale will be recorded in the Sales Journal as a credit entry. As we are operating a double entry system' the debit entry will be recorded in the Sales ledger in the personal account for that customer. The original entry in the Sales journal will help you keep track of your sales on a weekly or monthly basis, whereas the Sales ledger will tell you who owes you what.

In addition to keeping the books (ledgers), you also need to keep copies of the paper that was used to back up the transaction. For example, when you purchase products you intend to sell, you would get an invoice that shows how much you paid for those products. You should keep copies of all those invoices in case a question arises later. We talk more about what paperwork you need to keep and for how long you need to keep it in Chapter 6. We also talk about how to set up a filing system in that chapter, so you will be able to find everything when you need to do so.

Testing Your Work

At the end of an accounting period, you need to test to find out if you entered all the transactions in the books accurately and if your books are in balance. You start the process of testing for accuracy by checking your cash to be sure your cash balance is accurate.

Once you know your cash is right, then you test whether your books are in balance using a trial balance. If they're not in balance you'll need to do a worksheet to find the errors and prepare journal entries to correct them. We talk more about how to test your work and make any necessary corrections at the end of an accounting period in Chapters 12 and 13.

Naming the Financial Statements

After you take the time to put all your transactions into the books, you need to have a way to summarise the financial results of all these transactions. You do that by preparing financial reports about the business's activity. Two key reports that are prepared include the Balance Sheet and the Profit and Loss Statement.

- ✔ **The Balance Sheet,** which is based on the formula Assets equals Liabilities and Capital, shows a business's overall financial health at a particular date in time. In the UK, you can choose between two different formats, the Vertical format (the preferred method) and the horizontal format. Both layouts show the same information just laid out in a slightly different order. I show you how to prepare this statement in Chapter 14.

- ✔ **The Profit and Loss Statement,** which summarises the activity of a business during an accounting period, shows whether the business has made a profit or a loss. The accounting period can be a month, a quarter or a year. This statement starts with the Revenues, subtracts the costs of purchasing the goods or services you sell, then subtracts the expenses incurred operating the business. The bottom line of a Profit and Loss Statement is whether or not the company made a profit. We show you how to prepare this statement in Chapter 15.

Types of Business Organisations

Three main types of businesses exist: sole traders, partnerships and limited companies. This section takes you through their most important features.

Sole trader

This is how many small businesses start. A sole trader is simply an individual trading in his/her name, or under a trading name.

For example Jo Smith could set up a window cleaning business and trade under the name 'Smith's Window Cleaning'. The benefit of becoming a sole trader is that it is very quick to do, you could start trading tomorrow! One main disadvantage, is that you have to do everything yourself! You need to keep your own books, you're responsible for buying and selling your goods and if you need to take on some staff, you have to do the hiring and firing as well!

If things go 'pear shaped', as a Sole trader you are responsible for paying back all debts. This is why some people prefer the protection of a limited company – see the section later in this chapter.

Partnership

This is a group of at least two or more individuals who are trading in business. This can be regarded as a step up from being a sole trader in so much as there are more people involved in the business. It is very wise to get your solicitor to form a partnership agreement so that everyone knows what their responsibilities are. In the event of any problems between the partners, an agreement can help pave the way for a solution. Accurate records must be kept to ensure that all partners know how well the business is doing.

If the business is owned by a single person (Sole trader) or a group of people (partnership) money that the owners have put into the business is shown as capital introduced and money taken out as Drawings. Any profits kept in the business and not paid out to owners, would be shown in a Retained Earnings account.

As with a Sole trader, you will find that as partners, you are liable for all business debts. This can be resolved by setting up a limited liability partnership – but you would need to ask your solicitor how to do this.

Limited company

A limited company is actually a separate legal entity. It is owned by the shareholders and managed by directors. This is very different from sole traders and partnerships, as the business exists separately from its owners. The shareholders who have invested capital in the company have a limited liability, which means that they can only lose the amount of money they invested in the business and no more. They will not be called upon to pay any further monies if the company goes bust.

Many people prefer to use this option, as they feel more protected in the event that the company is not successful and needs to be closed. However, there are more administrative burdens placed upon the shareholders and directors of the company. Directors have legal obligations to send paperwork to Companies House and accounts to the Inland Revenue.

If the company is *incorporated*, (Limited) the owners' capital is shown as shares. Money paid out to shareholders would be found in a dividend expense account.

Limited companies tend to be slightly larger and have their own accounts departments and bookkeepers within that department. That said, there are many 'one man band' companies who are limited and require the services of bookkeepers, which they will source externally.

Basic Accounting Methods

There are two basic accounting methods, namely *cash-based accounting* and *accrual accounting*. The difference between the two methods is determined by the point at which you record the sales and purchases in your books. When setting up a business, the first major accounting decision that must be made is whether to keep the books using the cash-based accounting method or the accrual accounting method. If you decide to use the cash-based accounting method, you record all transactions only when cash actually changes hands. Cash can include payment by cash, cheque, debit card, credit card, electronic transfer, or any other means you use to pay for something you buy. If you decide to use the accrual accounting method, you record a transaction when the transaction is completed, even if cash has not yet changed hands.

For example, suppose if your company purchases products from a supplier, but doesn't pay for them until 30 days later. If you are using the cash-based accounting method, you would not record the purchase in your books until you actually paid for the products with cash. If you are using the accrual method, you would immediately record the purchase when you receive the product. You would record the purchase in an account called Purchases and you would record the liability (you are liable to pay the supplier invoice now that you have the products) in an account called Trade Creditors.

Her Majesty's Revenue and Customs (HMRC) will only accept the accrual method of accounting, so in reality you can't use cash-based accounting. There is however, a concession for smaller businesses which allows them to use cash-based accounting for VAT – this is called VAT cash accounting. More details on VAT can be found in Chapter 17.

Many not-for-profit organisations which have very simple accounting needs use cash-based accounting. They often only require an Income and Expenditure statement, which is produced using cash -based accounting methods. These organisations are not responsible to shareholders to demonstrate financial performance and will only need to satisfy their members that their subscriptions and funds are being used wisely. See Chapter 16 for more on not-for-profit organisations.

Q. You buy products for sale on June 15 on credit with the supplier and get an invoice with the purchase. You don't have to pay that invoice until July 1. How would you record this transaction in your books if you are using cash-based accounting and also how would you record it using accrual accounting?

A. For cash-based accounting, you would not record anything in the books until you pay for the products with cash on July 1. For accrual accounting you would record the purchase on June 15 in Trade Creditors, as well as in the account where you record purchases.

Exercise 3

You buy products you plan to sell paying cash on delivery on June 15. How and when would you record this transaction in your books if you are using cash-based accounting and how would you record it using accrual accounting?

Exercise 4

You contract with a painter to paint your shop front on June 15. He completes the work on July 1 and gives you an invoice. You pay the invoice in cash on July 5. How and when would you record this transaction in your books if you are using cash-based accounting and how would you record it using accrual accounting?

Exercise 5

You sell your products to a customer on credit on June 15. You send an invoice to the customer on July 1. You receive payment in cash from the customer on July 15. How and when would you first record this transaction in your books if you are using cash-based accounting and how would you record it using accrual accounting?

So which accounting method is better? The cash-based accounting method does a good job of tracking the flow of cash, but it does a poor job of matching your revenues to your expenses. The accrual accounting method does a good job of matching revenues and expenses, but does a poor job of tracking the use of cash. Companies that use accrual accounting also set up a system to monitor cash flow.

The main limitation to cash-based accounting is that it can't be used when your business allows customers to buy on credit. Your books will not show the revenue until the customers pay in cash. Also, you will have a more difficult time tracking how much is due from customers. When you make purchases for your company, the business only needs to record the transaction when it actually pays for the items bought. This means that revenues and expenses will not necessarily match up in the same financial year.

Cash-based accounting may be suitable for very small businesses who have a very simple business model – you have no stock, you start and finish a job within the same accounting period and get paid in the same period. However, in order to satisfy the requirements of HM Revenue and Customs, you will find it necessary to switch to accrual accounting.

It is advisable to start with accrual accounting, and as your business grows, you will have your accounting system already in place to cope with HMRC accounting requirements.

The biggest difference between these two methods shows up with transactions that occur at the end of one year and the beginning of the next year. As you work through these problems you will see how differently the transactions are handled at the end of a year for each accounting method and how the way they are handled can impact the profits and expenses you show on your financial statements, as well as the taxes you may have to pay on any profits at the end of the year.

Q. For example, suppose you are keeping the books for a carpenter who is contracted to do a job on December 15 for £15,000 and received 50 percent up front or £7,500.

He spent £5,000 in cash on materials December 16 and paid his workers £5,000 in cash on December 31 when the work was completed. The contractor did not meet with the customer for final approval of the work and final payment until January 3. How would you record these transactions using the cash-based accounting method and how would you record them using the accrual accounting method?

A. If you were keeping the books using the cash-based accrual method, you would record the cash received on December 15 of £7,500. You would record the £5,000 cash spent on materials on December 16 and you would record the payment to workers of £5,000 cash on December 31.

When you closed your books for the year on December 31, this job would show revenues of £7,500 and expenses of £10,000 or a loss of £2,500. You would then record the £7,500 cash received on January 3 and have no corresponding expenses, so at the end of that year you would have an additional £7,500 in profits for work performed for the previous year with the expenses for the work recorded in the previous year.

If you were using the accrual method, you would record the receipt of £7,500 revenue on December 15; you would record the £5,000 cash spent on materials on December 16. You would record the payment to your workers of £5,000 in revenue on December 31. You would also record the final payment of £7,500 due in an account called Trade Debtors, which tracks customer payments due. When you close your books at the end of the year, you would show a £5,000 profit on this job.

Exercise 6

Suppose you are keeping the books for a carpenter who contracted to do a job on December 15 for £15,000 and received 50 per cent up front or £7,500. He bought £5,000 of materials on credit on December 16 and paid his workers £5,000 in cash on December 31 when the work was completed. He will not be billed for the materials until December 31 and won't pay for them with cash until January 10. While the contractor submitted an invoice for the completed work on December 31, he did not meet with the customer for final approval of the work and final payment until January 3. How would you record these transactions using the cash-based accounting method and how would you record them using the accrual accounting method? Would the job show a profit or a loss on December 31?

Answers to Exercises on Deciphering the Basics

1 The fixed assets and current assets are as follows:

Fixed Assets	Current Assets
Plant & Machinery	Stock
Land & Buildings	Cash at Bank
Office Equipment	Debtors

2 A current liability is something that the business owes and is repayable within 12 months.

Examples are:

- ✔ Bank overdraft
- ✔ Trade Creditors (suppliers you owe money to)
- ✔ PAYE and National Insurance
- ✔ VAT

3 You would record the transaction the same way using cash-based or accrual accounting. Cash was paid on June 15, so the transaction would be recorded as a cash transaction in cash-based accounting. The transaction was completed on June 15, so the transaction would be recorded in accrual accounting as well.

4 You would record the money due the painter on July 1 when the work is completed in the Trade Creditors account to reflect the money that is due if you are using accrual accounting. You would not record the transaction until July 5 when you pay the painter in cash using cash-based accounting.

5 You would record the transaction on July 15 if you are using cash-based accounting. You would record the transaction on June 15 when you first make the sale in the Debtors Account, where you track sales to customers who buy on credit if you are using accrual accounting.

6 If you were keeping the books using cash-based accounting, you would record the cash revenue of £7,500 on December 15. You would record the cash payment to the workers on December 31. You would record the cash revenue on January 3 and you would record the payment for materials on January 10. At the end of the year the job would show a profit of £2,500 because only £5,000 had been paid to workers and the materials were not yet paid for. If you were keeping the books using accrual accounting, you would record the cash revenue of £7,500 on December 15. You would record the cash payments to workers of £5,000 on December 31. You would record the invoice for materials of £5,000 on December 31, and you would also record the revenue for the completed job now due from the customer of £7,500 on December 31 in the Debtors account on December 31. At the end of the year the job would show a profit of £5,000.

Chapter 2

Designing Your Bookkeeping System

In This Chapter

▶ Becoming familiar with the accounts

▶ Exploring the bookkeeping process

▶ Discovering double-entry accounting

▶ Understanding debits and credits

As a bookkeeper you serve as the eyes and ears of the accountant, so you have to understand the basics of accounting. In this chapter, we give you a brief overview of accounting basics and show you how to use that information to design a bookkeeping system. You also get a chance to practise the key concepts of bookkeeping, as well as the key functions of a bookkeeping system.

Introducing the Accounts

Your role as the bookkeeper requires you to track all the financial transactions of a business. Accounting provides the structure you must use to organise these transactions, as well as the procedures you must use to record, classify, and report information about your business.

On a day-to-day basis, you make sure that all transactions are entered accurately in the books. To be a bookkeeper you must be very detail oriented and love to work with numbers. Since you spend most of your day hunched over a computer inputting data, if you don't like working with numbers, forget about it – bookkeeping is not for you.

In the United Kingdom you don't have to have qualifications to undertake a bookkeeping role, and many people are qualified by experience. You don't have to belong to any professional accounting body, either. However, you might want to seek membership of The Institute of Certified Book Keepers, a worldwide organisation which strives to maintain the standards of Bookkeeping as a profession, and provides training and support to its members by way of a structured examination syllabus. For more information visit their website (www.book-keepers.org.) There are also four other professional accounting bodies about which you may be interested in finding out more: the contact details are available in Chapter 23.

As a bookkeeper, you'll probably work closely with the company accountant, who has set up the accounting system to make sure that the information generated by that system will be useable and meets the requirements of solid accounting principles. You'll probably get periodic visits from the accountant to review your system and be sure you're entering information correctly.

The business owner is dependent upon your work to know how well his company is doing. If you put garbage into the system (inaccurate data or data entered into the wrong accounts), you get garbage out of the system. The financial reports generated by a system with a lot of errors will be useless.

A bookkeeping system is designed based on the data needed for the two key financial reports – the *balance sheet* and the *profit and loss statement*. The balance sheet gives you a snapshot of a business as of a particular date. The profit and loss statement gives you a summary of all transactions during a particular period of time, usually a month, a quarter or a year.

Balance sheet basics

A few of the key balance sheet accounts that you need to be aware of include:

- **Assets:** Everything the business owns in order to operate successfully is considered an asset. *Fixed Assets* are items that are held for more than twelve months, and include buildings, land, tools, equipment, vehicles, and furniture. *Current assets* consist of stock, debtors (money due from customers who bought on credit) and cash. The first two are assets that can be easily liquidated into cash and always in less than twelve months, and cash is about as liquid as it gets!

- **Liabilities:** All the money the company owes to others (called *creditors*) are considered liabilities. These include mortgages, loans and unpaid bills.

- **Capital:** All the money invested in the company by the owners or stock holders is considered capital.

Profit and loss accounts

The key profit and loss accounts include:

- **Revenue:** All the money a business receives in selling its products or services is called *revenue* or *sales* and tracked in these accounts.

- **Cost of goods sold:** All money the company must spend to buy or manufacture the goods or services it sells to customers is tracked in these accounts. An account called Purchases is used to track goods purchased.

- **Expenses:** All money that is spent to run the company that is not related specifically to a product or service being sold is tracked in expenses accounts. For example, Office Supplies, Advertising, Salaries, and Wages are all types of expense accounts.

As the bookkeeper you will be responsible for identifying the account in which each transaction should be recorded. In Chapter 3, we give you a closer look at the types of accounts that fall under each of these categories.

Exercise 1

Have a look at the following list and decide whether the items described below belong in either the Balance Sheet or the Profit and Loss account:

Item	Profit and Loss or Balance Sheet?
Telephone bills	
Purchase of Motor Vehicles	
Bank Loan	
Petty Cash	
Sales	
Materials purchased for resale	

Learning the Lingo

In addition to learning the types of accounts and where the transactions should be recorded, you'll also need to learn an entirely new vocabulary. Some key terms you'll need to know include:

- **Accounting period:** This is the time period for which the transactions are being tracked. It can be a month, a quarter, a year or another period of time that is reasonable for the type of business. Most companies will prepare financial reports at least monthly and then prepare an annual report at the end of a 12-month accounting period.

- **Debtors (Also known as Accounts Receivable):** This is where you track customer sales for customers who buy on credit rather than pay by cash. (Read Chapter 8 for more detail about these types of transactions.)

- **Creditors (Also known as Accounts Payable):** This is the account you use to track invoices the company owes and has not yet paid. (Read Chapter 7 for more detail about these types of transactions.)

- **Depreciation:** This is how you track the use and aging of the equipment, furniture, buildings and other major assets the company owns. (Read Chapter 10 for more information about depreciation.)

- **Nominal Ledger:** This summarises all the financial transactions of a business. (Read Chapter 4 for more information about the Nominal ledger and how it is used.)

- **Interest:** Whenever the company borrows money, it will probably have to pay interest on the amount borrowed, just like you must do when you borrow money from the bank to buy a car or a house.

- **Stock:** Products that the company has available for sale to its customers. (Read Chapter 7 for more information about stock.)

- **Payroll:** All the money that is paid to the company's employees is tracked in a payroll account. (Read Chapter 9 for more detail about payroll management.)

Exercise 2

Do you know when your accounting period is? Make a note of it here. Check with your accountant if you are not sure.

Exercise 3

Now make a note of what your quarterly accounting periods will be. For example, if you have a year end of 31 December, then your quarterly periods will be March, June, September and December.

Write your quarterly accounting periods here:

Quarter 1:

Quarter 2:

Quarter 3:

Quarter 4:

Cycling Through the Bookkeeping Process

In addition to understanding all the new terminology and types of accounts, as a bookkeeper you'll also need to understand how the accounting cycle works. There are eight steps in the accounting cycle:

1. **Transactions:** The process starts with financial transactions. These can include the sale or return of goods, the purchase of goods or supplies, and the payment of salaries – essentially any time cash changes hands or the promise of payment is made, a transaction has occurred.

2. **Journal entries:** The first thing you do after a transaction has occurred is prepare a journal entry so you can record it in the books. (Read Chapter 5 for more on journal entries.)

3. **Posting:** After preparing the journal entry you post it to the books. we discuss posting financial transactions in Chapters 4 and 5.

4. **Trial balance:** At the end of an accounting period you'll test the books to see if they are in balance. we show you how to do a trial balance in Chapter 13.

5. **Worksheet:** Often on the first try you'll find the books are not in balance. A worksheet is used to figure out the problem. we show you how to do a worksheet in Chapter 13.

6. **Adjusting journal entries:** After you figure out what is wrong, you make adjustments to the books using Adjusting Journal Entries. we show you how to prepare these entries in Chapter 13.

7. **Financial statements**: Financial statements are prepared using the corrected trial balance.

8. **Closing:** At the end of an accounting period you close the books and get ready for the next accounting period. We talk about closing the books in Chapter 19.

When you close the books, everything starts again. The accounting cycle is more like a circle than a straight line – cycling from accounting period to the next accounting period.

Seeing Double with Double-Entry Bookkeeping

Every time you enter a transaction in your books you'll be entering it twice. This is called *double-entry bookkeeping* and, if you do it right, your books should be in balance on the first try. Even if you do make mistakes, double-entry bookkeeping helps to minimise those mistakes and increases your chance of your books being in balance without having to make corrections.

The key to double-entry accounting and the balance of the books is this formula:

Assets = Liabilities + Capital

That's the formula for the balance sheet, which we'll talk about in greater detail in Chapter 14 after you learn all the items that are used to make up the balance sheet.

Basically what you need to remember is that any time you enter a financial transaction, the transaction affects at least two accounts. An *account* is the place where financial transactions are recorded. For example, a bank account would record all of the banking transactions, such as payments in and out of the bank account. For each transaction, there will be a debit and a credit. If you can imagine an account as being a page in a book with a big thick line down the middle, the Debits are shown on the left hand side of the page and the credits are shown on the right side of the page. See Figure 2-1 as an example of a Sales account.

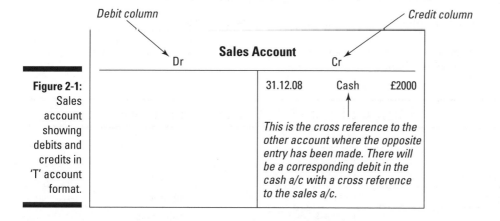

Figure 2-1: Sales account showing debits and credits in 'T' account format.

In Figure 2-1, you can see that the account is cross referenced from the sales account to the cash received account, and the date is shown for each transaction. The cross reference shows you the other account to look in for the opposite part of the transaction. This simple format for an account is often known as the 'T' account because if you draw a line under the title of the account and a thick line down the middle of the account, it resembles the letter T. T accounts are used mainly as a teaching aid, and it would be impractical to use them for every transaction that you record in a manual system. This book concentrates on the use of journals to record your transactions. Think of journals as separate books for accounts such as Sales, Purchases, Cash Received and Cash Paid. You should also use a General Journal which will pick up all other transactions. See Chapter 5 for more on dealing with miscellaneous transactions.

Now, you need to forget everything you ever learned about the meaning of debits and credits. From past experience you probably think of a debit as something that is subtracted from your bank account and a credit as something that is added to your bank account. You'll find debits and credits don't always work that way in accounting. For some accounts the debit will add to the account; for others it will subtract from the account. That's because it depends upon which side of the accounting formula the account is.

Bookkeeping Rules

All businesses use double entry bookkeeping to keep their books. It is so called because there are two entries for every transaction. You use a combination of debits and credits to adjust the balance of the accounts. There will be a corresponding debit and credit for every transaction. Certain rules exist that you must follow when applying double entry book keeping. If you learn these rules you won't go far wrong.

1. **If you want to increase an asset, you must debit the Assets account.**

2. **To decrease an asset, you must credit the Assets account.**

3. **To increase a liability, you credit the Liabilities account.**

4. **To decrease a liability, you debit the Liabilities account.**

5. **If you want to record an expense, you debit the Expense account.**

6. **If you need to reduce an expense, you credit the Expense account.**

7. **If you want to record income, you credit the Income account.**

8. **If you want to reduce income, you debit the Income account.**

It might be easier to remember these rules using table 2-1 below. You can copy this and keep it somewhere handy for you to refer to.

Table 2-1	How Credits and Debits Impact Your Accounts	
Account Type	*Debits*	*Credits*
Assets	Increase	Decrease
Liabilities	Decrease	Increase
Income	Decrease	Increase
Expenses	Increase	Decrease

First, we want you to practise the basics of developing a double entry.

Q. Suppose on the 1st January you bought furniture using cash totalling £1,000. You spent cash to buy the furniture, but you also added a new asset. How would you develop a journal entry to enter this financial transaction in your books?

A. Because you are buying furniture, you are increasing your assets, therefore you will be debiting the furniture account. But cash is also an asset which you are now reducing, thus you would be crediting the cash account.

The journal entries would be:

Debit   Furniture account   £1000

Credit   Cash Account   £1000

In a manual bookkeeping system, (I am demonstrating using 'T' accounts) you would show the transactions in their individual accounts as shown in Figure 2-2.

Using Journals

Whilst T accounts are a good way to demonstrate double entry bookkeeping, this book uses journals to present the transactions. We discuss these in greater detail in Chapter 4, but briefly you will probably have a separate book or pad for your sales, purchases, cash book and other general items. The book should contain columns for the date, details of the transaction and a column for debits and one for credits (much the same detail as is shown in the T accounts above). These journals will then be summarised at the end of each accounting period and it will be these totals that are used to post to the Nominal Ledger, more of which is discussed in Chapters 4 and 5.

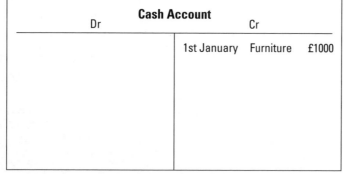

Furniture Account

Dr			Cr
1st January Cash £1000			

Cash Account

Dr		Cr	
		1st January Furniture £1000	

Figure 2-2:
This journal
entry is
shown in
'T' account
format.

Looking back at Figure 2-2, we will see how these journal entries affect the accounting equation. Both accounts are asset accounts, so a debit to the Furniture account will increase the ending balance of that account. The credit to the Cash account will decrease the total balance of the Cash account. (Remember the bookkeeping rules: when you decrease an asset, such as cash, you credit the asset account.). So the total value of the assets would not change and would keep the asset side of the equation equal to the liabilities and capital side.

In order to learn the basic rules of double entry bookkeeping you need to get some practice (the answers to all the questions are at the end of the chapter).

When writing your journal entry look back at the double entry rules shown in table 2.1 and consider whether you are increasing an asset, increasing a liability or vice versa or whether you are increasing expenses and income or vice versa. If it helps, write down the impact of each transaction in this way.

4. On 15th February, you buy new products (to be sold in your shop) on credit for £3,000. How would you enter this transaction in your books? Please write the journal entry as shown in the furniture question in the example in the previous section.

5. Write down the journal entry for the following transaction:

On 31st March you sold £5,000 worth of goods and received £5,000 in cash.

Date	*Account*	*Debit*	*Credit*

6. Write down the journal entry for the following transaction:

On June 30, you sold £3,000 worth of goods on credit. You didn't get cash. Customers will pay you after you bill them. How will your record the sales transaction?

Date	*Account*	*Debit*	*Credit*

7. Write down the journal entry for the following transaction:

On September 30, you buy office supplies for £500 using a cheque. How would you record the transaction?

Date	*Account*	*Debit*	*Credit*

Quick Quiz

1. In what two accounts would you record the cash purchase of goods to be sold?

2. In what type of accounts would you record the purchase of furniture for your office using a credit card?

3. In what type of account would you record the payment of rent to your landlord in cash?

4. If your accountant wants to know how many products are still on the shelves after you closed the books for an accounting period, which account would you show him?

5. If a customer buys your product on credit, in which account would you record the transaction?

6. You receive an invoice for some goods received. Where will you record the invoice in the accounting system, so that you can pay it in the future?

7. How do you record a transaction in your accounting system? (For the remainder of the questions, refer to Cycling through the Book Keeping Process for some clues)

8. What document would you prepare to ensure that your accounts are in balance?

9. If you find a mistake, what type of entry would you make to get your books back in balance?

Answers to Problems on Designing Your Bookkeeping System

1 **Telephone bill:** A telephone bill is usually considered to be an overhead of the business, as such it would be included in the Profit and Loss account and classified as an expense.

Purchase of Motor Vehicle: A motor vehicle is likely to be kept in the business for a long period of time, usually 3–4 years or more. This is categorised as a Fixed Asset and would be included in the Balance Sheet.

Bank Loan: The owner or directors of the business may have taken out a bank loan to provide funds for a large purchase. A bank loan is something that the business owes to a third party and it is considered to be a liability. As such it will be shown in the Balance Sheet.

Petty Cash: Although it may be a small amount of money held in a petty cash tin, it is still considered to be an asset. It will therefore be shown as an asset in the Balance Sheet.

Sales: Once your business starts generating some income through Sales, they must be entered into a Profit and Loss account. Sales is the first category of a Profit and Loss report, once costs are deducted from this, a profit or loss can be calculated.

Materials purchased for resale: You may buy goods and sell them on in their present state, or you may buy materials which can be used to manufacture a product. Either way these costs are considered to be *direct costs* (they are directly attributed to making the products you sell) and as such they will be shown as Cost of Goods sold in the Profit and Loss account.

2 The answers to Exercise 2 depend on the current practice in your business.

3 The answers to Exercise 3 depend on the current practice in your business.

4 In this transaction you would debit the Purchases account to show the additional purchases made during that period and credit the Creditors account. Remember if you are increasing a liability (such as creditors) you must credit that account. When recording an expense such as Purchases, you should debit that account. Since you are buying the goods on credit that means you will have to pay the bill at some point in the future.

Date	Account	Debit	Credit
15 Feb	Purchases	£3,000	
15 Feb	Creditors		£3,000

5 As you think about the journal entry you may not know whether something is a credit or a debit. As you know from our discussions earlier in the chapter, cash is an asset, and if you increase the value of an asset, you debit that account. In this question since you did receive cash, you know that the Cash account needs to be a debit. So your only choice is to make the Sales account the account to be credited. This is correct as all income accounts are increased by a credit. If you are having trouble figuring this out, look at table 2-1.

Date	Account	Debit	Credit
31st March	Cash	£5,000	
31st March	Sales		£5,000

6 In this question, rather than taking in cash, the customers were allowed to pay on credit, so you need to debit the asset account called Debtors. (Remember: When increasing an asset you debit that account.) You will credit the Sales account to track the additional revenue. (When recording income, you credit the income account).

Date	Account	Debit	Credit
30 June	Debtors	£3,000	
30 June	Sales		£3,000

7 In this question you are paying with a cheque, so the transaction will be recorded in your Cash account. The Cash account tracks the amount in your bank account. Any cash, cheques, debit cards or other types of transactions that will be taken directly from you bank account will always be entered as a credit. This is because you are decreasing an asset (i.e cash) therefore you must credit the cash account. All money paid out for expenses will always be a debit. When recording an expense you should always post a debit to the expense account.

Date	Account	Debit	Credit
30 Sept	Office Supplies	£500	
30 Sept	Cash		£500

Answers to the Quick Quiz

1 Record the goods purchased in a Cost of Goods Sold account called Purchases; record the cash spent in the cash account. Do not record the goods purchased in the Stock account. Stock is adjusted at the end of an accounting period after a physical count of the stock has been done. The one exception to this is a business that manages its stock system by computer. In most cases when stock management is computerised, the system automatically adjusts stock with each purchase of goods. But even with this type of system the initial entry would be to the Purchases account and the computer would then automatically update the Stock account.

2 Record the furniture in an asset account called Furniture, record the credit card transaction in a liability account called Credit Card. You would record the charge on the credit card in a liability account called Credit Card. Cash would not be paid until the credit card bill is due to be paid. Furniture is always listed as an asset on your balance sheet. Anything you buy that you expect to use for more than one year will be a Fixed Asset rather than an expense.

3. Record the rent payment in an expense account called Rent; record the cash used in a current asset account called Cash. Cash is always a current asset account (unless your bank account is overdrawn and then it would be considered a liability and would be shown in Current Liabilities). Rent is always an expense.

4 Stock Account. The Stock account is adjusted at the end of each accounting period to show the total number of products remaining to be sold at the end of the accounting period.

5 Debtors. This is the account that is used to track all customer purchases bought on credit. In addition to this account that summarises all products bought on credit, you would also need to enter the purchases into the individual accounts of each of your customers so you can bill them and track their payments.

6 Creditors: All unpaid invoices are recorded in Trade Creditors.

7 Journal entry. You would prepare a journal entry to get the transaction into your accounts, you take the time to think about the accounts impacted by the transaction. There will always be at least two accounts in the entry – one a debit and one a credit.

8 Prepare a trial balance. The trial balance is a working tool that helps you test whether your books are in balance before you prepare your financial statements.

9 Adjusting Journal Entries. At the end of an accounting period you correct any mistakes using Adjusting Journal Entries. These entries will also need to be in balance. You will always have at least one account that is a debit and one that is a credit.

Chapter 3

Sorting Out Your Chart of Accounts

. . . .

In This Chapter

▶ Mapping out your accounts

▶ Allocating your assets and liabilities

▶ Itemising your income

. . . .

*B*ookkeepers need a roadmap that helps them determine where to put the numbers. By developing a Chart of Accounts with clearly defined places for all your transactions, you can produce financial statements that accurately reflect your business activities for the year. This chapter introduces you to what goes into developing a chart of accounts and how to set it up.

Charting Your Accounts

A Chart of Accounts is organised to make it easier for you to produce two key financial statements:

> ✔ **The Balance Sheet,** which shows what your business owns and what it owes.

> ✔ **The Profit and Loss statement,** which shows how much money your business took in sales and how much money it spent to generate those sales (expenses).

You can find out more about Balance Sheets in Chapter 14 and Profit and Loss statements in Chapter 15. The Chart of Accounts should always start with the accounts you need to produce a balance sheet and then follow with accounts you need to produce an Profit and Loss Statement.

The basic order for your Chart of Accounts should start by listing the Balance Sheet accounts:

> ✔ **Current Assets:** Accounts for tracking everything the company owns and expects to use in the next 12 months, including cash, Trade Debtors (money collected from customers), stock, and any other current assets with a lifespan of less than a year.

> ✔ **Fixed Assets:** Accounts for tracking things the company owns that have a lifespan of more than 12 months, such as buildings, furniture and equipment.

> ✔ **Current Liabilities:** Accounts for tracking debts the company must pay over the next 12 months, such as Trade Creditors (bills from suppliers, contractors, and consultants), interest payable and credit cards payable.

> ✔ **Long-Term Liabilities:** Accounts for tracking debts the company must pay over a period of time longer than the next 12 months, such as mortgages payable and long term loans.

> ✔ **Capital:** Accounts for tracking company owners and their claims against the company's assets, which includes any money invested in the company, any money taken out of the company, and any earnings that have been reinvested in the company.

The rest of the chart is filled with Profit and Loss accounts, which you list in this order:

- ✔ **Revenue:** Accounts for tracking sales of goods and services as well as revenue generated for the company by other means
- ✔ **Cost of Goods Sold:** Accounts for tracking the direct costs involved in selling the company's goods or services
- ✔ **Expenses:** Accounts for tracking expenses related to running the businesses that aren't directly tied to the sale of individual products or services.

Exercise 1

Describe three types of Current Assets and state in which financial statement you would find them.

Exercise 2

In which Financial statement would you expect to see Expenses? List five different types of expenses.

Exercise 3

In which Financial statement would you find Current Liabilities? Describe some of the entries that you might find here.

Exercise 4

In which Financial statement would you expect to find Capital? As well as Capital introduced by the owner, what else would you expect to see here?

Detailing Your Balance Sheet Accounts

First, we want to take a closer look at the types of Balance Sheet accounts you would have in each of the five Asset sections of the Chart of Accounts – Current Assets, Fixed Assets, Current Liabilities, Long Term Liabilities, and Capital. Then we give you space to jot down your own list of Balance Sheet accounts for your business. Whatever you write down now is not carved in stone. You can add to and subtract from the Chart of Accounts. You can add an account at any time of the year, but you should only subtract accounts at the end of an accounting period to be sure you don't lose any transactions with the deletion.

Casting an eye over current assets

When thinking about the types of accounts you want to list as current assets, think about things your business owns that you expect to be used up in the next 12 months. The most common types of current asset accounts are:

- **Cash at Bank:** Your company's primary account that is used to deposit sales and pay expenses would be tracked in this account. You may have more than one cash operating account if your company has several divisions each with their own bank account.

- **Deposit Account:** Your company would use this account for surplus cash. Cash for which you have no immediate plans at the very least should be deposited in an interest-earning savings account until the company decides what to do with it.

- **Cash in Hand:** Your company would use this account to track any petty cash or cash kept in the cash registers.

- **Trade Debtors (Accounts Receivable):** If you offer your products or services to customers on credit given by your company, then you need this account to track the customers who buy on credit, so you can collect from them at a later date.

- **Stock:** You track all products you have on hand to sell to your customers.

You may also want to set up asset accounts for items that you prepay, such as insurance, which is usually paid for an entire year. You would track it as a current asset and gradually reduce its value as you allocate it as an expense month to month. This account would be called Prepaid Insurance. I talk more about how to handle prepaid items in Chapter 13.

___

Exercise 5

Think about the current assets you need to track for your business, and write down the accounts in this section.

Finding out about Fixed Assets

When thinking about the types of accounts you want to list as Fixed assets, think about the things your company owns that you use for more than 12 months. Here are some common Fixed Asset accounts:

- ✔ **Land:** You can track any land owned by the company in this account.

- ✔ **Buildings:** You can track the value of any buildings owned by the company in this account.

- ✔ **Leasehold Improvements:** If your company leases any facilities, you track the value of any improvements that made you to this leased space in this account. For example, if you lease a retail store, any improvements that you make to customise this space for your business would be traced in this account.

- ✔ **Vehicles:** Any vehicles your company owns would be tracked in this account.

- ✔ **Furniture and Fixtures:** You track any furniture or fixtures purchased for use in the business in this account.

- ✔ **Equipment:** You track any equipment that was purchased for use for more than one year, such as computers, copiers, tools and cash registers in this account.

In addition to these accounts, each Fixed asset account has an accumulated depreciation account to reflect the portion of the asset that already has been used up. We talk more about depreciation in Chapter 10.

Exercise 6

Think about the Fixed asset accounts you need to track for your business, and write down the accounts for those assets in this section.

Calculating Current Liabilities

Current Liabilities are debts due in the next 12 months. Some of the most common types of Current Liabilities accounts that appear on the Chart of Accounts include:

- ✔ **Trade Creditors (Accounts Payable):** You should track any money the company owes to contractors, suppliers, and consultants that must be paid in the next 12 months in this account.

- ✔ **VAT:** You may not think of VAT as a liability, but because the business collects taxes from customers and doesn't pay them immediately to the Inland Revenue, the taxes collected become a liability tracked in this account. You are allowed to deduct VAT on business purchases made and this reduces the overall VAT liability. The net amount is usually payable quarterly.

- ✔ **PAYE/NI:** You should use this account to track tax and national insurance collected from employees and paid across to the Inland Revenue the following month.

- ✔ **Credit Cards Payable:** You should track all your company's credit card accounts for which the business is liable.

How you set up your current liabilities and how many individual accounts you establish depends upon how detailed you want to track each type of liability.

Exercise 7

Think about the Current Liabilities accounts you need to track for your business, and write down the accounts for those liabilities in this section.

Looking at Long Term Liabilities

Long-Term liabilities include any debts that are due in more than 12 months. The number of Long-Term Liabilities accounts you maintain on your Chart of Accounts depends on your *debt structure*, in other words, the different elements of debt that the company has in its balance sheet. The main type of Long-Term Liability accounts are:

- **Loans Payable:** You use this account to track any long term loans, such as a mortgage on your business building. Most businesses have separate loans payable accounts for each of their long term loans. For example, you could have "Loans Payable – Mortgage Bank" for your building and "Loans Payable – Car Bank" for your vehicle loan.

- **Other Liabilities:** You may have other long term debts which perhaps don't require their own specific account but can be tracked in a general account called 'Other Liabilities.'

Exercise 8

Think about the Long term Liabilities accounts you need to track for your business, and write down the accounts for those liabilities in this section.

Contemplating Capital

Every business is owned by somebody. Capital accounts track owners' contributions to the business as well as their share of ownership. For a limited company, ownership is tracked by the sale of individual shares because each shareholder owns a portion of the business. In smaller companies that are owned by one person or a group of people, capital is tracked using Capital and Drawing accounts. Here are the basic Capital accounts that appear in the Chart of Accounts:

- **Ordinary Share Capital:** If your company is structured as a limited company, then this account reflects the value of outstanding ordinary shares sold to investors.

- **Retained Earnings:** Whether or not your company is limited, use this account to track any earnings that were kept in the business.

- **Capital:** You use this account if you are keeping the books for a small, unincorporated business. The Capital account reflects the amount of initial money the business owner contributed to the company as well as other owner contributions made after initial start-up.

- **Drawing:** This account is another that is necessary if you are keeping the books for a small, unincorporated business. The Drawing account tracks any money that a business owner takes out of the business. If the business has several partners, each partner gets his or her own Drawing account to track what he or she takes out of the business.

Exercise 9

Think about the Capital accounts you need to track for your business, and write down the accounts you need in this section.

Discovering Your Profit and Loss Accounts

The Profit and Loss Statement shows whether or not your business made a profit. Accounts that you set up to produce this statement can be grouped into three types of accounts:

- **Revenue:** These accounts track all money coming into the business, including sales, interest earned on savings, and any other methods used to generate income.

- **Cost of Goods Sold:** These accounts track the money spent to manufacture or buy the products you sell.

- **Expenses:** These accounts track all money that a business spends in order to keep itself afloat.

This section examines the various accounts that make up the Profit and Loss portion of the Chart of Accounts. You always start by listing the Revenue accounts, followed by the Cost of Goods Sold accounts and then the Expenses accounts.

Reviewing your Revenue

In the Revenue section, the accounts you set up track all money taken into the business from sales. If you choose to offer discounts or accept returns, that activity also falls in this section. The most common income accounts are:

- ✔ **Sales of Goods or Services:** You track all the money that the company earns selling its products, services, or both in this account.

- ✔ **Sales Discounts:** If you offer sales discounts, you track any reductions to the full price of merchandise in this account.

- ✔ **Sales Returns:** Every business ends up needing to accept returns from customers. You track any returns from customers in this account.

- ✔ **Other Income:** If your company takes in income from a source other than its primary business activity, you should record that income in this account. For example, suppose you decide to encourage recycling and earn income from the items recycled, record that income in this account.

Exercise 10

Think about the Revenue accounts you need to track for your business, and write down those accounts in this section.

Considering Cost of Goods Sold

Before you can sell a product, you must spend some money to either buy or make that product. You track these costs in accounts in the Cost of Goods Sold category. The most common Cost of Goods Sold accounts include:

- ✔ **Purchases:** Track all purchases of products in this account.

- ✔ **Purchase Discount:** If you get discounts on what you purchase, track them in this account. For example, a company may give you a 2 per cent discount on your purchase if you pay the bill in 10 days rather than wait until the end of the 30-day payment allotment.

- ✔ **Purchase Returns:** If you're unhappy with a product you've bought, record the value of any returns in this account.

- ✔ **Carriage Charges:** Any charges related to shipping items you purchase for later sale are tracked in this account.

- ✔ **Other Sales Costs:** Use this account for any costs that don't fit into one of the other Cost of Goods Sold accounts.

Exercise 11

Think about the Cost of Goods Sold accounts you need to track for your business, and write down those accounts in this section.

Evaluating Expenses

Your longest list of individual accounts are the Expense accounts. Any money you spend on the business that can't be tied directly to the sale of an individual product falls under the Expense account category. For example, advertising a shopwide sale isn't directly tied to the sale of any one product, so the costs associated with advertising fall under the Expense account category. The most common Expense accounts include:

- ✔ **Advertising:** Use this account to track all expenses involved in promoting a business or its products. In this account money spent on newspaper, television, magazine, and radio advertising is recorded as well as any money spent to print flyers and mailings to customers. Also, when a company participates in community events such as cancer walks or craft fairs, associated costs are tracked in this account as well.

- ✔ **Bank Charges:** Use this account to track any charges made by a bank to service a company's bank accounts.

- ✔ **Subscriptions:** Use this account to track expenses related to business club membership or subscriptions to magazines for the business.

- ✔ **Equipment Rental:** Use this account to track expenses related to renting equipment for a short-term project. For example, if you need to rent a van to pick up some new fixtures for the business, record that van rental in this account.

- ✔ **Insurance:** Use this account to track expenses for buying insurance.

- ✔ **Legal and Professional:** Use this account to track money paid for legal or professional advice.

- ✔ **Auditing and Accounting:** Use this account to track monies paid to your accountants, bookkeepers and auditors.

✔ **Miscellaneous Expenses:** Use this account for expenses that don't fit in other accounts. If you start recording expenses in this account and later decide you want to track them individually in their own account, you can choose to add an account to the Chart of Accounts and move related expenses into that new account by subtracting all related transactions from the Miscellaneous Expenses account and adding them to the new account. With this movement of transactions, it's important to carefully balance out the adjusting transaction to avoid any errors or double counting.

✔ **Office Expense:** Use this account to track any items purchased in order to run an office. For example, office supplies such as paper and pens or business cards fit in this account.

✔ **Employee Costs:** Use this account to track employee wages, employer's National Insurance contributions , employers pension costs, Statutory Sick pay (SSP), and Statutory Maternity Pay (SMP).

✔ **Postage:** Use this account to track any money spent on stamps, parcels, and other shipping.

✔ **Rent Expense:** Use this account to track rental costs for a business's office or retail space.

✔ **Supplies:** Use this account to track any business supplies that don't fit into the category of office supplies. For example, supplies needed for the operation of retail stores are tracked using this account.

✔ **Travel and Entertainment:** Use this account to track money spent for business purposes for travel or entertainment. Some businesses separate these expenses into several accounts, such as "Travel and Entertainment; Meals", "Travel and Entertainment; Travel," and "Travel and Entertainment; Entertainment" to keep a close watch. Entertainment can be further split into Staff Entertaining and Customer Entertaining. This is useful as there are differing tax implications as to whether an expense is allowable or not for tax purposes.

✔ **Telephone:** Use this account to track all business expenses related to the telephone and telephone calls.

✔ **Utilities:** Use this account to track money paid for utilities, such as electricity, gas and water.

✔ **Vehicles:** Use this account to track expenses related to the operation of company vehicles. This account is not used for the purchase of vehicles as that would be considered to be a Fixed asset. It is merely used to track the operating expenses of a vehicle, such as tax, insurance, servicing, fuel and so on.

Exercise 12

Think about the Expense accounts you need to track for your business, and write down those accounts in this section.

Setting Up Your Chart of Accounts

Use the lists you have developed through this chapter to set up your Chart of Accounts. You can see there really isn't a secret to how to set up these Charts of Accounts. You set them up based on how you believe your business will operate.

Your Chart of Accounts is not carved in stone. This is a chart that you can regularly update as your business grows and changes. But you should be very careful about adding and subtracting accounts in the middle of an accounting period.

If you want to add an account, you can do so at any time, but be sure you carefully transfer the funds from the old account in which you were posting the transactions to the new account you decide to set up. You do this with what is called an *adjusting journal entry*. I talk more about adjusting entries and reworking your Chart of Accounts in Chapter 13. If you want to delete an account, indicate in your books that no new transactions should be added to that account, but wait until the end of the year to delete the account.

When you set up the Chart of Accounts, plan for three columns. The column heads would be:

- **Account:** List all accounts by name.
- **Type:** List the type of account, such as asset, liability, capital, income, cost of goods sold, expense.
- **Description:** Describe the types of transactions that should be posted to that account.

Here is the basic format for the Chart of Accounts:

Account	Type	Description
Cash at Bank	Asset	Tracks all use of cash through transactions in the company's bank account

You should include as much detail as you need when describing the accounts, so that all employees who are involved in entering transactions in the books or coding a transaction to be entered into the books know which account to specify for the transaction. If transactions are not entered consistently, your financial reports won't be accurate.

Answers to Exercises on Sorting Out Your Chart of Accounts

1 Current Assets can be found in the Balance Sheet. The usual types of current assets are as follows:

- Stock
- Debtors
- Cash at Bank
- Cash in Hand
- Prepayments

The descriptions to all of the above can be found in this chapter – see section "Casting an Eye over Current Assets."

2 Expenses are found in the Profit and Loss statement. Typical expenses could be:

- Wages
- Office stationery
- Telephone costs
- Rent and Rates
- Heat, light and power
- Fuel expenses

More examples can be found in 'Evaluating Expenses' section of the chapter

3 Current Liabilities can be found in the Balance Sheet. Typical items include:

- Trade Creditors (suppliers you owe money to)
- Accrued expenses (costs you have incurred but you may not have an invoice for)
- HMRC payments due, such as PAYE/NI and VAT
- Overdrafts

More details can be found in the section 'Calculating Current Liabilities.'

4 Capital can be found in the Balance Sheet. As well as Capital Introduced, you will also find Drawings (cash taken out of the business for personal use) and Dividends, as well as retained profits which are profits made from previous periods but retained in the business. If your business is structured as a company, then you will also have Ordinary Share capital, which reflects each individuals share of the company.

5 The remaining exercises in this chapter did not have right or wrong answers. You should set up your Chart of Accounts with accounts that match how your business operates.

Part II
Putting It All on Paper

'This is real hell – The books
down here never balance!'

In this part . . .

You'll find the structure for entering business transactions into your books a bit weird at first, but there is a method to the madness that will help you keep your books in balance. We introduce you to the method used to correctly enter your financial transactions, how to post transactions to your Nominal Ledger (the granddaddy of your bookkeeping system) and how to track all the transaction details in your journals.

Chapter 4

Looking at the Ledgers

▶ Getting to the core of your finances

▶ Preparing ledger entries

▶ Entering data in the books

▶ Correcting what's there

Accountants and bookkeepers need one place they can go to review a summary of all business transactions during an accounting period and get a look at the big picture. The Nominal Ledger is that place.

This chapter introduces you to the Nominal Ledger and how it is used. You will practise how to create your own entries and how to post them to the Nominal Ledger.

Preparing the Core of Your Financial Details

Think of the Nominal Ledger as the core of a wide network of financial data. The accounts in the Nominal Ledger are based on your Chart of Accounts. Because it does include at least a summary of all financial transactions, the Nominal Ledger would become too massive and unwieldy if every piece of financial data was stored in that core.

Instead many of the details about your financial transactions are stored in journals, which we discuss in greater detail in Chapter 5. Most of the key entries in the Nominal Ledger are summaries of daily or monthly activity posted from one of the key journals where daily financial transactions are recorded.

The most common journals include:

✔ **Cash Payments Journal:** This tracks the daily use of cash.

✔ **Cash Receipts Journal:** Here's where you track daily cash received.

✔ **Sales Journal:** This tracks day to day sales.

✔ **Purchases Journal:** In which you track purchases of products for sale.

✔ **General Journal:** Used for tracking miscellaneous financial transactions that are not tracked in their own journal. These items are summarised and then posted to the Nominal Ledger.

Now this is by no means an exhaustive list of all the possible journals a business might have, but they are the five main ones. Each company determines the level of detail it wants to keep and how many different journals will be kept.

If your company has computerised your bookkeeping system, the journals are automatically generated by the system as you enter financial transactions into the computer. You can view the journals on the screen or print out them out.

Q. In which journal would you record a cash receipt of £500?

A. The Cash Receipts Journal

Exercise 1

In which journal would you record the purchase of new furniture for a business on credit?

Exercise 2

In which journal would you record the payment of invoices with cash?

Exercise 3

In which journal would you record the sale of goods to a customer on credit?

Developing Entries for the Ledger

Because you enter much of your financial transaction data into journals, you're probably wondering how the information makes it into the Nominal Ledger. At the end of each month you total the entries in each journal and develop summary entries for the Nominal Ledger. As you develop each entry for the Nominal Ledger, you must be sure the entry is in balance, which means the total of your debits must equal the total of your credits.

Those of you operating a manual bookkeeping system need a selection of accountancy pads for your journals, which can be purchased from any high street stationers. A good A4 six-column pad will normally suffice.

In Figure 4-1, we show you a sample page from a Purchases Journal. You can see that there is a column for the date of the transaction, the supplier, an invoice number, a Purchases debit, and a Trade Creditors credit. Each time products are purchased for sale the debit to the Purchases account will increase the amount of money spent on Purchases and the credit to the Trade Creditors account will increase the amount of money owed to suppliers.

At the end of the month, when it is time to develop an entry for the Nominal Ledger, you total the Purchases Journal columns. Then you develop a summary entry based on those totals.

Figure 4-1:
Sample page from a Purchases Journal showing total purchases for the month of May for a fictitious company, The Scrumptious Sweet Shop.

The Scrumptious Sweet Shop
Purchases Journal
May 2009

Date		Vendor	Invoice Number	Purchases Debit	Trade Creditors Credit	
1st	May	Ruth's Sweets	1780 –	2000 –	2000 –	
10th	May	Henry's Packaging Supplies	1525 –	1500 –	1500 –	
15th	May	Deb's Paper Goods	360 –	575 –	575 –	
25th	May	Karen's Grocery	2570 –	175 –	175 –	
				4250 –	4250 –	

Q Using the information from Figure 4-1, how would you develop an entry for the Nominal Ledger to record information from the Purchases Journal for the month of May?

A Note that you only need to record the totals for the transactions that month in the Nominal Ledger. You don't have to record all the information.

Account	Debit	Credit
Purchases	£4250	
Trade Creditors		£4250

Exercise 4

Using the information in Figure 4-2 how would you develop an entry for the Nominal Ledger to record transactions from the sales journal for the month of May?

Figure 4-2:
Sample page from a Sales Journal showing total sales for the month of May for a fictitious company, The Scrumptious Sweet Shop.

	Date		Customer		Invoice Number		Trade Debtors Debit		Sales Credit		
	1st	May	S. Smith		321 –		75 –		75 –		
	7th	May	John's Shop		322 –		250 –		250 –		
	15th	May	Pam's Shop		323 –		175 –		175 –		
	20th	May	Harry's Hotel		324 –		1550 –		1550 –		
	25th	May	Len's Restraunt		325 –		1325 –		1325 –		
							3375 –		3375 –		

The Scrumptious Sweet Shop
Sales Journal
May 2009

Exercise 5

Using the information from Figure 4-3, how would you develop an entry for the Nominal Ledger to record transactions from the Cash Payments Journal for the month of May?

Figure 4-3:
Sample page for a Cash Payments Journal for the month of May for a fictitious company, The Scrumptious Sweet Shop.

The Scrumptious Sweet Shop
Cash Payments Journal
May 2009

	Date		Account		General Debit		Trade Creditors Debit		Salaries Debit		Cash Credit
	1st	May	Rent		1500 –						1500 –
	3rd	May	Trade Creditors- Joe's Supplies				1250 –				1250 –
	4th	May	Trade Creditors- Ruth's Sweets				2000 –				2000 –
	10th	May	Salaries						800 –		800 –
	20th	May	Credit Card Payment		550 –						550 –
											6100 –

Exercise 6

Using the information from Figure 4-4, how would you develop an entry for the Nominal Ledger to record transactions from the General Journal for the month of May?

Figure 4-4:
Sample
page for
a General
Journal for
the month
of May for
a fictitious
company, The
Scrumptious
Sweet Shop.

Date		Account	General Debit	General Credit	Trade Creditors Debit	Trade Debtors Credit
6th	May	Sales Return	25 –			
		S. Smith				25 –
		Credit Memo 134				
15th	May	Henry's Packing			450 –	
		Purchase Return		450 –		
		Debit Memo 1235				
20th	May	Deb's Paper Goods			100 –	
		Purchase Return		100 –		
		Debit Memo 256				
25th	May	Office Furniture	700 –			
		(Inv. 1236)		700 –		
		Credit Card Payable				

The Scrumptious Sweet Shop
General Journal
May 2009

Posting Your Entries

After you develop your journal entries, you need to post them to the accounts in the Nominal Ledger. When you post entries to the Nominal Ledger, you must make sure you can track back those entries to their original location in the books. For example, if you are posting an entry that summarises activity from the Purchases Journal, you would want to include a reference to the page in that journal from which the summary was taken. That way if there are any questions about an entry posted to the Nominal Ledger, you have a way of tracing the source of the posted information and researching any questions that arise.

Q. The entry developed for the Nominal Ledger from the summary on Page 2 of the Purchases Journal on May 31 was:

Account	Debit	Credit
Purchases	£4,250	
Trade Creditors		£4,250

How would you record the entry into the Nominal Ledger accounts of Purchases and Trade Creditors?

A. Review Figures 4-5 and 4-6 to see how these entries would be posted to Nominal Ledger accounts.

Figure 4-5: Sample of a Nominal Ledger page for the Purchases account.

The Scrumptious Sweet Shop
Purchases
May 2009

Date		Description	Ref. No.	Debit	Credit	Balance
1st	May	Opening Balance				– 0 –
5th	May	From Purchases Journal	Page 2	4 2 0 0 –		

Figure 4-6: May 2009 Sample of a Nominal Ledger page for the Trade Creditors account.

The Scrumptious Sweet Shop
Trade Creditors
May 2009

Date		Description	Ref. No.	Debit	Credit	Balance
1st	May	Opening Balance				2 0 0 0 –
31st	May	From Purchases Journal	Page 2		4 2 0 0 –	

Each account in the Nominal Ledger needs to have a separate page or pages. Make entries from journals or directly to the Nominal Ledger throughout the month. At the end of the month total the account balance. We talk more about how to close the books out at the end of the month, or at end of another accounting period such as a quarter or a year, in Chapter 12.

You can see that the date of the entry is placed in the first column. Next you find a description indicating the source of the entry, followed by a reference number (which for a journal entry would be the page of the journal on which it is found); then you would post any debits to the debit column and any credits to the credit column.

Exercise 7

How would you post this journal entry developed using the information from page 2 of the Sales Journal on May 31 to the Nominal Ledger?

Account	Debit	Credit
Trade Debtors	£3,375	
Sales		£3,375

Trade Debtors

Date	Description	Ref. No.	Debit	Credit	Balance

Sales

Date	Description	Ref. No.	Debit	Credit	Balance

Exercise 8

How would you post this journal entry developed using the information from page 3 of the Cash Payments Journal on May 31 to the Nominal Ledger?

Account	Debit	Credit
Rent	£1,500	
Trade Creditors	£3,250	
Credit Card Payable	£550	
Salaries	£800	
Cash		£6,100

Rent Expenses

Date	Description	Ref. No.	Debit	Credit	Balance

Trade Creditors

Date	Description	Ref. No.	Debit	Credit	Balance

Credit Card Payable

Date	Description	Ref. No.	Debit	Credit	Balance

Salaries

Date	Description	Ref. No.	Debit	Credit	Balance

Cash

Date	Description	Ref. No.	Debit	Credit	Balance

Exercise 9

How would you post this journal entry developed using the information from page 5 of the General Journal on May 31 to the Nominal Ledger:

Account	Debit	Credit
Sales Return	£25	
Trade Creditors	£550	
Office Furniture	£700	
Purchases Return		£550
Trade Debtors		£25
Credit card payable		£700

Sales Return

Date	Description	Ref. No.	Debit	Credit	Balance

Trade Creditors

Date	Description	Ref. No.	Debit	Credit	Balance

Credit Card Payable

Date	Description	Ref. No.	Debit	Credit	Balance

Purchases Return

Date	Description	Ref. No.	Debit	Credit	Balance

Trade Debtors

Date	Description	Ref. No.	Debit	Credit	Balance

Office Furniture

Date	Description	Ref. No.	Debit	Credit	Balance

Adjusting for Errors

Entries that you make into the Nominal Ledger are not cast in stone. You can always adjust those entries. We talk more about how to do that in Chapter 13. Three of the most common reasons for making an adjusting entry include:

✔ **Depreciation:** This shows how an asset is being used up and allocates the cost of using that asset over the life of the asset. We talk more about depreciation in Chapter 10. Most companies post adjusting entries for depreciation once a year, but it can be done more frequently.

✔ **Prepaid expenses:** Expenses that you must prepay, such as a 12-month premium on an insurance policy, are expensed on a monthly basis using an adjusting entry. We talk more about how to do that in Chapter 13.

✔ **Adding an account:** When an account is added, you may need to move some transactions that were posted in one account to the new account. You do this using an adjusting entry, removing the sterling amount from the account where it was first posted, and then entering the amount into the new account. We talk more about this process in Chapter 13.

Answers to Exercises on Looking at the Ledgers

1 General Journal. The purchase of new furniture for the business would actually be an asset and not a cost for the purpose of purchasing or manufacturing items for sale. Therefore, you would not put it in the Purchases Journal, but instead in the journal for miscellaneous entries – the General Journal.

2 Cash Payments Journal. All cash payments are entered into the Cash Payments Journal.

3 Sales Journal. All sales are tracked in the Sales Journal.

4 See the following table for the answer:

Account	Debit	Credit
Trade debtors	£3,375	
Sales		£3,375

5 See the following table for the answer:

Account	Debit	Credit
Rent	£1,500	
Trade Creditors	£3,250	
Credit Card Payable	£550	
Salaries	£800	
Cash		£6,100

6 Note that in this case the accounts that were posted to a specific company are not listed. A Purchase Return is a product that you intended to sell but returned to a supplier. Therefore, you reduce the amount you owe that supplier by debiting Trade Creditors, which would reduce the amount due in Trade Creditors. When a customer returns a product to you, you must reduce the amount the customer owes. You would not only reduce the amount in that customer's account, but you would also credit Trade Debtors where you track payments due from customers.

Account	Debit	Credit
Sales Return	£25	
Trade Creditors	£550	
Office Furniture	£700	
Purchase Return		£550
Credit Card Payable		£700
Trade Debtors		£25

7 Here is how you would post the information to the Trade Debtors and Sales accounts of the Nominal Ledger:

Trade Debtors

Date	Description	Ref. No.	Debit	Credit	Balance
31/5	From the Sales Journal	Page 2	£3,375		

Sales

Date	Description	Ref. No.	Debit	Credit	Balance
31/5	From the Sales Journal	Page 2		£3,375	

8 Here is how you would post the information from the Cash Payments Journal:

Rent Expenses

Date	Description	Ref. No.	Debit	Credit	Balance
31/5	Cash Payments Journal	Page 3	£1,500		

Trade Creditors

Date	Description	Ref. No.	Debit	Credit	Balance
31/5	Cash Payments Journal	Page 3	£3,250		

Credit Card Payable

Date	Description	Ref. No.	Debit	Credit	Balance
31/5	Cash Payments Journal	Page 3	£550		

Salaries

Date	Description	Ref. No.	Debit	Credit	Balance
31/5	Cash Payments Journal	Page 3	£800		

Cash

Date	Description	Ref. No.	Debit	Credit	Balance
31/5	Cash Payments Journal	Page 3		£6,100	

9 Here is how you would post the information from the General Journal:

Sales return

Date	Description	Ref. No.	Debit	Credit	Balance
31/5	General Journal	Page 3	£25		

Trade Creditors

Date	Description	Ref. No.	Debit	Credit	Balance
31/5	General Journal	Page 5	£550		

Credit Card Payable

Date	Description	Ref. No.	Debit	Credit	Balance
31/5	General Journal	Page 5		£700	

Purchases Return

Date	Description	Ref. No.	Debit	Credit	Balance
31/5	General Journal	Page 5		£550	

Trade Debtors

Date	Description	Ref. No.	Debit	Credit	Balance
31/5	General Journal	Page 5		£25	

Office Furniture

Date	Description	Ref. No.	Debit	Credit	Balance
31/5	General Journal	Page 5	£700		

Chapter 5

Journaling – The Devil's in the Details

In This Chapter
▶ Understanding journals
▶ Following cash
▶ Monitoring sales
▶ Tracking purchases

*N*ot every business transaction can be found in the Nominal Ledger. Imagine how many volumes the Nominal Ledger would need to be if every single purchase, every single credit for the return of an item, and every other financial activity was individually listed in the Nominal Ledger. For a large business this can be thousands or even millions of transactions each month.

To keep the Nominal Ledger more manageable, bookkeepers keep journals for active accounts and only post their daily, weekly, or monthly summaries to the Nominal Ledger. In this chapter you can find the types of accounts for which journals are kept and how entries are made in these journals.

Defining Your Journals

Journals give you a place to look for the details on every transaction in your business. Rather than jumble all the thousands of transactions in the Nominal Ledger (see Chapter 4), which would make it difficult to find anything, bookkeepers set up a series of journals for the most active accounts, such as Cash Receipts, Cash Payments, Sales and Purchases.

Using these journals, you can easily find the detail about specific financial activity and post a summary of the day's, week's or month's activity to the Nominal Ledger so that you can do financial reporting. Think of the journals as a place for the details and the Nominal Ledger as the place you look for the big picture.

When entering a transaction in your books the first place you enter it is the journal for that type of transaction. Journals are kept in chronological order. For example you should enter sales transactions for the day into the Sales Journal.

Each entry should include information about the date of the transaction, the accounts to which the transaction will be posted, and the location of the source material used for developing the transaction. After posting to the Sales Journal, you then post the information to the accounts affected by the transaction. For example, suppose a customer bought an item on credit. You would post the information from the Sales Journal to the customer's account (in the Sales Ledger) in addition to the summary that you post to the Nominal Ledger.

Tracking Cash

Bookkeepers deal with cash transactions many times every day and you certainly want to keep track of every penny that goes in and out of your business. In fact, cash transactions are so numerous that bookkeepers keep two journals – one for incoming cash (Cash Receipts Journal) and one for outgoing cash (Cash Payments Journal). That way business owners can quickly get a summary of how much cash came into the business and how much cash went out of the business in any one day, week, or month.

Tracking the Receipts

The first place you enter cash receipts in your books is the Cash Receipts Journal. The majority of that cash will come from sales, but other possible sources of cash include deposits of capital from the company's owner, customer invoice payments, new loan proceeds and interest from savings accounts.

When you enter the cash in the books you must indicate how it was received and into which account it was credited. For example, when a customer pays an invoice the cash would be debited to the Cash account and credited to the Debtors account. You don't put it into the Sales account, because that account was credited when the sale was originally completed and the Debtors account was debited. Now you have to reverse that debit to Debtors with a credit to indicate that the money is no longer due. In addition, you would need to credit the payment to the customer's individual account as well (in the Sales Ledger).

In Figure 5-1, we show you a sample page in a Cash Receipts Journal. Note that there are seven columns of information:

- **Date:** Transaction date

- **Account Credited:** Account that will be credited

- **Folio or Page Reference (PR):** This information is filled in at the end of the month to indicate where in the Nominal Ledger the information is posted. As you post to the Nominal Ledger you indicate the completion of that post in the column so you can be sure you haven't missed anything. At the end of the month when the information is posted the columns will be totalled. You can post just the summary total of the Debtors, Sales and Cash accounts and put a tick mark next to the entries that are part of the summary total. Any entries that are not part of the summary total will need to be posted individually to the Nominal Ledger and an indication of where each entry was posted would be put in the Folio column.

- **General Credit:** This column is for transactions that are not tracked in their own column in the journal, since it involves an account that does not frequently involve a cash transaction. In Figure 5-1 you see that Anthony (one of the owners) made a cash deposit into the business of £1,500.

- **Debtors Credit:** All customer payments are credited to this column and will be summarised to the Debtors account at the end of the month.

- **Sales Credit:** Total cash sales for each day are credited to this column and will be summarised in the Sales account at the end of the month.

- **Cash Debit:** The total of this column will be debited to the Cash account at the end of the month. Remember a debit to the Cash account increases the balance of that account.

Figure 5-1: This sample page of a Cash Receipts Journal shows you how incoming cash transactions are first entered into the books.

Date		Account Credited	PR	General Credit	Trade Debtors Credit	Sales Credit	Cash Debit
		The Scrumptious Sweet Shop					
		Cash Receipts Journal					
		July 2009					
1st	July	Sales				300 -	300 -
2nd	July	Sales				250 -	250 -
3rd	July	Ck 125 from P. Smith			200 -		200 -
3rd	July	Sales				150 -	150 -
4th	July	Art's Capital		1500 -			1500 -
5th	July	Ck 320 – J. Johns			100 -		100 -
5th	July	Ck 575 – P. Post			200 -		200 -
5th	July	Sales				200 -	200 -

If you have another account with frequent cash inflows, you can add a column to track that account just as Debtors, Sales and Cash are tracked in Figure 5-1. The big advantage to having columns for active accounts is that you can post a summary entry into the Nominal Ledger at the end of the month, rather than an individual entry for each transaction. It saves a lot of time and minimises the bits of information that must be posted to the Nominal Ledger.

Q. Post these transactions in June 2009 to the Cash Receipts Journal page below:

June 1	Sales	£200
June 2	Sales	£350
June 3	Cheque 152 from Jane Smith (Customer)	£200
June 3	Sales	£220

A. Here is how the transactions would be posted:

The Scrumptious Sweet Shop Cash Receipts Journal – June 2009

Date	Account Credited	Folio	General Credit	Debtors Credit	Sales Credit	Cash Debit
1/6 ·	Sales				£200	£200
2/6	Sales				£350	£350
3/6	CQ 152, J. Smith			£200		£200
3/6	Sales				£220	£220

Exercise 1

Post these transactions in May 2009 to the Cash Receipts Journal page below:

May 1	Sales	£350
May 2	Sales	£300
May 3	Cheque 220 from John James, a customer	£250

May 3	Sales	£250
May 4	Cheque 225 from Anthony, an owner, for additional capital	£1,000
May 4	Sales	£325

The Scrumptious Sweet Shop Cash Receipts Journal – May 2009

Date	Account Credited	Folio	Nominal Credit	Debtors Credit	Sales Credit	Cash Debit

Exercise 2

Post these transactions in August 2009 to the Cash Receipts Journal page below:

August 1	Sales	£225
August 2	Sales	£125
August 3	Cheque 256 from Amy Smith, a customer	£150
August 3	Sales	£350
August 4	Cash from sale of unused office furniture	£750
August 4	Sales	£325

The Scrumptious Sweet Shop Cash Receipts Journal – August 2009

Date	Account Credited	Folio	Nominal Credit	Debtors Credit	Sales Credit	Cash Debit

Keeping an eye on outgoing cash

Cash sent out of the business is tracked in a similar way to Cash Receipts, using a Cash Payments Journal. In this journal, you track invoices you pay, salaries, rent and any other use of business cash. In this case all the accounts involved are debited and the Cash account is credited. A credit to the Cash account reduces the amount of cash you have available.

In Figure 5-2, you will see that some of the columns for the Cash Payments Journal look similar – the Date, Account Debited, Folio and General Debit (for miscellaneous debits) are the first four columns. You add Trade Creditors (Accounts Payable) debit (for bills paid) and Salaries Debit (for cash used to pay employees). The final column is for the Cash Credit. You can add more columns for accounts that experience frequent transactions during the month.

Figure 5-2:
A Cash Payment Journal keeps track of all transactions involving cash sent out of the business. This figure also shows how to summarise those transactions so that they can be posted to the nominal ledger.

The Scrumptious Sweet Shop
Cash Book (Payments)
June 2009

Date	Account Debited	Folio	Cheque No.	Nominal Debit	Trade Creditors Debit	Salaries Debit		Cash Credit
1st June	Rent		1065	800 —				800 —
3rd June	Trade Creditors - Henry's		1066		500 —			500 —
3rd June	Trade Creditors - Helen's		1067		250 —			250 —
4th June	Salaries		1068			350 —		350 —
10th June	Credit Card - Barclays		1069	150 —				150 —
				950 —	750 —	350 —		2,050 —

Exercise 3

Post these transactions in May 2009 to the Cash Payments Journal page below:

May 1	Rent	£1,500
May 2	Trade Creditors, Joe's Supplies	£2,000
May 3	Trade Creditors, Ruth's Sweets	£575
May 5	Salaries	£800
May 4	Credit Card Payment	£1,000

The Scrumptious Sweet Shop Cash Payments Journal – May 2009

Date	Account Debited	Folio	Nominal Debit	Creditors Debit	Salaries Debit	Cash Credit

Exercise 4

Post these transactions in August 2009 to the Cash Payments Journal page below:

August 1	Rent	£1,500
August 2	Trade Creditors, Joe's Supplies	£1,200
August 3	Trade Creditors, Ruth's Sweets	£325
August 5	Salaries	£800
August 5	Credit Card Payment	£250
August 4	Anthony, an owner, pays himself back for cash previous deposited in the business	£1000

The Scrumptious Sweet Shop Cash Payments Journal – August 2009

Date	Account Debited	Folio	Nominal Debit	Creditors Debit	Salaries Debit	Cash Credit

Managing Sales

If your business permits customers to buy on credit, then not all sales involve the use of cash. Non-cash sales are tracked in a Sales Journal. When you make an entry in the Sales Journal you credit sales, but you also must remember to update the customer's individual record so that you can bill the customer at the end of the month.

The most common columns you'll find in a Sales Journal include Date, Customer Account Debited, Folio, Invoice Number, Debtors Debit and Sales Credit. Note that in this journal you track both the customer name and the invoice, so that if the customer has a question when the invoice comes in, you will have enough detail in the Sales Journal to send out a copy of the transaction.

The Sales Journal allows the bookkeeper to project future cash inflows based on outstanding customer accounts. The owner can use the information to project possible cash shortage or plan for extra cash that can be used to grow the business when the money comes in.

Exercise 5

Post these transactions in July 2009 to the Sales Journal page below:

July 1	Sale to Susan Smith, Inv. #245	£500
July 2	Sale to Charlie's Café, Inv. #246	£1,200
July 3	Sale to Peter Perry, Inv. #247	£325
July 5	Sale to Jim Jones, Inv. #249	£125
July 4	Sale to Peter's Palace, Inv. #248	£2,500

The Scrumptious Sweet Shop Sales Journal – July 2009

Date	Customer Account Credited	Folio	Invoice Number	Debtors Debit	Sales Credit

Exercise 6

Post these transactions in August 2009 to the Sales Journal page below:

August 1	Sale to Susan Smith, Inv. #301	£150
August 2	Sale to Charlie's Café, Inv. #302	£750
August 3	Sale to Peter Perry, Inv. #303	£175
August 5	Sale to Jim Jones, Inv. #304	£ 95
August 5	Sale to Peter's Palace, Inv. #305	£1,500

Date	Customer Account Credited	Folio	Invoice Number	Debtors Debit	Sales Credit

Watching Purchases

A common way for business people to *obligate* (commit) to future cash purchases, without actually laying out any cash, is through purchase orders for supplies and other business needs. Bookkeepers track these non-cash obligations in the Purchases Journal. Using the Purchases Journal, the bookkeeper can quickly know the level of cash that will be needed to pay bills during the next month.

Common columns in the Purchases Journal include the date, Supplier Account Credited (where you indicate the company from where the items were purchased), Folio, Invoice Number, Purchases Debit (expenses from Purchases), and Creditors credit. When the Creditors account is credited, that means the account increases in value and additional money will be owed in the future.

Exercise 7

Post these transactions in July 2009 to the Purchases Journal page below:

July 1	Supplies from Ruth's Sweets, Inv. #1345	£500
July 2	Boxes from Henry's Packing Supplies, Inv. #275	£1,500
July 3	Supplies from Deb's Paper Goods, Inv. #356	£575
July 5	Food from Karen's Grocery, Inv. #1234	£125

The Scrumptious Sweet Shop Purchases Journal – July 2009

Date	Supplier Account Credited	Folio	Invoice Number	Purchases Debit	Creditors Credit

Exercise 8

Post these transactions in August 2009 to the Purchases Journal page below:

August 1	Supplies from Ruth's Sweets, Inv. #1345	£575
August 2	Food from Karen's Grocery, Inv. #1234	£315
August 3	Boxes from Henry's Packing Supplies, Inv. #275	£1,250
August 5	Supplies from Deb's Paper Goods, Inv. #356	£1,200

The Scrumptious Sweet Shop Purchases Journal – August 2009

Date	Supplier Account Credited	Folio	Invoice Number	Purchases Debit	Creditors Credit

Investigating invoices

Invoice numbers will not be consecutive for purchases because the number is supplied by the company from which you ordered. You can, if you wish, sequentially number the purchase invoices yourself and file in that order, so that you can easily access an invoice when necessary. Alternatively, if you don't do this, you must ensure that the purchase invoices are filed by supplier account in strict alphabetical order. You enter the transaction in the Purchases account when you receive the invoice for the goods ordered. Payment of the invoice will be made after you receive approval from the department that ordered the goods. Check for that approval before paying an invoice, in case there are any problems with the delivery.

Dealing with Miscellaneous Transactions

Not all of your transactions will fit neatly into one of these four main journals. If you have frequent transactions and you want to establish another journal, you can always create one developing the columns that can track the needed information. Otherwise, you can put miscellaneous transactions in a General Journal and post them to the Nominal Ledger at the end of the month.

Common columns in a General Journal include the Date, Account, Folio, General Debit (for most debits), and General Credit (for most credits). You will also find that these miscellaneous transactions usually impact Creditors (Accounts Payable) or Debtors (Accounts Receivable) accounts. It's good to add a column for each of those accounts.

The primary description of the transaction will be in the second column, called 'Account.' In this column you will probably need more detail about the transaction than with other journals because you will be posting so many different types of transactions impacting various accounts. In Figure 5-3, I show you a sample page from a General Journal.

Figure 5-3: This sample of a General Journal shows you how miscellaneous transactions are first entered into the books.

Note that in Figure 5-3, a Sales Return is entered in the General Debit column and will be posted to the Sales Return account in the Nominal Ledger, while the credit is posted in the Debtors Credit column because a returned item means the amount due from the customer is reduced. You will also need to use the information in the column to indicate details about whose account should be credited.

The Purchase Return to Henry's Packing shows debit memo detail. The Purchase Return account will be credited and Creditors (Accounts Payable) will be debited. The business owes less money to Henry's Packing. The same is true for the purchase return transaction and debit memo from Deb's Paper Goods.

The final transaction on that journal page is the purchase of office furniture with a credit card. In this case both the debit and credit are put in the general columns because neither the Creditors nor the Debtors accounts will be impacted by that transaction.

Exercise 9

Post these transactions in May 2009 to the General Journal page below:

May 1	Sales Return from Henry Hope, Credit Memo #346	£75
May 2	Sales Return from Sally Smith, Credit Memo #347	£120
May 3	Purchase Return to Henry's Packing, Debit Memo #1236	£525
May 5	Purchase of Office Supplies by Credit Card, Inv. #378	£575

The Scrumptious Sweet Shop General Journal – May 2009

Date	Account	Folio	General Debit	General Credit	Creditors Debit	Debtors Credit

Exercise 10

Post these transactions in August 2009 to the General Journal page below:

August 1	Sales Return from Pam Smith, Credit Memo #349	£35
August 2	Sales Return from Gary Green, Credit Memo #350	£25
August 3	Office Supplies purchase on credit card, invoice #678	£425
August 5	Purchase Return to Ruth's Sweets, Debit Memo #789	£125

The Scrumptious Sweet Shop General Journal – August 2009

Date	Account	Folio	General Debit	General Credit	Creditors Debit	Debtors Credit

Answers to Exercises on Journaling – The Devil's in the Details

1 The posts to the Cash Receipts Journal should be:

The Scrumptious Sweet Shop Cash Receipts Journal – May 2009

Date	Account Credited	Folio	General Credit	Debtors Credit	Sales Credit	Cash Debit
1/5	Sales				£350	£350
2/5	Sales				£300	£300
3/5	CQ 220 from J.James			£250		£250
3/5	Sales				£250	£250
4/5	Anthony's Capital		£1,000			£1,000
4/5	Sales				£325	£325

2 The posts to the Cash Receipts Journal should be:

The Scrumptious Sweet Shop Cash Receipts Journal – August 2009

Date	Account Credited	Folio	General Credit	Debtors Credit	Sales Credit	Cash Debit
1/8	Sales				£225	£225
2/8	Sales				£125	£125
3/8	CQ 256 from A. Smith			£150		£150
3/8	Sales				£350	£350
4/8	Office Furniture		£750			£750
4/8	Sales				£325	£325

3 The posts to the Cash Payments Journal should be:

The Scrumptious Sweet Shop Cash Payments Journal – May 2009

Date	Account Debited	Folio	General Debit	Creditors Debit	Salaries Debit	Cash Credit
1/5	Rent		£1,500			£1,500
2/5	Joe's Supplies			£1,200		£1,200
3/5	Ruth's Supplies			£575		£575
4/5	Credit Card Payment		£1,000			£1,000
5/5	Salaries				£800	£800

Note that we reordered the transactions so they would be in chronological order. All journal entries should be in chronological order.

4 The posts to the Cash Payments Journal should be:

The Scrumptious Sweet Shop Cash Payments Journal – August 2009

Date	Account Debited	Folio	General Debit	Creditors Debit	Salaries Debit	Cash Credit
1/8	Rent		£1,500			£1,500
2/8	Joe's Supplies			£1,200		£1,200
3/8	Ruth's Sweets			£325		£325
4/8	Anthony's Drawing		£1,000			£1,000
5/8	Salaries				£800	£800
5/8	Credit Card Payment		£250			£250

5 The posts to the Sales Journal should be:

The Scrumptious Sweet Shop Sales Journal – July 2009

Date	Customer Account Credited	Folio	Invoice Number	Debtors Debit	Sales Credit
1/7	Susan Smith		245	£500	£500
2/7	Charlie's Café		246	£1,200	£1,200
3/7	Peter Perry		247	£325	£325
4/7	Peter's Palace		248	£2,500	£2,500
5/7	Jim Jones		249	£125	£125

6 The posts to the Sales Journal should be:

The Scrumptious Sweet Shop Sales Journal – August 2009

Date	Customer Account Credited	Folio	Invoice Number	Debtors Debit	Sales Credit
1/8	Susan Smith		301	£150	£150
2/8	Charlie's Café		302	£750	£750
3/8	Peter Perry		303	£175	£175
5/8	Jim Jones		304	£95	£95
5/8	Peter's Palace		305	£1,500	£1,500

7 The posts to the Purchases Journal should be:

The Scrumptious Sweet Shop Purchases Journal – July 2009

Date	Supplier Account Credited	Folio	Invoice Number	Purchases Debit	Creditors Credit
1/7	Ruth's Sweets		1345	£500	£500
2/7	Henry's Packing Supplies		275	£1,500	£1,500
3/7	Deb's Paper Goods		356	£575	£575
5/7	Karen's Grocery		1234	£125	£125

8 Here are the posts to the Purchases Journal:

The Scrumptious Sweet Shop Purchases Journal – August 2009

Date	Supplier Account Credited	Folio	Invoice Number	Purchases Debit	Creditors Credit
1/8	Ruth's Sweets		1,345	£575	£575
2/8	Karen's Grocery		1,234	£315	£315
3/8	Henry's Packing Supplies		275	£1,250	£1,250
5/8	Deb's Paper Goods		356	£1,200	£1,200

9 Here are the posts to the General Journal:

The Scrumptious Sweet Shop General Journal – May 2009

Date	Account	Folio	General Debit	General Credit	Creditors Debit	Debtors Credit
1/5	Sales Return, Henry Hope, Credit Memo #346		£75			£75
2/5	Sales Return, Sally Smith, Credit Memo #347		£120			£120
3/5	Purchase Return, Henry's Packing, Debit Memo #1236			£525	£525	
5/5	Office supplies, purchase by credit card, Inv. #378		£575	£575		

10 The posts to the General Journal should be:

The Scrumptious Sweet Shop General Journal – August 2009

Date	Account	Folio	General Debit	General Credit	Creditors Debit	Debtors Credit
1/8	Sales Return, Pam Smith, Credit Memo #349		£35			£35
2/8	Sales Return, Gary Green, Credit Memo #350		£25			£25
3/8	Office Supplies, purchase on credit card, invoice #678		£425	£425		
5/8	Purchase Return, Ruth's Sweets Debit Memo #789			£125	£125	

Chapter 6

Designing Controls for Your Books, Your Records and Your Money

. . . .

In This Chapter

▶ Handling cash

▶ Maintaining records

▶ Avoiding theft and fraud

. . . .

*B*efore even opening the door of your business, establishing strong internal processes and controls for business operations is crucial. How employees will handle and monitor cash taken in or paid out can make or break a business.

In this chapter, you get to review the key concepts involved in setting up cash handling procedures. You will find ideas about how to design filing systems to be sure you keep all the proper records. You'll also discover how to develop internal control procedures for your company's assets.

Getting a Handle on Cash

Cash flows through your business in four key ways:

✔ Deposits into and payments out of your current bank accounts

✔ Deposits to and withdrawals from your savings accounts

✔ Petty cash transactions, where cash payments may be required

✔ Cash register transactions

You must be able to track when cash comes in and when cash goes out at any of these four locations. Without proper handling, you'll find cash finds ways to slip through the cracks and out of your business.

Current accounts

Most businesses will have at least one current account from which they operate their business. All money received from customers should be paid into this account, and consequently most payments to staff and suppliers will be made from this same account. It is therefore extremely important to keep a close eye on the balance of this account as it reflects the cash flow of the business.

Choosing the right bank

Your business needs to choose the right bank for your business needs. You want a bank that is open the hours you need it and that has a way to deposit funds easily. You also want a bank located near your business, so it will be convenient for you and your employees to conduct business.

In addition to location and times of operation, you want a bank that will offer you all the services you need. Check carefully to find out how much the bank charges for each of the services you expect to use. You will find service charges vary greatly among banks and you can save a lot of money if you shop carefully for a bank.

Make a note here about all the facilities that you require from your bank, such as online banking, opening hours and so on. For example, if you are rushed during the week, it is useful to know whether your branch is open on a Saturday morning, so that you can pay in last minute cheques.

Check to see if you can operate your banking via the internet. Charges are often much cheaper for transactions that are done online. For example, rather than writing out lots of cheques to pay suppliers (bank charges for writing out cheques can be expensive) try automating the payments to your suppliers by paying online. You don't necessarily have to subscribe to a fancy system, just pay your suppliers via your online banking system. As long as you have the sort code, account number and account name this is easy to do. It is often cheaper to make payments in this way. A word of caution: Make sure that you put a reference on the payment, so that the recipient knows who the money has come from and what it relates to.

Review your bank charges to see how much you could save by automating some of your payments rather than writing out lots of cheques.

Deciding on your cheque types

Once you have decided which bank to use, you must then consider whether you are going to manually write your cheques or use your computerised accounting system to print them.

Manual Cheques

If you are going to write manual cheques, then you will probably use a business cheque book, which is identical to a personal cheque book, with a cheque stub on the left, allowing you to write details of the payee, dates and amounts, and the main body of the cheque on the right.

Each cheque and counterfoil is numbered and this number can be used throughout your accounting system as a reference for that transaction. If someone makes a mistake in writing out, a cheque the voided cheque and voucher should be left in the chequebook, so you can account for all numbered cheques.

If you're paying a supplier by writing out a manual cheque, make sure that you write the supplier invoice number on the counterfoil of the cheque book. In addition, on the invoice itself, write the cheque number and stamp the invoice "PAID". This provides a cross reference between the bank and the supplier invoice.

Printing your cheques

If you plan to print your cheques, then order cheques based on the computerised bookkeeping system you use.

Your accounting software program (such as Sage 50 Accounts or Quickbooks), has a unique template for printing cheques. The information shown on the cheque is what you would expect, such as date, payee details, and amounts in both words and numbers. You don't have a counterfoil to fill in as you do for a manual cheque, but you don't need one: Your computer system will record details of all the cheques printed. Reports can be run, or on screen enquiries can be made to check details of cheques printed and issued.

Signing cheques

In addition to setting up a procedure for controlling the preparation of cheques, you also need to set up controls over who can sign cheques – and let the bank know the controls you have in place. For example, you may decide that certain people in the company are authorised to sign cheques of £1,000 or less and others can sign cheques between £1,000 and £10,000. You may want to require two signatures on all cheques over £10,000.

Your bank can help you establish cheque-signing authority and will have bank mandate forms which you need to complete to designate authorised employees as signatories to the account. Each authorised employee needs to sign the form, so that the bank has a copy of the signature on file in case a question about a cheque arises.

Handling deposits

When cash or cheques arrive at the business premises the details need to be recorded on a paying in slip and paid into the bank as soon as possible. Your bank will have provided you with pre-printed paying-in slips. If you have more than one account in which you deposit money, ensure that you have the correct paying-in slips for the required bank account. Details to write on the paying in slip include:

- ✔ The date.
- ✔ Details of who sent the cheque.
- ✔ The amount.

If a remittance advice note has been sent with the cheque, then you can note the invoice number on the paying-in slip as well. If you are using a computerised accounts system, you can post this information immediately.

Fill in the paying-in slip on the day the cash is received and make it part of your daily morning routine. You should try to pay in the money before 3.30 p.m. that day to ensure that the money is credited to your bank account that day.

Exercise 1

You work in the accounts department for a small business. Write a procedure for a new member of staff to follow, which shows them what to do when a cheque arrives by post into the business.

You should consider who opens the post, who writes up the paying in book and who ultimately takes the cheques to the bank. Try to remember that these responsibilities should be split up as much as possible to minimise any possibility of fraud. See the section Protecting Your Business from Theft and Fraud later in this chapter.

Savings accounts

If you do have extra cash that won't be needed for the daily operations of the business, you probably want to deposit this cash in an interest bearing account. You can set up a transfer between the current account and the savings accounts, but you should be very careful about who is authorised to access that transfer capability. For many small businesses, only the owner or the owner and his partners will have access to transfer money between current accounts and savings accounts. In a larger company, the transfer rights may be given to the chief financial officer.

Petty cash accounts

Many businesses find they have a need for small amounts of cash for unexpected needs during the week. For example, if a package arrives with postage due, the person at the reception desk may need a couple of pounds for the postman. Employees may have an urgent need for office supplies to finish up a project and draw from petty cash to run to a local shop rather than wait for the official office supply order.

Whatever the reason you can set up petty cash accounts that are handled by certain trusted staff, such as the office manager. You may designate that they keep £50 to £100 on hand for office cash emergencies.

Petty cash procedures

The business will normally assign an individual to be in charge of the Petty Cash. This person will be given a *float* (a pre-determined sum of money for petty cash purposes) of say £100 and will be given a lockable petty cash tin to keep it in. Petty cash duties include:

- ✔ Making payments to other members of staff
- ✔ Reimbursing staff members for business expenses
- ✔ Keeping records of payments made.

The individual in charge of the petty cash will also need to balance the petty cash tin at regular intervals. In order to carry out all these duties, the petty cash person will need to have a petty cash book to record all the payments and petty cash vouchers for petty cash claims to be made.

All petty cash vouchers must have the appropriate receipt attached to them so that the business can claim VAT when the VAT return is completed. See Chapter 17 for more on VAT. The person making the petty cash claim and the person authorising the payment should both sign the voucher.

This example illustrates the petty cash routine:

- Howard pays for a parcel to be sent via Special Delivery to a customer. He pays £4.80 for the parcel and obtains a receipt from the Post Office.
- Back at the office he hands the receipt to Joan the bookkeeper, who is responsible for the petty cash.
- Joan completes a petty cash voucher (these can be bought from all good stationers) and attaches the receipt to the back of the petty cash voucher.
- Joan authorises the petty cash payment by signing the voucher and carefully takes £4.80 from the petty cash tin and gives it to Howard.
- Joan will then write up the entry in the Petty Cash book.

Exercise 2

Review your petty cash procedure. If you do not have one, write one here.

Decide who is responsible for maintaining the petty cash tin, and how much the Petty cash float is going to be. Make sure that all staff are aware of the Petty cash procedure.

The imprest system

As we have already mentioned, many companies will give the petty cash person a float that can be used to make petty cash payments. Obviously, at some point this float is going to run out and will need to be replenished. Many companies operate what is known as the *imprest system* for their petty cash requirements. This system allows you to replenish the petty cash back to the agreed float amount by adding up the value of all the receipts in the petty cash tin and replacing that amount of money back into the tin, thus bringing the amount of cash back up to the float value. Please refer to the following example to see how an Imprest system would work.

Q. Joan needs to balance the petty cash tin on 31st January. Given the following transactions, how much money will be left in the Petty Cash tin on the 31st January, and how much will she need to reimburse the petty cash tin in order to replenish the petty cash float of £50?

January 1st	Float £50
15th Jan	Postage £5.01
21st January	Window cleaner paid £25
28th January	Jiffy bag purchased to parcel up customer item £2.40
29th January	Coffee and milk for the office £5.76

A. The total petty cash expenses are £38.17, this means that £11.83 should still be left in the tin. Joan will need to write a cheque for "Cash" for the sum of £38.17 to return the tin to its £50 float.

Exercise 3

Reconcile the following petty cash tin at 31 October. The float is £100 and the following expenses have been incurred:

1st October	Milk, tea and coffee for office use	£6.76
5th October	Envelopes purchased for office use	£3.99
10th October	Postage	£4.68
15th October	Window cleaners paid	£25.00
18th October	Donation to Church magazine	£10.00
25th October	Postage	£12.47

What is the petty cash balance at the end of October? By how much should the petty cash tin be replenished?

Cash registers

If you are running or working for a retail business, most of your cash comes into the business at your point of sale – the cash register. Of course, most people are honest, but as a business you do need to ensure that you have controls in place to be sure that cash makes it into the business and not into the pockets of people working the registers. For those of us who are as honest as the day is long, here are some of the ways the more unscrupulous members of the workforce can 'work the system' to make sure they can pocket cash without coming up short on the tills at the end of the day:

- ✔ **Don't record the sale and pocket the cash:** Make sure your cash register transactions match your sales receipts.

- ✔ **Don't provide a sales receipt and pocket the cash:** To avoid this make sure you post that a receipt is needed for all returns and exchanges. Customers will help you make sure a receipt is prepared for all sales.

- ✔ **Prepare a false credit voucher and keep the cash:** Establish procedures that require a manager's approval for all cash returned.

Whenever cash is involved, it is important that businesses review their systems to ensure that the staff who are handling the cash are trustworthy and that few opportunities are available for staff to be enticed by the apparently easy access to money. As the bookkeeper it is your responsibility to be involved in the design of sales receipts and cash vouchers and to be sure these vouchers are being used according to company policy.

If you are working for a small company, the deposit of money into and withdrawals out of a savings account is probably handled by the owner or partners. In a large company, the chief financial officer, or someone they specifically designate, will likely be responsible for major payments from a savings account.

Exercise 4

In the following space, jot down a few controls that you can put in place to ensure that fraud can be avoided when using cash registers.

Organising Your Record Keeping

Everything you do in your business is going to generate paperwork that you may or may not want to keep. You need to decide what to keep, and what you do keep you need to organise so you can access it quickly when you need it. If you computerise your accounting you may not need to keep as much paper, but you still want a paper trail in case something happens to your computer records or you need the backup information for a transaction that is questioned at a later date.

Obviously, filing cabinets are where you'll store most of your records for the current year and the prior year. Older files you may store in boxes in a warehouse or store-room if you don't have room in your filing cabinets. How you set up the files can be critical to your ability to find something when you need it. Many bookkeepers use four different methods to store accounting information:

- **File folders:** These are used for filing paperwork relating to payments, contract information about suppliers; information about individual employees, such as payroll related forms and data; and information about individual customer accounts. Even if you have a computerised system, you still need to file paperwork in hard copy form for employees, suppliers and customers.

- **Lever Arch Files:** Your Chart of Accounts (see Chapter 3), Nominal Ledger (see Chapter 4), and Journals (see Chapter 5) are usually kept in Lever arch files. Even if you do use a computerised accounting system, it's a good idea to keep a copy of this for the month most recently closed and the current month in hard copy in case your computer system goes down and you need to quickly check information.

- **Expandable files:** These types of files are good for managing outstanding bills and supplier activity. You can get alphabetical expandable files for managing pending supplier invoices and purchase orders. You can use 30-day and 12-month expandable files for managing outstanding invoices. As invoices come in you can place them in the 12-month file for the month they are due. Then move the current month's invoices to the 30-day file by the day they are due. You may be able to avoid using these files if you are using a computerised book-keeping system and set up the invoice pay reminder system in your accounting program. Careful thought should be given to your method of filing invoices. If you operate a computerised accounting system, you don't need to split invoices between those that have not been paid and those that have. As long as invoices are given a sequential number, they can all be filed in the same file. You can have one file for all your purchase invoices and another for your Sales invoices. Your computer system can then provide you with a list of outstanding payments due from your customers or to suppliers.

- **Media for storing backup computer data:** If you are keeping the books on a computer, be certain you make at least one backup copy of all your data daily and store it in a safe place – a place where the data won't be destroyed if there is a fire. A small fire safe is a good choice if your business does not have a built-in safe.

You'll find it doesn't take long to build up lots of paper and not have room to store it all. Luckily not everything has to be kept forever. Generally anything related to tax returns has to be kept for at least six years, this is the general rule that applies to most paperwork. You may wish to keep papers for longer, particularly if they relate to an asset that you still own. You also should keep any information about pending legal issues. It is wise to take advice from your accountant or legal professional if you are not sure about specific documentation. As far as employees are concerned, you are legally required to keep records for three years after they have left the company.

It is wise to keep the current years records and files in an accessible position and the more recent past years figure in easily located cabinets. Once a record is beyond the two year mark, you may wish to archive the data and box it up and put it into storage. You must ensure that the boxes are clearly marked showing the contents clearly on the outside of the box.

All important information should be filed in an easily accessible place that can be located quickly and easily. Each file should be clearly marked with a description of the contents, so that as little time as possible is wasted on looking for information.

Protecting Your Business from Theft and Fraud

Every business owner faces the possibility of theft or fraud. Too often business owners find out about an employee pocketing some assets when it's too late to do anything about it. Even the most loyal employee can be driven to steal if their personal financial pressures become too great. There are four basic types of financial fraud a business owner may face:

- ✔ **Embezzlement:** This involves the theft of funds by a person who actually has control of the funds, such as a bookkeeper.

- ✔ **Internal theft:** This involves the theft of company assets by employees, such as office supplies or merchandise on shop shelves.

- ✔ **Payoffs and kickbacks:** This involves employees accepting cash or other benefits for introducing suppliers to their business. For example a supplier may artificially inflate its sale price to the business and the employee would get a cut of this. A *payoff* is paid before the sale is made (effectively saying 'please') and a *kickback* is paid after the sale is made (saying 'thank you' to the employee for the introduction). Few businesses tend to report this problem, but when these type of deals are uncovered, it is usually considered a sackable offence.

- ✔ **Skimming:** This involves pocketing some of the company's sales receipts and not recording the revenue in the books.

Your best defence against theft and fraud is to put up barriers to discourage it. You do this by dividing staff responsibilities to reduce the possibility and opportunity for theft and fraud. Here are some key tips for controlling your cash and minimising theft and fraud:

- ✔ **Separate cash handlers:** Be sure that the person who accepts the cash is not the same person who records the transaction in the books.

- ✔ **Separate authorisation responsibilities:** Be sure that the person who authorises a cheque is not the same as the person who prepares the cheque. If possible a third person should be the one to sign the cheques. That way three people would have to collude to steal money using a company cheque.

- ✔ **Separate bookkeeping functions:** Don't put too much authority or trust in one person (unless that person is the business owner).

- ✔ **Separate operational responsibility:** Be sure you have one person who accepts the cash transactions and a second person who enters those transactions in the books. For example the person who handles the cash register should not be the one who makes the bank deposit.

✔ **Separate financial reporting:** Be sure that the person who prepares your financial reports is not the same person who is responsible for entering the data day-to-day in your books. Often an outside accountant is responsible for using the data entered to prepare the financial reports if a business does not have an accountant on staff.

Exercise 5

Imagine that you are setting up the accounting department. In the space below, jot down the types of tasks that require separation of duties.

Answers to Exercises on Designing Controls for Your Books, Your Records and Your Money

1   The following is an example of what you could have written.

Procedure for banking cheques:

   ✔ The person responsible for opening the post should ensure that all cheques and notifications of payments from customers (for example a Remittance Advice) are passed to the accounts department on the day that they are received.

   ✔ One person in the accounts department should be responsible for writing up the bank paying-in book and recording all the money received, along with details of the customer and which invoice they are paying. As much detail as possible should be written on the paying-in slip stub.

   ✔ If possible, a different individual should ensure that the paying in book is taken to the bank and the money deposited, **the same day it is received.**

   ✔ Once the bank paying in book has been returned to the accounts department, the customer receipts should be entered into your bookkeeping system. If you have a computerised system, you should enter the customer receipts against the appropriate account, using the bank paying-in reference and details shown on the paying-in book to identify which invoices the payment should be allocated to. Tick the paying in slip, once you have entered the information into your book-keeping system.

2   Here are the main elements of a petty cash procedure:

Petty cash procedures

   ✔ Designate a member of staff to be responsible for petty cash. Ensure that all members of staff know who this is.

   ✔ Complete petty cash vouchers for all petty cash payments detailing the type of expenditure and noting VAT if applicable. Attach the receipts to the vouchers, so that VAT may be claimed at a later date.

   ✔ Ensure that the individual claiming money from petty cash signs the petty cash voucher to acknowledge receipt of the money and also ensure that the petty cashier authorises the payment by signing the voucher accordingly.

   ✔ Number each petty cash voucher so that it can be filed and easily located later if necessary.

   ✔ Write up the petty cash book, or enter the petty cash vouchers onto your computerised system, using the number mentioned in the previous step as a reference.

   ✔ Petty cash should be counted and balanced on a regular basis. This is usually done when the float needs topping up.

3   The total petty cash expenses are £62.90.

   The amount of cash left in the tin prior to balancing is £37.10.

   The petty cash tin should be replenished by £62.90, to bring the float back up to £100.

4 The following controls should be put in place when using cash registers:

✔ Ensure that your cash register transactions match your sales receipts. A manager should help the cashier with this checking process.

✔ Credit notes should be issued for all sale returns. A manager should authorise the credit note at the time the transaction is taking place.

✔ Make sure the appropriate refund methods are in place:

• If the customer cannot supply a receipt, then a credit note must be given.

• If the customer paid by credit card, then the customer must be refunded on the credit card, not with cash.

• If the customer paid by cash and can provide a valid receipt, then cash can be returned to the customer.

5 The following are the types of duties which you should consider separating amongst different members of staff. Obviously in a very small company this may not be possible, so common sense should prevail.

✔ The person who opens the post and accepts the cash should not enter the transaction in the books.

✔ The person who enters the data in the books on a daily basis should not prepare the financial statements.

✔ The person who prepares the cheques should not have the authority to sign the cheques.

✔ The person who pays the money into the bank should not be the person who completes the paying in slips.

Part III
Tracking Day-to-Day Business Operations with Your Books

'Brother Cedric's doing the abbey's books now – they should be ready for your inspection in five years.'

In this part . . .

Do you want to know every single financial transaction that happens in your business each and every day? You should. That's the only way you'll be able to put all the pieces together and see how well your business is doing financially.

We show you how to track your day-to-day business operations by recording sales and purchases, as well as any discounts and returns. You'll also need to pay your employees, so we show you the basics of setting up and managing employee payroll and all the government paperwork you must do once you employ staff.

Chapter 7

Purchasing Goods and Tracking Your Purchases

....

In This Chapter
▶ Tracking purchases
▶ Controlling stock
▶ Paying for what you get

....

*E*very business must have something to sell. Whether selling products or services, you do spend money on items that will later be sold, which become stock until sold. You also need supplies to run the business.

This chapter reviews how to track your purchases, manage stock, and pay for items you buy. You also get to practise how to value your stock and pay your invoices.

Detailing and Managing Your Stock

Bookkeepers track their stock in two different accounts – Purchases and Stock. When you initially buy goods to sell, those transactions are tracked in the Purchases account, which is an expense account and shown on the Profit and Loss Statement (see Chapter 15 for more information on the Profit and Loss Statement). When you prepare your financial reports at the end of the month, any goods still on the shelves are then tracked in an asset account called Stock, which is shown on the Balance Sheet (see Chapter 14 for more information on the Balance Sheet).

When tracking that stock, companies do so in two different ways – *periodic stock count* and *perpetual stock count*:

- ▸ **Periodic stock count:** When goods on hand are tracked using a periodic stock system, a physical count is conducted of the goods in the shop as well as in the warehouse. This count can be done on a daily, monthly, quarterly or yearly basis. In an active retail environment, shop counts are often done daily. You've probably seen signs on shop windows indicating that the shop is closed for an entire day to count stock. That usually happens at the end of the year as a company prepares its financial statements, or in the process of a company audit.

- ▸ **Perpetual stock count:** When goods on hand are tracked as they are sold, that's called a perpetual stock system. This type of system must be implemented using a computer software program that is integrated with the accounting system. You'll see this today in many major retail shops where bar codes are used and the actual item purchased shows on your receipt. Stock counts are adjusted automatically. Even when you use this type of system, you need to make a physical count of stock periodically to verify that the stock numbers in the computerised database actually match what's on the shelf and in the warehouse. Some goods are lost to theft; others are lost to damage. The only way the computer system can be adjusted to actual numbers on hand is through a physical count.

Q. If you purchase goods with cash and plan to sell them to customers, which two accounts would be impacted by that transaction?

A. Purchases and Cash. You would enter a debit to the Purchases account, which would increase the balance in the account and show the additional expense. You would enter a credit to the Cash account, which would decrease the balance in that account.

Determining stock value

When you first enter a purchase in the books, you enter its value based on the cost that you paid for those goods. But, the way you track the value of that stock is often not the same as the actual cost. For example, a hardware shop that buys and sells hammers can't possibly keep track of how much it paid for each individual hammer on the shelf. One week when an order comes in, the price from the manufacturer may be £5 for the hammer and the next week it may be £5.50. It would be a nightmare for the shop owner to have to keep track of the price of each hammer and then calculate exactly how much profit was made on each hammer.

Instead of trying to track each individual item, bookkeepers use various methods for valuing stock. Your company must choose one method and follow that method all the time. If you decide to change your method, you must inform both Her Majesty's Revenue and Customs (HMRC) and your accountants, as the method you use will affect your financial
statements at the year end. The value of stock sold can affect how much profit a company makes, as the rest of this section demonstrates.

The are five methods of valuing stock:

✔ **LIFO (Last In, First Out):** With this method of valuing stock, a shop owner assumes that the last product put on the shelf is the first product sold when he's calculating the value of his stock for the books and his financial report. LIFO is most often used by a business that does not have to worry about perishable goods. For example, a hardware shop that receives new hammers is not likely to carefully empty the shelves, put the newest hammers at the back of the shelf and then put the oldest hammers in the front. Instead, when a new delivery arrives the shop owner puts the newest hammers out front, so they get sold first. The actual price at which the shop owner sells his hammers to customers will be the same no matter when he put them on the shelves.

✔ **FIFO (First In, First Out):** With this method of valuing stock, a shop owner assumes that the first in (oldest item) is the first one sold when he's calculating the value of his stock for the books and his financial records. Food shops commonly use this system because they must worry about perishable goods. When you go to the shop, you know that you will always find the oldest milk (the milk that will expire first) at the front of the shelf and the newest milk (the milk with a longer time until expiration) will be at the back. That shop is using a first in, first out method of counting stock – trying to get the product that came in first to sell first.

✔ **Averaging:** With this method of valuing stock, a company doesn't worry about what came in first or last. Instead it averages the cost of stock when calculating stock value.

✔ **Specific identification:** With this method of valuing stock, the shop owner does keep track of how much he paid for each individual item. This type of stock method is only used when high value items are sold. For example, a car dealer will keep track of how much he paid for each car and for how much each car sold.

✔ **Lower of Cost or Net Realisable Value (NRV):** The stock is valued on whichever is lower: the original amount paid for the goods, or the market value (otherwise known as NRV). Businesses that deal in precious metals, commodities or publicly traded securities are likely to use this method, as these goods tend to fluctuate wildly in value. Your accountants will use this method to value the stock at the year end, to ensure that the Balance Sheet shows a true and fair representation of the stock value.

Calculating the value of ending stock and cost of goods sold is different with each method. Take a look at this example of how to do the calculations for averaging, LIFO, and FIFO and then try to calculate a problem on your own.

A hardware shop owner purchased hammers several times during the month of April. (He doesn't have a warehouse, so all new goods purchased are put on the shop shelves.)

Date	Quantity	Per Hammer Price
April 1	150	£5.00
April 10	150	£7.50
April 20	200	£8.00

He started the month with 50 hammers worth £250. At the end of the month, when he counts what is left on the shelf, he has 75 units left. What is the value of his ending stock and what was the cost of goods sold?

To calculate stock value, start with the number of items of stock at the beginning of the month. Then add the purchases made during the month. That total will give you the number of goods you had available for sale. Then you subtract the amount of stock left on the shelf. The stock left on the shelf would be the ending stock and the difference between stock available for sale and ending stock would be the cost of goods sold. The ending stock would be the value that you would put in the asset account Stock shown on the Balance Sheet and the cost of goods shown would be an expense on the Profit and Loss Statement.

Here is how you would calculate the cost of goods sold and ending stock using the Averaging method:

Beginning Stock	50	£250.00
Purchases	150 @ £5.00	£750.00
	150 @ £7.50	£1,125.00
	200 @ £8.00	£1,600.00
Total Goods Available for Sale		£3,725.00
Average Cost per Unit	(£3,725/550)	£6.77
Ending Stock	(75 @ £6.77)	£507.75
Cost of Goods Sold	(550–75 = 475 goods sold @ £6.77)	£3,215.75

Exercise 1

Harry's Hardware started the month with 25 wrenches on the shelf with an average per unit value of $3.25. During the month Harry made these additional purchases:

April 1	100 wrenches @ $3.50
April 10	100 wrenches @ $3.75
April 20	150 wrenches @ $4.00

At the end of the month he had 100 wrenches on the shelf. Calculate the value of the ending stock and the cost of goods sold using the Averaging method.

Using the same purchase information for the hammers shown in the preceding example, how would you calculate the value of the ending stock and cost of goods sold using the FIFO stock method? Remember, the beginning stock was 50 hammers purchased at $5 each, the ending stock was 75 hammers. Additional purchases were:

Date	*Quantity*	*Per Hammer Price*
April 1	150	$5.00
April 10	150	$7.50
April 20	200	$8.00

Since FIFO is first in, first out, you would start the calculation with the beginning stock of 50 hammers at $5 and assume those were sold first.

Beginning Stock	50 @ $5.00	$250.00
Next in: April 1	150 @ $5.00	$750.00
Next in: April 10	150 @ $7.50	$1,125.00

Then of the last 200 purchased, 125 were sold and 75 are left.

Next in: April 20	125 @ $8.00	$1,000.00
Cost of Goods Sold		$3,125.00
Ending Stock	75 @ $8.00	$600.00

Note that the ending stock has a greater value than when the Averaging method is used and the cost of goods sold is lower. That's because the remaining stock are the most expensive hammers that were bought.

Exercise 2

Harry's Hardware started the month with 25 wrenches on the shelf with an average per unit value of $3.25. During the month he made these additional purchases:

April 1	100 wrenches @ $3.50
April 10	100 wrenches @ $3.75
April 20	150 wrenches @ $4.00

At the end of the month he had 100 wrenches on the shelf. Calculate the value of the ending stock and the cost of goods sold using the FIFO method.

Using the same purchase information for the hammers shown in the example above, how would you calculate the value of the ending stock and cost of goods sold using the LIFO stock method? The beginning stock was 50 hammers purchased at $5 each, the ending stock was 75 hammers. Additional purchases were:

Date	*Quantity*	*Per Hammer Price*
April 1	150	$5.00
April 10	150	$7.50
April 20	200	$8.00

Since LIFO is last in first out, you would start the calculation with the beginning stock of 50 hammers at $5 and assume those were sold last. The first hammers sold are the ones that were received last, so you would start with the 200 hammers bought on April 20.

| First sold: April 20 purchase | 200 @ $8.00 | $1,600.00 |
| Next sold: April 10 | 150 @ $7.50 | $1,125.00 |

Then knowing that you had 75 hammers left, 50 of them would be the oldest units at $5 from the beginning stock and 25 would be from the purchase on April 1 at $5.

Next sold: April 1	125 @ $5.00	$625.00
Cost of Goods Sold		$3,350.00
Ending Stock	75 @ $5.00	$375.00

Note that the ending stock using the LIFO method has the lowest value of the three and the cost of goods sold is the highest.

Exercise 3

Harry's Hardware started the month with 25 wrenches on the shelf with an average per unit value of $3.25. During the month he made these additional purchases:

April 1	100 wrenches @ $3.50
April 10	100 wrenches @ $3.75
April 20	150 wrenches @ $4.00

At the end of the month he had 100 wrenches on the shelf. Calculate the value of the ending stock and the cost of goods sold using the LIFO method.

As the bookkeeper, it is critical for you to know the stock valuation method the owner of the company uses. Depending on the stock valuation method chosen, the cost of goods sold total could be comparatively higher than if the averaging method had been chosen. If cost of goods sold is higher, then the expenses for the period will be higher and the profit will be lower. That means the owner will pay less tax because he shows a lower profit. A lower cost of goods sold total will mean the profit will be higher and the tax will be higher. The Averaging method falls in between these two stock valuation types.

Buying and Monitoring Office Supplies

In addition to purchasing items for sale, your company also buys office supplies and other items that are needed for the everyday operation of the business. You are most likely to record these purchases by debiting an expense account called Office Supplies and crediting the Cash account (if the purchase was made using cash) or Trade Creditors (Accounts Payable), if the purchase was made on credit.

How carefully you need to monitor the use of the office supplies depends on your company. Many companies don't require the bookkeeper to monitor anything but the actual expenses and require the management of office supplies to be done by the office manager or supply manager.

Paying Your Invoices

After recording the purchases, the bookkeeper takes primary responsibility for making sure that the invoices are paid for both the stock and the supplies purchased. Usually, you will post the invoices to the Trade Creditors (Accounts Payable) account when they arrive, file them in the month or day to be paid, and pay them when they are due.

There are five key functions you must carry out in order to pay invoices properly:

✔ Entering the invoices into the accounting system

✔ Preparing the cheques for paying the invoices

✔ Signing the cheques

✔ Sending out the payment to the suppliers

✔ Reconciling the bank account

One person should not be responsible for all these tasks. In fact the person who enters the invoices into the accounting system and prepares the cheques, should never be the one with the authority to sign the cheques. To be even more careful about cash control, it's a good idea to have a third person review the cheques against the invoices due and actually send the signed cheques out to the suppliers. By separating these tasks you minimise the risk that business funds will be misused.

A key function of a Purchase Ledger Clerk (Accounts Payable) is to keep track of any discounts your company may be able to take. For example, sometimes a company will offer a 2 per cent discount on an invoice if paid within 10 days and expect payment in full between 10 days and 30 days. Then, there could be a late penalty of 1.5 percent interest for payments received after 30 days. The Purchase Ledger clerk should organise the invoices to pay them in time to take advantage of the discount and save his company money.

Q. Suppose a company received a invoice for £100,000 on March 31 that said 'Settlement Discount of 2 per cent if paid within 10 days of invoice date'. How much discount would you receive and what date should the invoice be paid to receive this discount?

A. The company can take a 2 per cent discount if paid by April 10; otherwise the full amount is due if paid after April 11. To calculate the discount you would multiply the total amount of the invoice by 2 per cent and then subtract that amount from the invoice total to find the discounted amount due.

£100,000 @ 2 per cent = £2,000

So the company would save £2,000 if it paid the invoice by April 10. Companies can save a lot of money during the month by taking advantage of supplier discounts.

Exercise 4

Suppose a company received an invoice for £500,000 on March 31 that said 'Settlement Discount of 3 per cent if paid within 10 days of date of Invoice'. How much discount would you receive and by what date should the invoice be paid to receive this discount?

Exercise 5

Suppose a company received an invoice for £100,000 on March 31 that said 'Settlement Discount of 2 per cent if paid within 15 days of the date of invoice'. How much discount would you receive and what date should the invoice be paid to receive this discount?

Quick Quiz

1. If you keep track of the amount of stock you have on hand by physically counting how much product is on your shop shelves and in your warehouse on a regular basis, what kind of stock system is this called?

2. If your stock is counted each time you ring up a sale on your register, what kind of stock system is this called?

3. If you work in a grocery shop and carefully place the newest loaves of bread at the back of the shelf and bring the older loaves of bread to the front of the shelf, what type of stock system does your shop probably use?

4. If you work at a car dealership and you must track the sale of a car using the original invoice price, what type of stock system does your dealership probably use?

Answers to Exercises on Purchasing Goods and Tracking Your Purchases

1 Here is how you would calculate the ending stock and cost of goods sold using the averaging method:

Beginning Stock	25 wrenches @ £3.25	£81.25
April 1	100 wrenches @ £3.50	£350.00
April 10	100 wrenches @ £3.75	£375.00
April 20	150 wrenches @ £4.00	£600.00
Total Goods Available for Sale	375 wrenches	£1,406.25
Average Cost per Unit	£1,406.25/375	£3.75
Ending Stock	100 @ £3.75	£375.00
Cost of Goods Sold	275 @ £3.75	£1,031.25

2 Here is how you would calculate the ending stock and cost of goods sold using the FIFO method:

Beginning Stock:	25 wrenches @ £3.25	£81.25
Next in:		
April 1	100 wrenches @ £3.50	£350.00
April 10	100 wrenches @ £3.75	£375.00
April 20	50 wrenches @ £4.00	£200.00
Cost of Goods Sold		£1,006.25
Ending Stock	100 wrenches @ £4.00	£400.00

3 Here is how you would calculate the ending stock and cost of goods sold using the LIFO method:

First Sold purchased April 20:	150 @ £4.00	£600.00
Next Sold purchased April 10:	100 @ £3.75	£375.00
Next Sold purchased April 1:	25 @ £3.50	£87.50
Cost of Goods Sold		£1,062.50
Ending Stock		
75 from April 1	@ £3.50	£262.50
25 from Beginning	@ £3.25	£81.25

4 The company would receive a 3 per cent discount if it paid the invoice in 10 days – by April 10. The discount will be £15,000 if paid by April 10. So the bookkeeper should pay the invoice by April 10.

5 The company would receive a 2 per cent discount if it pays the invoice in 15 days – by April 15. The discount will be £2,000 if paid by April 15. So the bookkeeper should pay the invoice by April 15.

Answers to Quick Quiz

1 If you physically count your stock on a regular, monthly, quarterly or yearly basis, this is known as a periodic stock count system.

2 If your business operates a system whereby the till adjusts your stock each time a sale is made, then this is called a perpetual stock system.

3 A grocery shop would want the first product in (oldest item) to be the first product out (first sold). This describes the FIFO method.

4 A car dealership usually wants to maintain a specific identification system because each car in the stock probably has different options and will have a different cost. This describes the Specific Identification method.

Chapter 8

Calculating and Monitoring Sales

· ·

In This Chapter

▶ Getting cash

▶ Accepting credit

▶ Cashing up your cash register

▶ Calculating discounts

▶ Tracking sales returns and allowances

▶ Acknowledging non-payers

· ·

You love to take in money when you run a business. Everyone does. But once money starts coming in the door you need to track that cash and credit properly.

Tracking the cash is not enough, you also must:

✔ Record transactions in your books

✔ Track individual customer accounts

✔ Record any discounts that were offered

✔ Track any returns or allowances that were given to customers

✔ Collect from customers to whom you sell on credit

✔ Monitor customer accounts to be sure they pay on time

✔ Write off accounts from customers who just won't pay

This chapter helps you practise the key elements of tracking your sales, recording them properly in the books, and monitoring all the accounts related to your sales.

Taking in Cash

First you need to know what is cash and what is not. That may sound strange but cash does not only include the pound notes and coins that you receive. You also count customer cheques as cash, as well as items bought on credit cards, as long as those credit cards were not issued by you.

When it comes to buying on credit for the purposes of your bookkeeping, the only sales that need to be tracked in Debtors (Accounts Receivable) are those that involve credit issued by your business. Credit card sales on credit cards issued by banks or other financial institutions should be listed as cash. In fact today, with the electronic transfer of funds, many companies will see the money show up in their bank account almost immediately after the sale. It all depends upon how you have set up to receive your money through the bank that handles your credit transactions.

As a bookkeeper, you can get all the information you need to enter cash transactions in the books from your sales receipts. Suppose you are the bookkeeper for a bakery: Figure 8-1 shows what a sales receipt might look like:

```
BENSONS Bakery

Sales Receipt 15/2/2009

Item _____ Quantity    Price      Total

Meat Pie _____ 10          £2.50      £25.00

Cornish Pasty _____ 10          £1.00      £10.00

Sausage Rolls _____ 10          £1.00      £10.00

Subtotal Sales _____ £45.00

VAT at 17.5% _____ £7.88

Total Sales _____ £52.88

Cash Paid _____ £55.00

Change _____ £2.12
```

Figure 8-1: A typical till receipt.

Q. How would you use the information in Figure 8-1 to develop an entry for your bookkeeping system that would enable you to record this sales transaction in your books?

A. The The key numbers you need to use are Total Sales, Subtotal Sales, and VAT. Here is what the bookkeeping entry would look like:

	Debit	*Credit*
Cash received	£52.88	
Sales		£45.00
VAT @ 17.5%		£7.88

Cash receipts for 25/2/2009

The information from this journal entry, would be recorded in your Sales Journal. For more information about Sales Journals and other types of journals you need to maintain, read Chapter 5. Note that you would enter a Debit to the bank account and a Credit to the Sales and VAT accounts. An equal amount was posted to both the Debits as to the Credits. That should always be true. Your bookkeeping entries should always be in balance. These entries would increase the amount in all three accounts. To understand more about how Debits and Credits work read Chapter 2.

Most likely when you work for a company, you will get a summary of total sales for the day and may not necessarily need to add up each receipt. It all depends on the types of cash registers used in your business. The entry into your books would most likely be a total of cash sales on a daily basis.

The VAT rate used at the time of writing is 17.5 per cent. The rate prior to this was temporarily reduced to 15 per cent.

Exercise 1

How would you record this transaction in your books, if you were the bookkeeper for a hardware business?

HANDSONS Hardware			
Sales Receipt 25/2/2009			
Item	**Quantity**	**Price**	**Total**
Hammer	1	£15.00	£15.00
Paint Brushes	5	£5.00	£25.00
Paint	2 Gallons	£10.00	£20.00
Subtotal			£60.00
VAT @ 17.5%			£10.50
Total Sale			£70.50
Paid by Visa Credit Card			£70.50

Exercise 2

How would you record this transaction in your books, if you were a bookkeeper for an office supply business?

SIMPLY STATIONERY

Sales Receipt 05/03/2009

Item	Quantity	Price	Total
Paper	2 boxes	£10.00	£20.00
Print Cartridge	1	£15.00	£15.00
Hanging Files	2 boxes	£5.00	£10.00
Subtotal			£45.00
VAT @ 17.5%			£7.88
Total Sale			£52.88
Paid by Personal Cheque			£52.88

Figure 8-3:
Sales
Receipt
for Simply
Stationery
on
05/03/2009.

Exercise 3

How would you record this transaction in your books, if you were a bookkeeper for an office supply business?

Simply Stationery Sales Summary for 05/03/2009			
Item	*Quantity*	*Price*	*Total*
Paper	10 boxes	£10.00	£100.00
Print Cartridges	5	£15.00	£75.00
Hanging Files	7 boxes	£5.00	£35.00
Envelopes	10 boxes	£7.00	£70.00
Pens	20 boxes	£8.00	£160.00
Subtotal			£440.00
VAT @ 17.5%			£77.00
Total Cash Sales			£517.00

You can also track stock using the information collected in the sales receipt. We talk more about that in Chapter 7.

Selling on Credit

All of the examples we've mentioned in this chapter so far have referred to Cash sales. The customer has paid for the goods at the time he or she receives the goods. However, many businesses also decide to allow their customers to buy using credit offered directly by the business. In these cases the account is not offered by a bank, but instead by the business owner. This gives the business owner the ability to be more flexible about the credit terms and may help to attract customers who otherwise couldn't buy items in the business. Buying on credit means that the customer can collect the goods, but does not have to pay for them immediately. The business which has sold the goods to the customer will issue a sales invoice to the customer and will expect that invoice to be paid in 30 days time. (30 days is the norm but other terms may be agreed at the point of sale and these terms should be documented on the invoice).

If you are the bookkeeper for a company that does allow customers to buy on credit, you will be responsible for recording the sales transactions, as well as maintaining the individual records of customers who buy on business credit.

As a bookkeeper, you can get all the information you need to enter credit transactions in the books from your sales invoices. On the invoice, you will find information regarding the customers name and address and account number, the date and value of the sale and any VAT associated with it, and also any discount that may have been given.

Suppose you are the bookkeeper for a stationers, which does allow customers to buy on credit. You sell some A4 Copy paper for £46 to The Village Shop on 21 April 2009. See Figure 8.4 which shows the invoice that has been prepared for The Village Shop.

Invoice
Simply Stationery

32 High Street, Benton, Digbyshire. DG17 2LD
Tel: 01234 567890 Fax: 01234 567891
Email: Sales@simplystationery.co.uk
WWW.simplystationary.co.uk
VAT Reg: 862 113 49

Invoice to: **Invoice No: 105**

The Village Shop,
69 Bradbury Way,
Benton,
Digbyshire
DG17 4LY

Date: 21.04.09

Description	Qty	Price	Total	Discount	Net
A4 Copy Paper	20	£2.00	£40.00	£0.00	£40.00

Terms 30 Days

Goods Total	**£40.00**
Less Discount	**£00.00**
Net Sales	**£40.00**
VAT@ 17.5%	**£7.00**
Total Sales	**£47.00**

Figure 8-4:
A sales invoice from Simply Stationery.

Q. Using details from the invoice shown in figure 8.4, here's how you would make the following entries in your bookkeeping system to record this sales transaction:

A. The key numbers you need to use are Total Sales, Net Sales and VAT. You also need the customer name and account number. Here is what the bookkeeping entry would look like:

	Debit	*Credit*
Debtors (Accounts Receivable)	£47.00	
Sales		£40.00
VAT @ 17.5%		£ 7.00

In addition to recording the sales transaction in your Sales Journal, you also need to record the transaction in the customer's account. You can maintain that account on a computer worksheet, in a paper journal, or on cards for each customer. Whichever way your company tracks individual customer accounts, here's the entry that you would need to make to the account of The Village Shop:

21/04/2009   A4 copy paper Invoice No 105   £47.00

When you record a transaction in a customer's account, you want to be sure you have enough identifying information to be able to find the original sales transaction in case the customer questions the invoice. Each sales invoice will be given a sequential number and it is sensible to file the sales invoices in that order. It is then very easy to locate an invoice if the customer can provide you with the invoice number.

Exercise 4

Using the invoice shown in figure 8.5 below, how would you record this credit transaction in your books, if you were the bookkeeper for Handsons hardware?

Invoice
Handsons Hardware

Unit 10 Leestone Industrial Unit, Newtown, Digbyshire. DG14 7PQ
Tel: 01234 123456 Fax: 01234 123457
Email: Sales@handsonshardware.co.uk
WWW.handsonshardware.co.uk
VAT Reg: 978 654 49

Invoice to:

Jo Tester,
74 Acacia Avenue
Benton,
Digbyshire
DG17 4GH

Invoice No: 4567
Account No: 789

Date: 25.02.09

Description	Qty	Price	Total	Discount	Net
A4 Copy Paper	1	£15.00	£15.00	0.00	£15.00
Paint brushes	5	£5.00	£25.00	0.00	£25.00
Paint	2 Gall	£10.00	£20.00	0.00	£20.00

Terms 30 Days

Goods Total	**£60.00**
Less Discount	**£00.00**
Net Sales	**£60.00**
VAT@ 17.5%	**£10.50**
Total Sales	**£70.50**

Figure 8-5:
Sales invoice for Handson's Hardware.

Exercise 5

Using the invoice shown in figure 8.6 below, how would you record this credit transaction in your books, if you were a bookkeeper for an office supply business?

Invoice
Simply Stationary

32 High Street, Benton, Digbyshire. DG17 2LD
Tel: 01234 567890 Fax: 01234 567891
Email: Sales@simplystationary.co.uk
WWW.simplystationary.co.uk
VAT Reg: 862 113 49

Invoice to:

Sues Insurance Agency,
23 High Street,
Benton,
Digbyshire
DG17 4LU

Invoice No: 124

Date: 05.03.09

Description	Qty	Price	Total	Discount	Net
A4 Copy Paper	2	£15.00	£30.00	0.00	£30.00
Print cartridge	1	£25.00	£25.00	0.00	£25.00
Hanging Files	2	£10.00	£20.00	0.00	£20.00

Terms 30 Days

Goods Total	£75.00
Less Discount	£00.00
Net Sales	£75.00
VAT@ 17.5%	£13.00
Total Sales	£88.25

Figure 8-6: Sales invoice for Simply Stationery.

Checking Your Register

You want to be sure that none of your cashiers make mistakes during the day in giving change to customers. You also want to be sure that your cashiers don't decide to pocket any of the cash for themselves.

You monitor cash by knowing exactly how much cash was in the register at the beginning of the day and then checking how much cash is left at the end of the day. You should count the cash at the end of the day as soon as all sales transactions have been completed. You should also print out a summary of all transactions. In many companies the sales manager will actually cash up the register at night working with the cashiers and give you the copy of the completed cash register summary.

After you get that information you can complete a cash summary form that looks something like this:

Cash Register: _____	Date: _____	
Receipts	**Sales**	**Cash in Register**
Beginning Cash	------------	
Cash Sales		
Credit Card Sales		
Credit Account Sales		
Total Sales		
Minus Credit Sales		
Total Cash Received		
Total Cash that Should be in Register		
Actual Cash in Register		
Difference		

Using the following sales summary and knowing that you began the day with £100 in the register and ended the day with £316.25 in the register we can check whether the ending cash total is correct.

Sales summary for 05/03/2009

Item	Quantity	Price	Total
Paper	10 boxes	£15.00	£150.00
Print cartridges	5	£25.00	£125.00
Hanging Files	7 boxes	£10.00	£70.00
Envelopes	10 boxes	£7.00	£70.00
Pens	20 boxes	£8.00	£160.00
Subtotal			£575.00
VAT @ 17.5%			£100.63
Total cash sales			£225.63
Total Credit Card sales			£200.00
Total Business credit sales			£250.00
Total Sales			£675.63

We need to complete the following cash summary form, to check whether the cash in the till at the end of the day is correct.

Cash Register: Sales Summary		Date: 5/3/2009
Receipts	**Sales**	**Cash in Register**
Beginning Cash		£100.00
Cash Sales	£225.63	
Credit Card Sales	£200.00	
Credit Account Sales	£250.00	
Total Sales	£675.63	
Minus credit Sales	(£450.00)	
Total Cash Received		£225.63
Total Cash that Should be in Register		£325.63
Actual Cash in Register		£330.63
Difference		Overage of £5.00

So in this example, with the cash remaining in the cash register, the cashier actually took in £5 more than needed. This was most likely an error in giving change.

Exercise 6

Use the information in the Cash Register summary shown below to complete the blank cash summary form below. Also assume that the cash register had £100 at the beginning of the day and £416.50 at the end of the day. Is there a difference between how much should be in the register and how much is in there?

Cash Register Summary for Jane Doe on 15/3/2009			
Item	**Quantity**	**Price**	**Total**
Paper	20 boxes	£15.00	£300.00
Print Cartridges	10	£25.00	£250.00
Envelopes	10 boxes	£7.00	£70.00
Pens	20 boxes	£8.00	£160.00
Subtotal			£780.00
VAT @17.5 %			£136.50
Total Cash Sales			£316.50
Total Credit Card Sales			£200.00
Total Credit Account Sales			£400.00
Total Sales			£916.50

Cash Register: _____		Date: _____
Receipts	**Sales**	**Cash in Register**
Beginning Cash		_____
Cash Sales	_____	
Credit Card Sales	_____	
Credit Account Sales	_____	
Total Sales	_____	
Minus Credit Sales	_____	
Total Cash Received		_____
Total Cash that Should be in Register		_____
Actual Cash in Register		_____
Difference		_____

Discounting Sales

You may find one other twist to recording sales. Sometimes a business will offer discounts during a sale. You want to keep track of your sales discounts separately, so you know how much money your company lost to discounting over the year. While sales discounts certainly generate traffic, it's important to carefully track how frequently you needed to offer these discounts to encourage traffic or stay competitive with other similar retail businesses.

You may find you need to adjust your retail prices to better meet the actual going price on the market, which means you may need to adjust your anticipated profit levels for the year. If your project does come in below what you expect, you will then have the detailed information you need to determine what impacted your sales revenue.

As you record a transaction in your books, you will add an account called Sales Discounts to track any discounts you offer throughout the year.

This is how you would record this sales transaction for Handsons Hardware.

Invoice

Handsons Hardware

Unit 10 Leestone Industrial Unit, Newtown, Digbyshire. DG14 7PQ

Tel: 01234 123456   Fax: 01234 123457

Email: Sales@handsonshardware.co.uk

WWW.handsonshardware.co.uk

VAT Reg: 978 654 49

Invoice to:

Jo Tester,
74 Acacia Avenue
Benton,
Digbyshire
DG17 4GH

Invoice No: 4567
Account No: 789

Date: 25.02.09

Description	Qty	Price	Total
A4 Copy Paper	1	£15.00	£15.00
Paint brushes	5	£5.00	£25.00
Paint	2 Gall	£10.00	£20.00

Terms 30 Days

Goods Total	**£60.00**
Less Discount	**£6.00**
Net Sales	**£54.00**
VAT@ 17.5%	**£9.45**
Total Sales	**£63.45**

Figure 8-7:
Sales
Invoice with
discount.

Looking at the invoice you will see that there is a discount amount shown. You need to enter the total sales before discount (in this case £60) and then post the discount amount to a sales discount account.

Here is what the bookkeeping entry would look like:

	Debit	*Credit*
Cash in bank	£63.45	
Sales Discount	£6.00	
Sales		£60.00
VAT Collected		£9.45

Note the rules of double entry book keeping ensure that the total of both the debit and credit entries are equal – both total to £69.45.

Exercise 7

Using the sales receipt below. How would you record this transaction in your books, if you were a bookkeeper for an office supply business? Design a sales invoice using the information supplied and show the book keeping transactions. Be as creative as you wish with the name and address of the office supply business. Use the examples of previous sales invoices shown in figures 8.4 to 8.7 to help you with the design of the invoice.

Sales Receipt 05/03/2009

Item	Quantity	Price	Total
Paper	2 box	£15.00	£30.00
Print Cartridge	1	£15.00	£15.00
Hanging Files	2 boxes	£5.00	£10.00
Subtotal			£55.00
Sales Discount @ 20%			£11.00
Sales after discount			£44.00
VAT @ 17.5%			£7.70
Total Cash Sale			£51.70

Exercise 8

How would you record this credit transaction in your books, if you were a bookkeeper for an office supply business?

Sales Summary for 05/03/2009

Item	Quantity	Price	Total
Paper	10 boxes	£15.00	£150.00
Print Cartridges	5	£15.00	£75.00
Hanging Files	7 boxes	£5.00	£35.00
Envelopes	10 boxes	£7.00	£70.00
Pens	20 boxes	£8.00	£160.00
Subtotal			£490.00
Sales Discount @20%			£98.00
Sales after discount			£392.00
VAT @ 17.5%			£68.60
Total Cash Sales			£135.60
Total Credit Card Sales			£150.00
Total Credit Account Sales			£175.00
Total Sales			£460.60

Recording Sales Returns and Allowances

Some customers decide they don't want the products they bought and return them to the business. You must track these sales returns separately in your books. Another type of transaction you must track separately is sales allowances, which include sales incentive programme such as gift cards.

Sales returns

Although it might be easier to decide on a no-return policy, that would surely result in very unhappy customers; instead, a business owner must decide what the rules will be for sales returns and how they will be handled logistically. Here are common rules for sales returns:

✔ Returns will only be allowed within 30 days of purchase.

✔ You must have a receipt to return an item.

✔ If you return an item without a sales receipt, you will receive a credit note

The person who owns the business for which you are doing the bookkeeping can set up whatever return policies he sees fit. After the policies are determined, the critical issue is how the sales returns will be monitored internally to be sure the return process is not used by cashiers to pocket extra cash. In most businesses, a manager's approval is required for a sales return and the manager should carefully check to see how the customer paid for the item. A customer who paid with cash can receive cash back, but a customer who paid by credit card can only get a credit to that card. Only after a manager approves a return can the cashier give that customer either the cash or the credit to their card. If the business's policy is only to give credit notes on returns, then a copy of the credit note would be given to the customer.

Have a look at Figure 8.8 for an example of a credit note that has been issued by Handsons Hardware for some paint that has been returned.

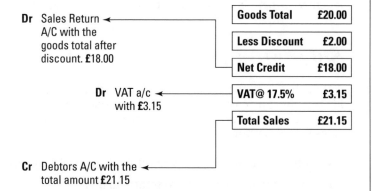

CREDIT NOTE

Handsons Hardware

Unit 10 Leestone Industrial Unit, Newtown, Digbyshire. DG14 7PQ
Tel: 01234 123456   Fax: 01234 123457
Email: Sales@handsonshardware.co.uk
WWW.handsonshardware.co.uk
VAT Reg: 978 654 49

Invoice to: **Invoice No: 4567**
                                                          Account No: 789
Jo Tester,
74 Acacia Avenue
Benton,
Digbyshire
DG17 4GH

Date: 25.02.09

Description	Qty	Price	Total
Paint	2	£10.00	£20.00
Reason: Wrong Colour			

Terms 30 Days

Dr Sales Return ◄─────────────── | **Goods Total** | **£20.00** |
A/C with the
goods total after | **Less Discount** | **£2.00** |
discount. £18.00
                                        | **Net Credit** | **£18.00** |

Dr VAT a/c ◄─────────── | **VAT@ 17.5%** | **£3.15** |
with £3.15
                             | **Total Sales** | **£21.15** |

Cr Debtors A/C with the ◄─────────────
total amount £21.15

Figure 8-8:
An example
of a credit
note,
annotated
with double
entry trans-
actions.

When you look at the credit note, you'll see that a reason has been given for the return: the wrong colour paint was sent. You'll also notice that the credit note layout looks very similar to an invoice layout. You must be careful when entering invoices and credit notes into your bookkeeping system. Some people separate all their credit notes and enter them all in one go – this ensures that you are not swapping and changing between both invoices and credit notes where a mistake could easily be made in the double entry bookkeeping required. A credit note requires the opposite bookkeeping entries to an invoice as it is effectively cancelling out the original invoice value for the item(s) concerned.

Sales allowances

Sales allowances are sales incentives programme to get the customer to come back to the business again. The most popular type of sales allowance today is the gift card. With a gift card the customer pays cash up front and gets a gift card that can be used by the customer or any other person that gets the card. Gift cards are actually a liability for the business because the business got the cash, but the customer is still owed an item in exchange for that cash at some time in the future.

Tracking sales returns and allowances

Often sales returns and allowances are tracked using one account called Sales Returns and Allowances that is subtracted from total Sales. When you see an Profit and Loss Statement you usually see the term "Net Sales." That means that adjustments were made to total sales, which includes this subtraction for sales returns and allowances.

A customer returns a blouse she bought for £40 using cash. She has a receipt showing when she made the original purchase. The rate of VAT is 17.5 per cent. Here is how you would record the transaction in the books:

	Debit	Credit
Sales Returns and Allowances	£34.04	
VAT	£5.96	
Bank Account		£40.00

When you return the amount of the purchase to the customer you must also adjust that amount by adding the taxes the customer paid and subtracting those taxes from the VAT control account. This transaction would increase the balance in the Sales Returns and Allowances account, would decrease the balance in the VAT control account, and would decrease the amount in the Bank account.

Exercise 9

A customer returns a pair of trousers he bought for £35 using a credit card. He has a receipt showing when he made the original purchase. The rate of VAT is 17.5 per cent. How would you record that transaction in the books?

Exercise 10

On December 15 Jean Jones, a customer of Simply Stationery, returns a filing cabinet she bought on 1 December for £75 on credit. She has already been issued with a sales invoice but has not yet paid for it. Design a credit note for this transaction and state how you would record that transaction in the books.

Note: The rate of VAT is 17.5 per cent.

Monitor Collections from Your Customers

Whenever your company sells to customers on credit, you will need to monitor how quickly your customers are paying their invoices. You also need to keep track of customers who aren't paying on time. As you do your invoices at the end of the month, make a list of all your customers and how much money they have outstanding in their accounts and the date on which the original charge was made.

Here is a list of five customers who bought on credit from the office supply business and have not yet paid their invoices as of 31/03/2009:

Customer	Date of Purchase	Amount Purchased
Sue's Insurance Company	05/03/2009	£79.50
Joe Tester	25/02/2009	£64.20
Chapstone's Coffee Shop	15/2/2009	£85.60
Jane Doe	15/01/2009	£49.50
Harry Man	23/03/2009	£89.20

In addition to sending out invoices on April 2, you should also prepare an Aged Debtors Summary for your manager that summarises all your customers that owe you money. It is so called, because it groups the invoices into different ageing categories, for example, current, 31–60 days, 61–90 days and 90+ days.

You would group this summary based on time of purchase.

Here is an example of an Aged Debtors Summary report as of March 31 for all outstanding customer accounts:

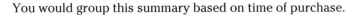

Aged Debtors Summary: As of March 31, 2009				
Customer	Current	31–60 Days	61–90 Days	90+ Days
Sue's	£79.50			
Tester		£64.20		
Chapstones		£85.60		
Jane Doe			£49.50	
Harry Man	£89.20			
Totals	£168.70	£149.80	£49.50	

You can quickly see who is behind in their invoices and how much old debt you have on your books. You should give a copy of this information to your manager, as well as the sales or business manager so they can make decisions about whether or not they want to continue offering credit to customers who aren't paying their invoices. Your company will also need to establish a collections process.

Exercise 11

Use the information from the account list below to set up an **Aged Debtors Summary as of 30/04/2009:**

Customer	Date of Purchase	Amount Purchased
Sarah Smith	05/04/2009	£37.85
Joe James	15/03/2009	£63.20
Manny's Restaurant	20/03/2009	£135.20
Manny's Restaurant	15/04/2009	£128.75
Harry Harris	25/02/2009	£49.50
Maury Man	05/01/2009	£89.20

Writing Off Bad Accounts

Sometimes your company will have to accept the fact that you'll never collect the money from some customers. When that happens you'll need to write off the loss as a bad debt. Each company sets its own policy on how long they will keep an account on the books before it is written off as bad debt.

Q. Suppose your company determines that it will write off bad debt after it's six months past due. After completing your Aged Debtors Summary on 30/04/2009, you find that you have two accounts totalling £157.45 that are more than 6 months past due. You would record that information in your books as follows:

A.

	Debit	*Credit*
Bad Debt	£157.45	
Debtors		£157.45

Accounts written off for bad debt as of 30/04/2009

Exercise 12

You discover after compiling your Aged Debtors Report for 30/06/2009 that you have an account that is more than six months past due for a total of £125.65. Your company policy is that you write off bad debt once an account is more than six months late. How would you record this transaction in your books?

Answers to Problems on Calculating and Monitoring Sales

1   Note: You may have a seperate bank account you use to record credit card recieipts. In the interestes of simplicity we have used a basic bank account. Handson's Hardware would record the sales receipts transactions as follows:

	Debit	*Credit*
Bank Account	£70.50	
Sales		£60.00
VAT		£10.50

Cash receipts for 25/2/2009

2   Simply Stationery would record the sales receipts information as follows:

	Debit	*Credit*
Bank account	£52.88	
Sales		£45.00
VAT		£7.88

Cash receipts for 05/03/09

3   Simply Stationery would record the information from their sales summary as follows:

	Debit	*Credit*
Bank Account	£517.00	
Sales		£440.00
VAT		£77.00

Cash receipts for 05/03/09

4   You would record the sales invoice details as follows:

	Debit	*Credit*
Debtors	£70.50	
Sales		£60.00
VAT		£10.50

Credit receipts for 25/02/2009

5   You would record the sales invoice details as follows:

	Debit	*Credit*
Debtors	£88.13	
Sales		£75.00
VAT		£13.13

Credit receipts for 05/03/2009

6 Here is how you would complete the cash out form.

Cash Register: Jane Doe		Date: 15/3/2009
Receipts	*Sales*	*Cash in Register*
Beginning Cash		£100.00
Cash Sales	£316.50	
Credit Card Sales	£200.00	
Business Credit Sales	£400.00	
Total Sales	£916.50	
Minus Sales on Credit	(£600.00)	
Total Cash Received		£316.50
Total Cash that Should be in Register		£416.50
Actual Cash in Register		£406.50
Difference		Shortage of £10.00

The manager would need to investigate why the till was down by £10.

7 You can use figures 8.4– 8.7 to guide you in designing your invoice for these transactions. The book keeping entry will be as follows:

	Debit	Credit
Bank account	£51.70	
Sales Discount	£11.00	
Sales		£55.00
VAT		£7.70

Cash receipts for 05/03/09

8

	Debit	Credit
Bank account	£285.60	
Debtors	£175.00	
Sales Discount	£98.00	
Sales		£490.00
VAT		£68.60

Cash receipts for 05/03/09

9 The entry would be

	Debit	Credit
Sales Returns and Allowance	£29.79	
VAT	£5.21	
Bank Account		£35.00

Even though the customer is receiving a credit on his credit card, you would show this refund by crediting your bank account. Remember when a customer uses a credit card the card is processed by the bank and cash is deposited in the business's bank account.

10 The double entry book keeping would be:

	Debit	*Credit*
Sales Returns and Allowances	£63.83	
VAT	£11.17	
Debtors		£75.00

11 Here is what an Aging Summary report would look like:

Aging Summary: As of April 30, 2009

Customer	*Current*	*31–60 Days*	*61–90 Days*	*>90 Days*
Sarah Smith	£37.85			
Joe James		£63.20		
Manny's	£128.75	£135.20		
Harry Harris			£49.50	
Maury Man				£89.20
Totals	£166.60	£198.40	£49.50	£89.20

12

	Debit	*Credit*
Bad Debt	£125.65	
Debtors		£125.65

Accounts written off for bad debt as at 30/06/09.

Chapter 9

Paying Your Employees

· ·

In This Chapter

▶ Establishing payroll

▶ Paying taxes

▶ Calculating pay

· ·

Most businesses do employ a number of people. Unless the business has only one employee (the owner), it probably pays some employees, offers benefits, and manages a payroll. In this chapter you will explore employee staffing issues the bookkeeper may need to manage. In addition you'll practise key aspects of the payroll function that fall to the bookkeeper.

Setting Up Payroll

In many small companies, the bookkeeper takes the responsibility for being certain that all the necessary payroll forms are completed when a new person is hired.

One of the best places to look for information when setting up a new payroll, or even just employing a new person, is the Her Majesty's Revenues and Customs (HMRC) website which can be found at www.hmrc.gov.uk. If you click on the 'new employers' link, you will be taken to the help area for new employers. If you are a bit of a technophobe, and prefer to use the phone, dial 0845 607 0143 and talk to someone on the New Employer Helpline.

Before you even start to pay your staff, you need to make sure you have the following:

✔ **PAYE tax reference**: Any company operating a payroll scheme must have an Employer's PAYE reference in order to employ staff. Without this reference you will be unable to legally pay staff and deduct PAYE (Pay As You Earn) tax and NI (National Insurance). This reference is typically a three digit number (this signifies the tax office) and is then followed by four alpha characters (to identify the employer). Contact HMRC to obtain an employer reference number.

✔ **National Insurance Number**: Every person you pay must have an National Insurance Number. This number enables HMRC to track the amount of money you pay this individual, as well as the amount of PAYE tax and NI you have collected and paid across on their behalf.

In addition to receiving your new employer's tax reference, you should also receive a New Employers Guide. This includes a CD which includes details of online help and a PAYE and NI calculator to help you work out how much to pay people. Obviously this is only relevant if you are operating a manual payroll system: For those of you lucky enough to be operating a computerised payroll system, the computer will work out how much tax and National Insurance to deduct automatically. The system is, however, only as good as the information you enter, so you need to make sure you have accurate details of individuals' tax codes and cumulative amounts paid to date.

New Starter Forms

Each new member of staff should be required to fill in a New Starter Form with the company. This form will provide the information needed to set up the employee on a payroll system (whether it be manual or computerised). Details such as name, address, date of birth and NI number are required, but also information about the job, such as the department, rate of pay or annual salary and start date. The payroll department also need to know how that person is to be paid, such as weekly or monthly.

Requesting a P45

In addition to the usual personal details, the employee needs to provide a P45, which should be given to her when she leaves her previous employment. The information contained on the P45 will allow the new employer to deduct the correct amount of tax and National Insurance.

A P45 contains 4 parts (carbon copies).

- ✔ **Part 1:** This shows details about the person at the point at which they left their last job. It includes the name, address, National Insurance number and leaving date of the employee, along with the tax codes and amount of tax paid to date. The previous employer completes this form and sends the top copy (part 1), to the local Inland Revenue office. This ensures that the tax office is informed that the employee has left his/her job.

- ✔ **Part 1a:** This is an exact copy of part 1 which the employee can keep for his/her records.

- ✔ **Part 2:** This contains information that you as a new employer need to know about your new employee. It will include details of the tax code used by the previous employer and the cumulative pay and tax paid to date, this information can be used, provided you are still in the same tax year.

- ✔ **Part 3:** You need to complete this section as a new employer. The information in parts 1 to 7 has already been completed by the previous employer, need to complete sections 8 to 16 and then sign the declaration in box 17 and send the form back to your local Inland Revenue office.

Completing a P46 for employees without a P45

You might find that your new employee doesn't have a P45 to give you. They may have lost it, or they may simply have taken on an extra job, to give them some extra money. In this instance they must complete a P46.

The P46 is a substitute for the P45. The new employee should complete section 1 and the new employer (you) completes section 2. You then send the completed form to your local tax office as soon as possible.

For those of you operating a manual payroll, make sure you have enough copies of P45 and P46 forms for the foreseeable future. Check your New Employer Guide for any copies that may have been included. If not, phone the Employer Orderline on 0845 7 646 646.

If you are running a computerised payroll system such as Sage Payroll, you can print off copies of completed P45's from the software. You can even send these directly to HMRC if you have set up the online PAYE service. Check the website www.hmrc.gov.uk for more details of the online services available.

Completing forms for foreign workers

It is your responsibility as an employer in the UK to verify that any person you hire is a UK citizen or has a right to work in the UK.

If you are in any doubt, you must ask to see his/her passport or Home Office Work Permit.

Exercise 1

Design a New Starter Details form. What information should be included on this form to help you set up a new employee?

Determining pay periods

Companies can operate using different pay periods. As the bookkeeper you will need to keep track of how frequently each employee is paid. Often a company will pay hourly employees (employees paid based on an hourly rate) on a weekly or fortnightly basis and salaried employees (employees paid based on a set monthly income rather than based on the number of hours worked) on a monthly basis. See details below:

- **Weekly:** Employees receive their pay each week and payroll must be done 52 times a year.

- **Fortnightly:** Employees receive their pay every two weeks and payroll must be done 26 times a year.

- **Monthly:** Employees receive one payment per month and payroll must be done 12 times a year.

Whichever pay period is selected, it must be kept consistently. The payroll department will usually learn about the pay period for each employee from the New Starter form which is required to be completed in order to set up new members of staff on the payroll.

Ensure that you put the pay period on your new starter form.

Exercise 2

Design a payroll checklist identifying who should be paid weekly and monthly and tick off as you complete each payroll.

Collecting Employee Payroll Taxes

Another key responsibility of the bookkeeper when preparing payroll is to collect all the government taxes due from the employees. Yes, employers do play tax collector when they dole out salaries, and must reduce those cheques by the amount of taxes due. In fact, you will collect both PAYE (Pay As You Earn taxes) and National Insurance contributions.

As a bookkeeper, you need to know how to calculate tax and National Insurance deductions and all the other intricacies of payroll. It is often money well spent to employ a payroll bureau who will operate the payroll for you. This will free up a lot of your time, particularly if you were thinking of adopting a manual payroll system. The cost of using a payroll bureau is not prohibitive and may well be the best money you ever spent.

If you are still adamant about doing it yourself, then at least consider one of the off-the-shelf payroll packages such as Sage. These are very easy to use and make operating payroll a much more accurate and speedier process than doing it by hand.

Calculating National Insurance Contributions (NICs)

The easiest way to calculate the NI contributions, assuming you are not using a computerised system, is to use the NICs calculator on the Employer CD that is sent to you as part of the welcome pack.

The NICs are made up of two parts:

✔ **Employees contribution**: The part deducted from your employees' pay.
✔ **Employers contribution**: The part your business must pay.

Several different categories of NICs exist depending on the age of the employee. If you are not sure of the category, then seek advice from HMRC at its website www.hmrc.gov.uk.

Most women between the ages of 16 and 59 and most men between the ages of 16 and 64 fall into category A, which we refer to later in this chapter as Table A. If you are not going to use the Employer CD and wish to calculate the NI manually, you will need booklet CA38, National Insurance Contribution tables A & J, from HMRC. You must make sure the tables you have are for the correct year.

To use the tables you must:

1. Look up the employees gross pay on the left hand column of the table 'Employees earnings up to and including the UEL (Upper Earnings Limit)'. If the exact amount is not shown, then use the lower amount closest to the exact gross pay.

2. Record these figures in each column of the table onto the employees form P11 Deductions Working Sheet. Available from the Employer Orderline.

Q. Dora is paid £182.62 for week 39 in the tax year 08/09.

Using the NI tables how much NI should she pay?

A. Total of employers and employees contributions is £18.44, with Dora's employee contribution being £8.52.

Using the National Insurance tables which can be found on www.hmrc.gov.uk/nitables/ca38.pdf or using the NI calculator on the CD ROM answer the following exercises.

Exercise 3

Using tables for the tax year ended 5 April 2009. Daniel earns £310.53 in week 42. How much is the employer NIC contribution?

Exercise 4

Using tables for the tax year ended 5 April 2009. Jilly earns £1500 per month. For month 5, how much NI should she pay?

Working out PAYE tax

This is even more complex than working out the National Insurance contributions, as you have to take into account an individual's tax code (of which many different ones exist!)

A tax code is normally made up of one or more numbers followed by a letter. The number indicates the amount an employee is able to earn tax free in each tax year. For example an employee with a tax code 500L can earn £5000 in the current tax year before becoming liable to pay tax.

If the tax code is followed by a Week1/month1 or an X, instead of keeping a running total of the pay to date, you should treat each payment as though it were the first week or month of the tax year.

Tax codes work on an annual cumulative tax allowance. For example, a tax code of 603L means that the employee can earn £6030 tax-free in a complete tax year. If they are paid weekly, this amounts to £115.96 per week tax free. By the end of week 8 the employee will have been entitled to 8/52 of £6030, in other words £927.69.

If an employee is given a tax code BR (Basic Rate) this means that all the pay is liable to tax. There is no tax-free allowance. The BR code can also be followed by a week 1 or month 1 which means you are working on a non-cumulative basis. If a week 1 or month1 does not apply, you work on a running total basis of 'total pay to date' at the end of each pay day.

The basic rate of income tax is currently 20 per cent.

The easiest way to calculate tax is to use the tax calculator on your employer CD. The calculator provides you with the columns you need to complete the P11 deduction working sheet.

Calculating the PAYE deduction for a weekly paid employee

Looking at the same example as earlier, Dora is paid £182.62 for week 39 in the tax year 08/09. You need to calculate the amount of tax to be paid. You have a copy of her P45 and this states:

- ✔ Her tax code is 603L
- ✔ The pay year to date is £6939.56.
- ✔ The total tax to date is £505.00

You must enter the above information onto the P11 Deduction Sheet.

- ✔ **Column 2:** This shows this weeks pay of £182.62

- ✔ **Column 3:** This shows the *cumulative pay* (£6939.56 + 182.62) = £7122.18

- ✔ **Column 4a – Total Free Pay to date:** Find the page in Tax Table A for week 39 and read off the amounts. For week 39 the tax free amount is £4536.48 (made up of £3756.87 & £779.61). Because of the way the tax tables are set up, you need to read what 500 is and then 103 for week 39, as the tables only go up to 500. This explains the two figures in the brackets earlier. Enter £4536.48 into column 4a for week 39.

- ✔ **Column 5 – Total taxable pay to date:** This is a straight forward calculation, taking column 3 and deducting column 4a. In this example you should enter £2585.70 (£7122.18 - £4536.48).

- ✔ **Column 6 – Total tax due to date:** You will need your Taxable Pay Tables, Calculator Method. See www.hmrc.gov.uk. For weekly paid staff see pages 2,3 & 4. For monthly paid, see page 5. In our example, the taxable pay figure is £2585.70, we need to round down this amount to the nearest pound and multiply by 0.20. This gives us £517, which should be entered in column 6 against week 39.

- ✔ **Column 7 – Tax deducted or refunded:** We have to assume that the 'Total tax to date' figure on the P45 is correct. If the figure in column 6 week 39 is greater than the figure in column 6 for week 38, then that tax is to be deducted. In this exercise, the total tax paid to date up to week 38 is £505.00 and for week 39 it has been calculated as £517. Thus a tax payment of £12 is due.

Exercise 5

Using the Inland Revenue tax calculator (or tax tables if you are feeling masochistic) work out how much tax and National Insurance Debbie Day should pay.

- ✔ Start date 1 September 2008
- ✔ Paid £1500 monthly
- ✔ P45 pay to date £7500
- ✔ P45 tax paid to date £996.60
- ✔ Tax code 603L

Statutory Payments

In addition to being able to calculate tax and National Insurance deductions, you also need to be aware of the following statutory payments and how they are calculated.

Stationary Sick Pay (SSP)

Employees who are off sick for more than three consecutive days are entitled to statutory sick pay. The first three days off are called *waiting days* and don't qualify for SSP.

Statutory Maternity Pay (SMP)

For the tax year ended 5 April 2009, all employed women are legally entitled to a total of 52 weeks maternity leave regardless of their length of service. Statutory maternity pay is a legal entitlement to a certain amount of pay to help the mother take time off around the birth of a baby, and can last for up to 39 weeks.

The new rates for SMP from 6 April 2008 are:

- ✔ First 6 weeks: 90 per cent of average weekly earnings then
- ✔ The lower of the above or £117.18

Statutory Paternity Pay

New dads are legally entitled to take a certain amount of pay to take time off to care for a baby or support the mother in the first few weeks after birth.

SSP rates from 6 April 2008 are:

- ✔ 90 percent of average weekly earnings
- ✔ Or the lower of the above and £117.18.

You will be pleased to know that help calculating all of the above is given on the Inland Revenue CD Rom.

Once you have calculated how much tax and National Insurance to deduct, you then need to calculate how much to pay your employees. This is covered in the next section.

Figuring Out Net Pay

Net pay is the amount of money left over after subtracting all deductions including tax and national insurance from gross pay.

In the absence of gross pay, an employee may be paid statutory payments such as maternity pay or sick pay.

In its most simple terms:

Gross pay – PAYE & NI = Net pay

However, life is never that simple and there can be a whole host of different types of deductions in addition to PAYE and NI, including pensions, child support payments, county court payments and so on.

Calculating Payroll

Calculating paycheques will vary depending upon pay period, whether an employee is hourly or salaried. You also may have some employees that are paid by commission or by partial salary and commission. These variations in pay can make preparing payroll a nightmare for the bookkeeper.

Calculating pay for hourly employees

When you are calculating paycheques for hourly employees, you need to know their hourly rate and the number of hours they worked each week in the pay period.

Q. Suppose Jack, who is paid weekly, earns £12 per hour and worked 48 hours last week. How would you calculate his gross pay? You can assume that his normal working week is 40 hours and any time over this is classified as overtime.

A. You would separate the amount of timed work at standard rate pay, 40 hours, from the time worked at overtime pay 8 hours. The gross pay is then calculated as follows:

40 hours regular pay @ £12 per hour = £480

8 hours overtime pay @ £12 per hour × 1.5 overtime rate = £144

Gross pay = £480 + £144 = £624

Exercise 6

John, who gets paid fortnightly, earns £15 per hour. He worked 40 hours in the first week of the pay period and 45 hours in the second week of the pay period. How much was his gross pay? Again, we will assume that John works a standard week of 40 hours.

Calculating pay for salaried employees

Calculating pay for salaried employees can be much easier than hourly employees, since most are not eligible for overtime pay. If you do have salaried employees that are eligible for overtime pay, then you would need to calculate an hourly pay rate for these employees and use that pay rate to calculate the overtime pay.

For example if John earns £30,000 per year and is paid monthly, his gross pay is £2,500 per month.

Exercise 7

Suppose Ann earns £42,000 per year and is paid monthly. How much would her gross pay be each pay period?

Calculating pay for commissioned employees

Some employees' pay is based on their sales performance and they receive a commission based on that performance. The employee can be paid on full commission, which means all his pay is based on the volume of sales, or he may have a base salary plus commission.

If the employee has a base salary plus commission, then he gets a set amount per month plus a commission based on his sales volume. Full commission employees usually get a greater percentage of their sales volume in commission than employees who earn a base salary plus commission.

To calculate pay for a commissioned employee you need to know his commission percentage, the volume of his sales, and whether or not he has a base salary.

Q. Suppose Jack is a full commission sales person and he earns 10 per cent commission on his sales volume, what would be the amount of his gross pay if he is paid on a monthly basis and his monthly sales volume was £60,000?

A. Jack's pay would be calculated by multiplying the sales volume times his commission percentage:

£60,000 × 10 per cent = £6,000

Exercise 8

Jane earns a basic salary of £1,000 per month plus 5 per cent on her sales volume. She is paid on a monthly basis. What would her gross pay be if her sales volume was £30,000?

Calculating pay for employees who earn tips

One other complication to calculating payroll involves employees who earn tips. In most places where tips are earned, such as a restaurant, tips can sometimes count towards the national minimum wage.

There are three levels of minimum wage and the rates from 1st October 2008 are as follows:

- ✔ £5.73 for employees aged 22 years and older

- ✔ A development rate of £4.77 per hour for employees aged 18 to 21

- ✔ £3.53 per hour for all employees under the age of 18 who are no longer compulsory school age

A tip is a payment freely given by the customer in return for services. If tips are given directly to you by the customer, you are legally obliged to declare those tips to the Inland Revenue via a tax return. You'll have to pay tax on them but not NI. If your restaurant operates a *tronc* (a pool of tips) and then shares them out amongst the staff, they will be legally obliged to deduct tax from these tips, but it depends on how the tips are allocated as to whether NI is paid or not.

In simple terms, if the tronc master (the person allocating the tronc) decides who gets the tips, then you have to pay NI on them. If your employer doesn't decide or influence how the tips are paid out, then NI is not due.

For tips that are paid via debit card or credit card, it is relatively easy for the restaurant to split out the tips money and pay it either directly to you or transfer it to the tronc.

When you prepare the payroll for employees who earn tips you must pay tax on the hourly rate plus tips.

Q. If Ann earns £3.00 per hour plus £3 per hour in tips, calculate her rate of pay and gross pay? Please assume a 40 hour week.

Her gross pay would be:

£6 x 40 hours work = £240

Her taxes would be calculated based on her pay plus tips or £6 per hour.

A. Her rate of pay would combine both the tips and standard rate of pay, which would be £6 per hour, thus ensuring she is over the minimum rate of pay.

Exercise 9

Sally earns £4.00 per hour plus makes £7 per hour in tips. If she works 40 hours, what will her weekly gross pay be and what would be the total pay used to calculate her taxes?

Settling up with Revenue and Customs

Each month, you are required to pay across to HMRC all taxes and NIC collected on behalf of your employees. Each company is given what is commonly known as a 'yellow book' (Employer Payslip Booklet) containing one payslip for each payroll month. Once you have calculated the employers NIC, employees NIC, PAYE tax and any student loan repayments, you should complete a payslip voucher and accompany this with a payment to HMRC. They helpfully provide you with envelopes that are pre addressed which you can send your payment to your designated accounts office (usually to Cumbernauld in Scotland).

If you are operating a computerised payroll system, you can simply print of a P32 for the relevant payroll month and all the necessary information will be summarised for you, so that you can complete your payslip booklet with ease.

As you can see payroll can be a mind-boggling task. Many small companies avoid the headache of managing payroll and benefits by outsourcing payroll to a company that specialises in handling it. If you are responsible for payroll, you may want to research the cost of contracting these services and make a case to outsource the work.

Answers to Exercises on Paying Your Employees

1 The following information should be included on a New Employee Details Form (New Starter Form):

- ✔ Full name and address.
- ✔ Date of Birth.
- ✔ National Insurance Number.
- ✔ Date of starting employment.
- ✔ Pay period (for example monthly, fortnightly or weekly).
- ✔ Payment method, for example, cheque, cash or BACS. (Bankers Automated Clearing Service).
- ✔ Bank account information if paid by BACS. This should include sort code, account number and account name.
- ✔ Pay amount. (For example rate per hour or annual salary).
- ✔ P45 information. (Note: a P46 form must be completed if a P45 is not made available to the employer). A simple tick box (P45 Yes/No) would suffice as long as the P45 or P46 is attached to the new starter form.
- ✔ Details of any pension contributions or pension schemes that may be applicable to that employee.
- ✔ Details of any deductions that may need to be made, such as County Court payments or Child Support payments that the employee is required to pay.
- ✔ The department that this employee is going to be working in. This is sometimes necessary to code the employee costs to specific departments.

2 Payroll checklist should include the following:

- ✔ Enter new starter details and set up new employees (if required).
- ✔ Using timesheets or other input mechanism, enter the pay details for the period.
- ✔ Check for any new tax codes to apply in the month, or any other legislation that may require a tax code change (for example changes in the Budget).
- ✔ Calculate the tax and NI due (if using manual system).
- ✔ Write or print out your pay slips.
- ✔ Update your payroll if you are operating a computerised system.
- ✔ Complete a P32 form to record details of deductions for all employees including PAYE, student loans, National Insurance, Statutory Sick Pay, Statutory Maternity Pay, Statutory Adoption pay for each tax month.
- ✔ Complete your Yellow book (otherwise known as P30BC) and send your payment voucher detailing PAYE and NI due along with a cheque HMRC.

3 Daniel has earned £310.53 in week 42. Using the tables, we can see that £310 will mean that £48.90 will be the total employee and employer contribution, with the employer paying £26.30.

4 Using the NI tables, look at the £1,498 row as this is the nearest amount to £1,500. Casting out eyes across the table, the total employee and employer NI contributions is £249.19 with the employee contribution being £115.17.

5   Having used the Inland Revenue P11 calculator for the tax year 08/09 we can provide the following information:

> ***For Month 6:***

Cumulative pay to date:	£9000
Total tax free pay to date:	£3019.56
Taxable pay to date:	£5980.00
Tax due to date:	£1196
Tax paid to month 5:	£996.60
Tax due for month 6:	**£199.40**
National Insurance:	**£115.17**

6   Calculate John's gross pay

> ***Week 1***

40 hours at £15	£600

> ***Week 2***

40 hours at £15	£600
5 hours overtime at 1.5 times	£112.50
Total gross pay	**£1312.50**

7   Ann earns £42000 per annum. Her monthly gross pay is £42000/12 = £3500

8   Jane's gross pay would be:

Basic pay per month:	£1000
Commission (0.05 × £30,000)	£1500
Total gross pay	**£2500**

9   Sally's combined tips and basic rate will mean that she will be earning a rate of £11 per hour.

Based on a working week of 40 hours her gross pay will be:

40 hours × £11 per hour = £440.

Part IV
Getting Ready for Year's (Or Month's) End

'I hate the end of the financial year.'

In this part . . .

Eventually every accounting period has an end. When that end comes, whether it's the end of a month, a quarter or a year, you'll need to check your work and get ready to close out the period.

We introduce you to the process of preparing your books for closing out the accounting period. You also learn about the key adjustments needed to record depreciation of your assets (a process which tracks the use of your tangible assets, such as cars and buildings), which must be done before you close the books. Plus, you learn how to calculate and record your interest payments and income in your books.

Then we show you how to make sure your books are correct by checking your cash, testing your book's balance and making any needed adjustments or corrections.

Chapter 10

Depreciating Your Assets

. . . .

In This Chapter

▶ Understanding depreciation

▶ Figuring out an assets useful life

▶ Depreciation methods

▶ Setting depreciation schedules

. . . .

*A*ll businesses operate using assets which they hold for the long term (defined as more than a year). These assets include land, buildings, plant and machinery and motor vehicles. These assets are commonly known as Fixed Assets and have a useful life of more than 12 months.

Due to the nature of fixed assets, they tend to be large and expensive items. Following generally accepted accounting principles you are not able to *write off* (set off against profits) the expense of these items in the year that they were purchased, and instead have to depreciate the value of each asset over a number of years. Effectively this means charging a proportion of the value of the fixed assets to the Profit and Loss account over their estimated useful life. This means that you are spreading the cost of these assets and matching your costs to revenues.

This chapter introduces you to depreciation and the various methods that are used to calculate it. You get to practise the various depreciation methods and learn how to track them within your bookkeeping system.

Understanding Depreciation

You probably think of depreciation as something that happens to a new car when you drive it off the forecourt after buying it. All of a sudden your shiny new motor is worth 20 to 30 per cent less than you paid for it: that's depreciation. Well, for bookkeeping purposes depreciation is not quite the same thing. Accountants use depreciation to spread the cost of the asset over its estimated useful life to the business. As a bookkeeper, you record the full transaction when the asset is bought, but you then subtract a portion of the value of that asset as a depreciation expense. This reduces the value of the asset gradually. If you keep monthly management accounts, you record depreciation on a monthly basis, but many small businesses prepare accounts on an annual basis and therefore only do this at the end of the year, prior to preparing the year end accounts.

Not everything can be depreciated. Any item that you expect to use up in a year is not eligible for depreciation. These types of items are written off as expenses instead. You also don't depreciate land. Land does not get used up, it tends to appreciate in value. While you can't depreciate a building or car you rent or lease, if you do major renovations to a leased property you can depreciate the value of those improvements.

You cannot depreciate assets that you use outside of your business such as a personal car or computer, but you can claim a proportion of their capital allowances on your tax return. This is discussed more fully in the 'Tackling Taxes and Depreciation' section of this chapter.

Exercise 1

List three categories of assets that can be depreciated. Note: If you want to be more specific about an asset – then also state what category it would be included in.

Exercise 2

List three types of assets that cannot be depreciated and make a note of them below:

Working out the useful life of an asset

The first thing you must determine when you need to calculate the depreciation for an asset is how long that asset remains useful to the company.

Your accountant is able to advise you on the best practice for depreciation of your assets. Once you have determined a depreciation policy then you must adhere to it consistently.

Common rates of depreciation for fixed assets are as follows:

Life/Depreciation rate	*Description of asset*
10 years/10 per cent per annum	Plant and Machinery
5 years/20 per cent per annum	Office equipment, fixtures and fittings
4 years/25 per cent per annum	Motor Vehicles
3 years/33.33 per cent per cent per annum	Computers

You may find that if items such as computers need replacing more regularly then you depreciate at a much higher rate. For example, if you felt that you would only get one year's use out of your computers before you needed to upgrade, then you could depreciate at 100 per cent and write them off within the first year.

Review your business assets and make a note of the assets, depreciation rates and estimated useful life in the space below:

Determining the cost basis

The other key factor in calculating depreciation is the cost basis of an asset. The equation for cost basis is:

Cost of the fixed asset + disallowed VAT + Shipping and delivery costs + Installation charges + Other costs (such as commissions or finder's fees) = Cost basis

✔ **Cost of the fixed asset** is what you paid for that equipment, furniture, building, vehicle, or any other asset you intend to use for more than 12 months.

✔ **Disallowed VAT** is any VAT charged on the purchase of the asset that you cannot reclaim.

✔ **Shipping and delivery** includes any charges that you paid to get that asset to your place of business.

✔ **Installation charges** include any charges you paid to get that asset working in your business. That could include new electrical outlets, carpentry work, or any type of work that was needed to install the new asset.

✔ **Other costs** include any other costs involved in the purchase of the asset. This can include commissions or finder fees, as well as additional hardware such as wiring or monitors to put a new piece of equipment into operation.

Q. Calculate the cost basis of a new desk for your office. You bought the desk for £700 and you paid £50 to have it delivered.

A. Cost basis = £700 + £50 = £750

Exercise 3

Calculate the cost basis of a new piece of machinery for your factory. You bought the machine for £25,000 and paid £2000 for transportation of the machine and a further £3000 for setting up the machine in your factory.

Exercise 4

Calculate the cost basis for the renovations of the office space you just leased. You paid £20,000 for new carpet, you paid £30,000 for new office furniture, you paid £5,000 for painting the space, and you paid a contractor £15,000 to install dry wall to build out the offices.

Depreciating Your Assets

Once you know your asset's anticipated life span and its cost basis, you can then calculate how much you should write off for depreciation. Depreciation is not a cash expense. The cash expense happens when you buy the asset – or a cash inflow can happen when you sell the asset. Depreciation just shows the use of that asset, so it does not involve the use of cash. We show you how to record depreciation in the books in the section, 'Recording Depreciation Expenses.'

There are two methods of calculating depreciation: *straight-line* and *reducing balance*. We show you how to calculate each and then give you a chance to practise.

Straight-line method

Straight-line depreciation spreads out the cost of the asset over the entire useful life of an asset. It's the simplest type of depreciation to calculate. The formula is:

Cost of the asset / Estimated useful life = Annual depreciation expense

Or

Cost of asset × Depreciation rate = Annual depreciation expense

For example, a car with a value of £20,000 is estimated to have a useful life of four years. This equates to a depreciation rate of 25 per cent. The depreciation charge for each year would be: £20,000/4 = £5,000 or could also be written as £20,000 × 0.25 = £5,000.

Exercise 5

Calculate the annual depreciation expense for a copier with a cost basis of £5,000 and a depreciation rate of 20 per cent using the straight line depreciation method.

Exercise 6

Calculate the annual depreciation expense for a computer with a cost basis of £1500 and a useful life of 3 years using the straight line method of depreciation.

Reducing balance method

The reducing balance method works slightly differently to the straight line method, and comes closer to the HMRC method of calculating capital allowances. (These are discussed later in this chapter). This method does not apply the same amount of depreciation each year as the straight line method would. Instead it operates a gradually reducing amount of depreciation as each year goes by. A depreciation rate is set, usually on the useful life basis as outlined above, but rather than splitting the depreciation evenly, after the first year of depreciation the rate is applied to the net book value of the asset.

Net Book Value = Cost less accumulated depreciation

For example, using the car example from earlier in the chapter:

Cost of asset:	£20,000
Depreciation rate:	25 per cent

Year 1

Cost of asset	£20,000
Depreciation charge	£5,000 (£20,000 × 25 per cent)
Net Book Value	£15,000

Year 2

Depreciation	£3,750 (£15,000 × 25 per cent)
Net Book Value	£11,250 (£15,000 - £3,750)

Year 3

Depreciation	£2812.50 (£11,250 × 25 per cent)
Net Book Value	£8,437.50 (£11,250 - £2812.50)

And so on forever . . .

In theory the asset never gets fully depreciated, the depreciation expense just gets smaller and smaller each year.

Exercise 7

John has just bought a photocopier costing £8000. He intends to depreciate it at a rate of 20 per cent using the reducing balance method. Calculate the depreciation charges for the next three years and then write down the net book value at the end of the three year period.

Bookkeeping entries for depreciation

In terms of the bookkeeping entries, as usual there are two entries for the depreciation transaction. The depreciation charge is treated as an expense in the Profit and Loss account, so you will be debiting the Depreciation account. The opposite entry is a credit to the Accumulated Depreciation account in the Balance Sheet. This ensures that the Balance Sheet shows the reduced value of the Fixed Asset as depreciation is applied.

The journals are:

Debit	Depreciation Account (in Profit & Loss Account)
Credit	Accumulated Depreciation Account (in Balance Sheet)

Setting Schedules

Remembering how much to depreciate for each asset you have in your business can be an overwhelming task. The best way to keep track of what you need to expense each year is to set up a depreciation schedule for each type of asset that lists the date it was put into service, the description of the asset, the cost basis, the useful life, and the annual depreciation. Table 10-1 is a sample of this type of schedule.

Table 10-1	Depreciation Schedule: Vehicles			
Date Purchased	*Description*	*Cost*	*Useful Life*	*Annual Depreciation*
01/05/2009	Ford Transit FR51 CRW	£16,000	4 Years	£4,000
31/09/2009	Vauxhall Corsa FV58 TRC	£9,000	4 Years	£2,250

Note: The annual depreciation in this schedule has been calculated using the straight line basis.

Computerised systems, such as Sage 50 Accounts, have a Fixed Asset register which you can use (available in Plus and Professional models). This allows you to record all the fixed asset details in one place, such as the costs and depreciation methods and rates and then Sage calculates the depreciation for you, and even posts the journals! This makes life a lot simpler and eliminates the need for you to keep schedules for all assets as shown in Table 10-1.

Tackling Taxes and Depreciation

You need to be aware that HMRC does not recognise depreciation as being a valid business expense. This is because a business can set the rate of depreciation for any asset, and could set a very high rate of depreciation to post as much expense as possible through the Profit and Loss account for that year, thus artificially reducing the amount of taxable profit and therefore potentially reducing the tax liability for that year. Instead, HMRC insist that you use Capital Allowances, which can be set off against business profits.

In order to calculate your taxable profit for the year, HMRC states that you must *add back* your depreciation charges to your taxable profit and then deduct Capital allowances.

Capital allowances are split into categories, one of them being Plant and Machinery. However, plant and machinery also includes cars, furniture and computers as well as the usual plant and machinery. The standard allowance from April 2008 is 20 per cent of the asset value, but sometimes HMRC allow you to use First Year Allowances which can allow you to deduct from 40 per cent and sometimes 100 per cent of the asset value as capital allowances during the first year of the asset's life. You need to check the current rules with your accountant as these can change from time to time.

Quick Quiz

1. What is the purpose of depreciating assets?

2. If you wanted to apply an even amount of depreciation each car against your asset, which depreciation method would you use?

3. If you have a machine with a useful life of 4 years, what depreciation rate would you use?

4. How do you calculate net book value?

5. Which method of depreciation uses net book value in it's calculations?

Answers to Problems on Depreciating Your Assets

1   The following assets are ones that can be depreciated (this list is not exhaustive):

     ✔ Plant and machinery

     ✔ Motor vehicles

     ✔ Office equipment

     ✔ Furniture and fittings

     ✔ Computers

2   The following items are not normally depreciated:

     ✔ Small value assets – for example under £1000. Treat these as expenses for that year,

     ✔ Land

     ✔ Treat any asset with a short term life of less than one year as an expense for that year.

Any type of current asset would not be depreciated. (Eg Stock, Debtors & Cash).

3

Purchase price of machinery:	£25,000
Transportation costs	£2,000
Installation costs	£3,000
Total cost of asset	£30,000

4   The cost basis for office renovations would be:

New carpet	£20,000
Painting	£5,000
Dry wall installation	£15,000
Total cost	£40,000
New office furniture should be set up in a separate depreciation schedule with a cost basis of	£30,000.

5

Cost price of photocopier	£5,000
Depreciation (0.20 × £5,000)	£1,000

6

Cost price of computer	£1,500
Depreciation (£1500/3 years)	£500

* This equates to a depreciation rate of 33.33 per cent (100 per cent / 3 years)

7 *Year 1*

Cost of photocopier	£8,000
Depreciation at 20 per cent	£1,600 (0.20 × £8,000)
Net Book Value	£6,400

Year 2

Depreciation at 20 per cent	£1,280 (20 per cent of £6400)
Net Book Value	£5,120 (£6,400 – £1,280)

Year 3

Depreciation at 20 per cent	£1,024 (20 per cent of £5120)
Net Book Value	£4,096 (£5,120 - £1,024)

Answers to the Quick Quiz

1 The purpose of depreciation is to spread the cost of the fixed assets across their useful lives. The value of a fixed asset is shown as decreasing gradually in the accounts.

2 Straight line

3 25 per cent (100 per cent / 4 years)

4 Cost of fixed assets less accumulated depreciation

5 Reducing balance

Chapter 11

Paying and Collecting Interest

· ·

In This Chapter

▶ Exploring types of interest

▶ Calculating credit card interest

▶ Recording credit card interest

▶ Paying long-term debt interest

▶ Recording interest income

· ·

*M*ost businesses carry some debt and most pay interest on that debt. Some businesses loan money or other assets and receive interest payments.

This chapter reviews the debt types and how to calculate and record interest expenses for each type. You also get to practise how to perform interest calculations and how to track and enter interest payments into the bookkeeping system.

Determining Interest Types

Financial institutions use two different types of interest calculation when determining how much to pay you in interest for money you have on deposit, or when calculating how much you need to pay them on a loan or credit card. These two types are *simple interest* and *compound interest*.

Simple interest

Simple interest is easy to calculate. Here's the formula for calculating simple interest, where *n* represents the number of years of the loan.

Principal × Interest rate × *n* = Interest

Q. Calculate the simple interest earned over three years for a £10,000 savings account earning 3 per cent interest per year.

A. £10,000 × 0.03 × 3 = £900

Exercise 1

What is the simple interest earned over five years for a £20,000 savings account at 3 per cent?

Exercise 2

What is the simple interest earned over seven years on a £5,000 savings account at 5 per cent?

Compound interest

Compound interest is more complicated to calculate because interest is not only charged on the amount you have on deposit, it is also calculated on the interest earned during the time you have it on deposit. So when you calculate compound interest you must add the interest earned in the previous period to the balance before calculating the interest earned during the new period. Here's the formula for calculating compound interest for a three-year deposit:

Principal × Interest rate = Interest for year one

(Principal + previous accumulated interest earned) × Interest rate = Interest for year two

(Principal + previous accumulated interest earned) × Interest rate = Interest for year three

You would repeat this method of calculation for the life of the deposit.

Q. Calculate the compound interest on a £10,000 deposit at 3 per cent for three years.

A. Year one interest: £10,000 × 0.03 = £300

Year two interest: £10,300 × 0.03 = £309

Year three interest: £10,609 × 0.03 = £318.27

Total interest earned in three years = £927.27

Exercise 3

What is the compound interest earned over five years for a £20,000 savings account compounded annually at 3 per cent?

Exercise 4

What is the compound interest earned over six years for a £5,000 savings account compounded annually at 6 per cent?

When you are taking a loan, you always want to be sure you are paying simple interest. When you are opening a savings account or any other type of savings instrument with a financial institution you always want to be sure you earn compound interest. Even compound interest can be paid differently. Some banks compound your earnings monthly, which means interest earned is added to your balance before the next monthly interest calculation. For other types of accounts interest is only compounded annually. So always look for a bank that compounds your savings monthly.

Determining Interest on Debt

Businesses borrow money for both short-term (less than 12 months) and long-term business needs. Short-term debt usually includes credit cards and bank overdrafts. Long-term debt can include a 3 or 4 year car loan or 20 years or more for a mortgage. Any money paid toward interest in the current year is shown as an interest expense on the Profit and Loss Account (see Chapter 15). In this chapter we review how to calculate that interest expense.

Credit cards

As you know from your personal credit cards, if you pay the bill in full at the end of each month, you don't have any interest charges. But, if you don't pay the balance in full each month, interest is charged based on a daily periodic interest rate, which means you start paying interest from the day you make a purchase. The daily periodic rate is calculated by dividing the annual rate by 365 days. Table 11-1 shows you a typical credit card interest charge. You can find a similar table on your credit card bills, but the actual interest rates may be different depending on your credit card agreement.

Table 11-1	Credit Card Interest Calculation				
	Average Daily Balance	*Daily Periodic Rate*	*Corresponding Annual Rate*	*Daily Rate*	*Equivalent Monthly charge*
Purchases	£500	0.0340%	12.4%	£0.17	£5.27
Cash	£1000	0.0764%	27.9%	£0.76	£23.56

Q. Using Table 11-1, calculate the interest for a purchase of £1,500 made on April 15. The month closes on April 30. Assume the bill is not paid in full each month.

A. £1,500 x 0.0340 per cent × no of days= £0.51 × 15 days = £7.65

Exercise 5

Using Table 11-1, if you have purchased goods on the 1st December worth £3000, how much interest would be charged at the end of the month?

Exercise 6

Using Table 11-1, calculate the interest for a cash advance of £2,000 made on April 15. The month closes on April 30. Calculate how much interest you pay by the end of April.

You should now be able to see that interest compounded daily can be a lot more expensive than simple annual interest rate. Credit cards are definitely the most expensive way to carry a loan. Thankfully, you won't be the person calculating interest: This will have already been done for you on the monthly credit card bill. You will, however, have to post the interest that you have been charged as an interest expense in your accounts.

Recording payments on a credit card

Normally businesses have a direct debit payment set up to pay their credit cards. The amount is usually deducted from their current bank account. The actual payment of the credit card is simply a transfer of funds between the bank current account and the credit card account. An example of paying £100 off a credit card would be as follows:

	Debit	*Credit*
Credit card account	£100	
Bank Current account		£100

Obviously purchases made on the credit card which show as charges in the month to the credit card. Interest payments also accrue on the card.

Payments and interest charges have to be recorded in the accounts as well as the amount repaid each month.

For example, Bob purchases some stationery for his business costing £250. To record this purchase on the credit card:

	Debit	*Credit*
Office stationery account	£250	
Credit Card account		£250

This example is applying the traditional rules of double entry, to record an expense you debit that account and to record an increase in liability you credit the account.

You record interest charges in a similar manner. For example, you'd record interest charges of £25 on a credit card as follows:

	Debit	*Credit*
Interest charges	£25	
Credit Card account		£25

Exercise 7

Dick pays £75 off his credit card. Record the journal that he needs to make to record this transaction.

Exercise 8

Part of Dick's credit card shows that the interest accrued this month is £22.57. How would he write this journal to show this transaction?

Businesses may seek better rates for short-term borrowing by using an overdraft facility with their bank. This may prove to be slightly cheaper than credit card funding, although the bank probably requires some cash flow calculations to prove when the overdraft might be repaid.

Any money that is regarded as short term debt, such as an overdraft, is shown on the Balance Sheet as a Current Liability. Any interest that is paid on the borrowings is shown as an expense on the Profit and Loss statement.

Utilising an overdraft facility does not involve you receiving money in the same way as a bank loan would, it simply means that the bank balance becomes a negative in the balance sheet and should be shown as a current liability.

Recording Interest on Bank Loans

Sometimes it is better to have a bank loan than an overdraft. Loans are used mainly when purchasing large items such as machinery and vehicles. These items tend to be bought with long term loans, as they are often used for more than 12 months. Record the loan in the Balance Sheet as a Long Term Loan in the Long Term Liabilities section.

When the money is first received in the bank, you need to record both the cash received and the increase in liability. For a bank loan of £3,000, the journal entries should be recorded like this:

	Debit	*Credit*
Cash	£3,000	
Bank Loan		£3,000

You are usually provided with a schedule of bank payments that need to be made. The repayment schedule probably only shows you how much money per month you need to repay. However, some of the amount is repaying capital (the original amount of the loan) and the remaining portion is interest. You need to know the split between the principal amount and the interest amount, as they are recorded in different places within the accounts.

A repayment of £105 for a bank loan would be recorded as follows:

	Debit	*Credit*
Long Term Loan	£75	
Loan Interest	£30	
Bank		£105

As we mentioned, bank loans are used mainly for the purchase of large items – a car, for example. It is quite likely that you'd put down an initial deposit, with the balance being paid via a bank loan.

John buys a company van costing £15,000. He agrees to pay a cash deposit of £5,000, with the remaining balance being funded by a bank loan.

He would record the purchase of the van as follows:

	Debit	*Credit*
Motor Vehicles	£15,000	
Cash		£5,000
Bank Loan		£10,000

He would then record the repayments as follows:

	Debit	*Credit*
Bank loan	£500	
Interest expense	£100	
Cash		£600

A traditional bank loan usually involves the bank opening a loan account for you. You record this as though it's a separate bank account. The intial lump sum loaned to you appears as an overdrawn account. Repayments are made monthly and this reduces the loan amount. Interest is charged to the loan account, often on a quarterly basis. The interest rate is usually linked to the bank base rate, so you don't know how much interest is due until a couple of weeks before your account is charged. At this point, you can record the interest charges to the profit and loss interest account.

Some people purchase assets such as vehicles or machinery using a hire purchase agreement. Here the accounting treatment is very different. You must account for the full liability of the hire purchase agreement at the outset. For example, if Bob buys a car using hire purchase (HP) for £13,000, and finance costs associated with the agreement total £2,500, then a liability of £15,500 should be recorded in the books.

The double entry would be:

	Debit	Credit
Fixed Assets	£13,000	
Accrued HP Interest	£2,500	
HP Loan account		£15,500

As you make each repayment, you need to record two separate journals:

1. Record the actual payment against the loan account;

   Debit: Loan account

   Credit: Bank account

2. Recording the interest element of the loan against your profit and loss account.

   Because you have already accrued the HP interest in the balance sheet at the outset the double entry is as follows:

   Debit: Interest Charges

   Credit: Accrued HP Interest

Exercise 9

Deborah buys a piece of machinery for £20,000. She agrees a cash deposit of £2,000 and then agrees to fund the balance using a bank loan. She discovers that her repayments is £370 per month with £70 being the interest element. Write the journals she needs to complete for these transactions.

If you have any bank loans or credit card loans, check the interest rates that you are paying and see if you can prove the interest payments.

Booking Interest Income

Many businesses earn interest from money in savings accounts, money market accounts, certificates of deposit or other investment vehicles. You need to record any interest earned for the business in an Interest Income account, which appears on the Profit and Loss statement.

Luckily you shouldn't have to calculate that interest. Your bank statement indicates the amount of interest earned.

Q. When you get the statement from the bank you find that your business account earned $25 in interest income. How would you record that transaction in the books?

A. The entry would look like this:

	Debit	Credit
Cash	$25	
Interest Income		$25

Exercise 10

When you get the statement from the bank you find that your business account earned $53 in interest income. How would you record that transaction in the books?

Answers to Exercises on Paying and Collecting Interest

1 £20,000 × 0.03 × 5 = £3,000

2 £5,000 × 0.05 × 7 = £1,750

3 Year 1 = £20,000 × 0.03 = £600.00

Year 2 = £20,600 × 0.03 = £618.00

Year 3 = £21,218 × 0.03 = £636.54

Year 4 = £21,854.54 × 0.03 = £655.64

Year 5 = £22,510.18 × 0.03 = £675.31

4 Year 1 = £5,000 × 0.06 = £300.00

Year 2 = £5,300 × 0.06 = £318.00

Year 3 = £5,618 × 0.06 = £337.08

Year 4 = £5,955.08 × 0.06 = £357.30

Year 5 = £6,312.38 × 0.06 = £378.74

Year 6 = £6,691.12 × 0.06 = £401.47

5 £3000 × 0.0340 per cent × 31 days = £31.62

You can see that with the interest compounded daily on a credit card you pay a lot more interest on your money.

You will also have to factor in your repayment amount. Usually credit card companies request a minimum repayment of 3 per cent of the balance, to be paid each month. If you only pay off the minimum repayment each month, it is going to take a lot longer to pay off the balance.

6 £2000 × 0.0764 per cent × 15 days = £22.92

7

	Debit	Credit
Credit card	£75	
Bank		£75

8

	Debit	Credit
Interest	£22.57	
Credit card		£22.57

9 To purchase the machinery, the double entry is:

	Debit	Credit
Machinery	£20,000	
Cash		£2,000
Loan		£18,000

To repay the loan, the double entry is:

	Debit	Credit
Loan interest	£70	
Capital	£300	
Cash		£370

10

	Debit	Credit
Cash	£53	
Interest income		£53

Chapter 12

Checking Your Books

· ·

In This Chapter

▶ Counting the cash

▶ Finalising journals

▶ Reconciling your bank accounts

▶ Ledger posting

· ·

*M*ost businesses count the cash on hand each day, as well as at the end of an accounting period. In addition, you must review each of the journals and close it at the end of the accounting period.

In this chapter, we explain how businesses test to be sure the cash counts are accurate. We also discuss how to handle any errors that you find, as well as start the closing process and post results to the Nominal (General) Ledger.

Checking Cash

At the end of each month, as businesses close their books for the month, they start by checking their cash balance. In any business cash can be found in several different places — the cash registers, incoming post (for example, cheques from customers paying invoices), petty cash accounts, and the business's bank accounts. Transactions involving cash can be found in the Cash Receipts Journal (cash coming into the business) and the Cash Payments Journal (cash going out of the business). We talk more about this in the next section called 'Checking You've Accounted for All Your Cash Transactions'.

First you need to review the cash on hand. In Chapter 8, we talk about how to balance the cash registers. As a bookkeeper, you should receive a report of the cash remaining in each register with any records of deposits from the shop managers. Tallying all those records gives you a total of cash on hand in the retail outlets. The closing process for any business can take a week or more. You can't even start the process until you have the reports from all the cash registers the day after the last day of the month.

In addition you need to track any other place cash is kept in the business, such as petty cash accounts. Many businesses have several people, such as office managers, assigned to manage small petty cash accounts for paying things like postal charges or small supply needs. You also want to tally the total of cash on hand at the bank. In the section later in this chapter called 'Reconciling Bank Accounts', we discuss how to reconcile all these accounts. Finally, you need to check the post for any payments received on the last day of the month to be sure those cheques are deposited and recorded before you close the books for the month.

Exercise 1

Make a list of all the accounts in your business that you need to reconcile at the end of each accounting period. Remember to include all bank accounts and petty cash accounts, as well as any credit card accounts that have been used in the month. (We provide a general answer at the end of this chapter).

Exercise 2

What is the purpose of a petty cash account? List some typical items that may be paid through petty cash.

Checking You've Accounted for All Your Cash Transactions

After counting the cash on hand, you next want to find out where all the cash went that was used during the accounting period. Any cash that came into the business should be tracked in the Cash Receipts Journal and any cash that was paid out of the business should be tracked in the Cash Payments Journal. These journals need to be summarised at the end of each period, and we show you how to do this in Chapter 4.

After recording the cash from the last day's receipts in the Cash Receipts Journal, you need to be sure all other charges have been recorded in the journal. For example, if you allow your customers to use credit cards, you need to record any customer disputes charged back by the credit card companies.

Understanding credit card fees

Every company must pay fees to the banks that process their credit card charges. These fees lower the amount you actually take into the business, so you must adjust your credit card receipts and record the fees. Possible fees include:

- **Address verification service:** This service is used to verify credit card identities so you can avoid accepting fraudulent credit cards. This is particularly important if your business accepts payment from customers by telephone or by the Internet when you don't actually see the credit card being used. Banks charge a fee for every transaction verified.

- **Discount rate:** All businesses that accept credit cards must pay for the services of the bank that handles the transactions. These costs are reflected in the discount rate, which is a percentage of each transaction. The amount of this fee varies depending on the contract rates agreed between your business and the bank that processes your credit cards. Fees are usually set based on volume of sales.

- **Secure gateway fee:** If you are selling products over the Internet, this fee secures transactions. Businesses that use this service pay for it on a monthly basis.

- **Customer support fee:** This fee is charged to companies that want customer support 24 hours a day, 365 days a year. Mail order catalogues or Internet web sites that want this round-the-clock support for orders pay this fee. Sometimes companies may make arrangements for overnight support only if they accept orders internationally, so they don't need to staff their customer service centres 24 hours a day.

- **Monthly minimum fee:** All banks set a minimum monthly fee no matter how many transactions are handled. This fee is paid even if your business processed no credit card transactions during the month. The fee is often £10 to £30 per month. Your business won't have to worry about these fees as long as enough credit card transactions are processed. For example, if you pay a 2 per cent discount fee on all credit card transactions and process £500 in transactions during the month, you pay £10. If your monthly minimum fee is £10 then you are covered and won't have to pay the minimum. But if your monthly minimum is £30 and you only generate enough transactions for £10 in fees, then you would need to pay an additional £20 for the credit card services. If your business is just starting to think about accepting credit cards, you must be certain you generate enough business to cover the monthly minimum fee.

- **Transaction fee:** Each time you submit a credit card transaction for approval you incur a transaction fee, even if the credit card is denied.

✔ **Equipment and software fees:** This fee is charged based on the type of equipment and software your company uses to process credit transactions. Most businesses have a small machine through which a credit card is swiped. Some companies have software added to their computerised cash registers. Whichever your company uses, there is likely to be a fee for buying or leasing the equipment or software.

✔ **Chargeback and retrieval fees:** If a customer disputes a transaction, then you may see a chargeback to your account when you get your invoice. You need to reverse the money entered for that sale in your books.

Exercise 3

If you allow customers to pay by credit card, check your system to ensure that you understand how to account for monies received by the credit card company. Have you got a system in place to be able to identify which customers are paying you? For instance, the credit card company will probably deposit a lump sum from credit card payments into your bank account. You need to ensure you have a method of indentifying which customers have paid you via credit card, so that you may update your accounts.

If you don't have procedures in place, write some now.

Reconciling your credit card statements

As a bookkeeper you would go nuts trying to figure out the fees for each credit card transaction individually. Instead, you should adjust the cash taken in from sales using *adjusting journal entries*. The entries debit (which reduces) the Sales account and credit (which reduces) the cash account.

In most cases the actual credit sales transactions are deposited in the company's bank account on the day the sales took place. Fees charged, as well as any *chargebacks* (credit due to customer disputes), are calculated monthly and sent to the company in a bank statement. As the bookkeeper, when you get the credit card statement from the bank, you then total the fees and enter those fees in the books. You also enter any chargebacks.

Q. When you get the credit card statement at the end of May, you see that there are a total of £125 in fees for the month and find that one customer disputed a charge of £35. How do you make that adjustment in the Cash journals?

A. You make two adjusting entries – one to reverse the sale recorded in the Cash Receipts Journal and one to record the fees in the Cash Payments Journal. The credits reduce the amount of cash in the books. The cash has already been subtracted from your bank account. So you must reconcile what's in your books with what is in your bank account.

You would make this entry in your Cash Receipts Journal to reverse the sale:

	Debit	*Credit*
Sales	£ 35	
Cash		£35

You would make this entry in your Cash Payments Journal to record the fees:

	Debit	*Credit*
Credit Card Fees	£125	
Cash		£125

Exercise 4

When you get your credit card statement you find a total of £225 was charged in fees and you find three chargebacks for customer disputes totalling £165. How do you record this information in your books?

Exercise 5

When you get your credit card statement you find a total of £275 in chargebacks from customer disputes and £320 in fees. How do you record this information in your books?

Accruing your invoices

At the end of the month you're likely to get invoices that you have not yet paid. If the invoices represent expenses incurred during the month, you want to record those expenses so you can match cash receipts with the expenses incurred. For example, if you took an advertisement in the newspaper for a sale on May 15 and receive the invoice for that advertisement on May 30 with a due date of June 10, you want to record that invoice as a May expense. This is called *accruing invoices*.

As you close the books for the month, you want to be sure that you have accrued all invoices for the expenses of that month even if you haven't paid them.

Q. Suppose you advertised a sale in *your* local paper on May 17. The advertisement cost £500 and you receive a invoice for it on May 30. You have ten days to pay the invoice. Would you need to record that invoice before closing the books for May? How would you record that invoice in the books?

A. Since it is a May expense, you do need to record the invoice before closing the books. You would record the invoice by entering a debit to Advertising expenses (to increase the amount you spent on advertising for the month) and a credit to Trade Creditors otherwise known as Accounts Payable (to record the liability that must be paid). Here is what the entry would look like:

	Debit	*Credit*
Advertising	£500	
Trade creditors		£500

Exercise 6

On June 30 you receive a invoice for £2,500 for advertising during the month of June. You won't have to pay the invoice until July. When should you record the invoice? How would you record the invoice?

Exercise 7

You receive a invoice for £375 for office supplies for the month of May on May 30. You won't have to pay the invoice until June 10, but the supplies were used primarily in May. When should you record the invoice? How would you record the invoice?

Reconciling Bank Accounts

One of the biggest jobs each month is reconciling your bank statement to be sure it matches your bank account in your books. Often the bank statement does not come in on the last day of the month, so you reconcile your bank accounts at a different time from when you are closing the books.

You've probably had to reconcile your personal account. Well reconciling a business bank account is not much different, even though it probably includes a lot more transactions than your personal account. Table 12-1 shows you a common format for reconciling a bank account.

Table 12-1	Bank Reconciliation			
Transactions	*Beginning Balance*	*Deposits*	*Payments*	*Ending Balance*
Balance per bank statement	£	£	(£)	£
Deposits in transit (those not shown on statement)		£		£
Outstanding cheques (cheques that haven't shown up yet)			(£)	(£)
Total	£	£	(£)	£
Balance per bank account or Cash book (which should be the same)				£

Q. You've just received your bank statement in the post. You find your balance at the bank is £1,200 beginning balance, £4,000 in deposits, £4,300 in Payments, and your ending balance is £900. You review the deposits and find that a deposit of £1,000 does not show on the statement. You find that cheques totalling £600 have not yet cleared. The balance in your bank account is £1,300. Does your bank account reconcile to the balance on your bank statement?

A. Using the bank reconciliation chart, here is the answer:

Transactions	*Beginning Balance*	*Deposits*	*Payments*	*Ending Balance*
Balance per bank statement	£1,200	£4,000	(£4,300)	£900
Deposits in transit (those not shown on statement)		£1,000		£1,000
Outstanding cheques (cheques that haven't shown up yet)			(£600)	(£600)
Total	£1,200	£5,000	(£4,900)	£1,300
Balance per cashbook or bank account (which should be the same)				£1,300

The bank statement and your bank account do reconcile.

Exercise 8

You've just received your bank statement in the post. You find your balance at the bank is £1,500 beginning balance, £6,000 in deposits, £6,500 in Payments and your ending balance is £1,000. You review the deposits and find that a deposit of £2,000 does not show on the statement. You find that cheques totalling £1,700 have not yet cleared. The balance in your bank account is £1,300. Does your bank account reconcile to the balance on your bank statement?

Transactions	Beginning Balance	Deposits	Payments	Ending Balance
Balance per bank statement	£	£	(£)	£
Deposits in transit (those not shown on statement)		£		£
Outstanding cheques (cheques that haven't shown up yet)			(£)	(£)
Total	£	£	(£)	£
Balance per bank account or Cash book (which should be the same)				£

Exercise 9

You've just received your bank statement in the post. You find your balance at the bank is £1,800 beginning balance, £7,000 in deposits, £6,500 in Payments and your ending balance is £2,300. You review the deposits and find that a deposit of £1,000 does not show on the statement. You find that cheques totalling £2,500 have not yet cleared. The balance in your bank account is £1,200. Does your bank account reconcile to the balance on your bank statement?

Transactions	Beginning Balance	Deposits	Payments	Ending Balance
Balance per bank statement	£	£	(£)	£
Deposits in transit (those not shown on statement)		£		£
Outstanding cheques (cheques that haven't shown up yet)			(£)	(£)
Total	£	£	(£)	£
Balance per bank account or Cash book (which should be the same)				£

Sometimes you find the balance in the bank account or cash book does not match the balance on your bank statement. When that happens you need to find out why. You need to check a few things if you find a difference in your accounts.

✔ **If the bank balance is higher than your balance,** the first thing you should look for are deposits on the bank statement that are not in your Bank/Cash account in your books. If you do find a deposit for which you don't have an entry, you'll need to research what that deposit was for and add it appropriately to your books. For example, if you find a bank deposit of £1,500 on May 15 and in reviewing your books don't see one that day for sales, you might want to review your sales receipts for that day and see if they were recorded. If the sales weren't recorded, it's an easy fix to do a journal entry for the sales. You also may find that you missed a cheque you should have listed in your outstanding cheques. When you add the amount of the missing cheques, you may find yourself in balance. If that's the case then you don't need to make any entries to the books.

✔ **If the bank balance is lower than your balance**, the first thing you should check to see is that all the cheques listed by the bank are recorded in your Bank/Cash account in your books. You may have sent out a cheque that wasn't recorded properly. If that's the case then record the cheque and redo your reconciliation to be sure it reconciles. Another possibility is that a deposit you did make does not show up on your bank statement. If that happens you'll need to find proof of the deposit and contact the bank.

If all deposits and cheques are correct, you'll then need to check your maths. Make sure all cheques and deposits were entered correctly as well.

Once you find the error, you need to create a journal entry to correct the books and make sure all affected accounts are adjusted.

Q. Suppose you could not reconcile your bank statement. As you reviewed the deposits you see that a deposit of £1,000 is not recorded in your books. After researching the deposit you find that the £1,000 was a payment from a Joe Smith that did not get recorded in the books. How would you record the payment?

A. You need to reduce the amount in Debtors (Accounts Receivable), because the payment is not due. You would also need to increase the cash balance because you do have additional money in the bank.

	Debit	*Credit*
Cash	£1,000	
Debtors		£1,000

In addition to this entry, you also need to update the records of Joe Smith to indicate he paid his invoice.

Exercise 10

Suppose you could not reconcile your bank statement. As you review the cheques you see there is a cheque written for £2,500 that is not recorded in your books. As you research the cheque, you find it is a payment made to Olive's Office Supplies. How would you record that in the books?

Exercise 11

Suppose you could not reconcile your bank statement and you find that a deposit of £5,300 is not recorded. As you research the deposit you find the sales receipts were not recorded for May 15. How would you record that in the books?

Closing Journals and Posting to the Ledger

After you have checked all the cash accounts as discussed in this chapter, you can then summarise your cash journals. we show you how to summarise journals in Chapter 4.

Essentially you total the journals and then prepare a summary entry that appears in the Nominal Ledger. Remember the Nominal Ledger is the main ledger within your accounting system (see Chapter 4 for more information on the Nominal Ledger).

Suppose you summarised your Cash Receipts Journal and got these totals from page 6 for the end of May:

Sales Credit	£100,000
Debtors Credit	£25,000
Sale of Furniture	£5,000
Cash	£130,000

What would you enter into the Nominal Ledger accounts?

	Debit	*Credit*
Cash	£130,000	
Sales		£100,000
Debtors		£25,000
Furniture		£5,000

The individual nominal accounts would be shown as follows:

Cash account

Date	*Description*	*Ref. No.*	*Debit*	*Credit*	*Balance*
	Opening Balance				£90,000 DR
31/5	Cash receipts journal	Page 6	£130,000		
	Closing balance				£220,000 DR

Sales account

Date	*Description*	*Ref. No.*	*Debit*	*Credit*	*Balance*
	Opening Balance				£180,000 CR
31/5	Cash receipts journal	Page 6		£100,000	
	Closing balance				£280,000 CR

Debtors account

Date	*Description*	*Ref. No.*	*Debit*	*Credit*	*Balance*
	Opening Balance				£70,000 DR
31/5	Cash receipts journal	Page 6		£25,000	
	Closing balance				£45,000 DR

Furniture account

Date	*Description*	*Ref. No.*	*Debit*	*Credit*	*Balance*
	Opening Balance				£20,000 DR
31/5	Cash receipts journal	Page 6		£5,000	
	Closing balance				£15,000 DR

With this entry your Cash account would increase by £130,000. Your Sales account would increase by £100,000. Your Debtors (Accounts Receivable) account would decrease by £25,000 to reflect the payments by customers and the fact that the money was no longer due. Your Furniture account would decrease by £5,000 to reflect the sale of furniture and an asset you no longer have.

You can see that we have included opening and closing balances on the nominal accounts. You must have the closing balances at each period end, when you come to prepare your trial balance. This is described in Chapter 13.

Exercise 12

Suppose you summarised your Cash Receipts Journal and got these totals on page 10 for the month of June:

Sales Credit	£150,000
Debtors Credit	£45,000
Owner's Capital	£50,000
Cash	£245,000

What would you enter into the Nominal Ledger Accounts?

Exercise 13

Suppose you summarised your Cash Payments Journal and got these totals on page 15 for the month July:

Rent Debit	£1,500
Trade Creditors Debits	£150,000
Salaries Expenses Debits	£35,000
Credit Card Payable Debit	£5,000
Cash	£191,500

What would you enter into the Nominal Ledger Accounts?

In addition to summarising your cash journals as described in the previous section, you also need to summarise the sales, purchases and general journals. As you are summarising, you should be looking out for blatant errors, because you need to ensure that the entries accurately reflect the transactions that your business has made.

Any errors you find in the journals should be corrected before the journals are totalled up and then posted to the nominal ledger. Chapter 13 continues the process of checking and correcting your books, should you have missed anything at this stage.

You notice that in the answers to Exercise 12 and 13 we have included an opening balance and closing balance. You need the closing balance to prepare a Trial Balance, which is discussed in Chapter 13. These answers only show information specific to the question, so for your information we show you an example of a more likely scenario of the debtors account closed off at the end of a period.

Debtors account

Date	Description	Ref. No.	Debit	Credit	Balance
Opening Balance					£50,000 DR
31/5	Cash receipts journal	Page 6		£130,000	
31/5	Sales journal	Page 3	£230,000		
Closing balance					£150,000 DR

In this example you can see the postings from both the sales journal and the cash receipts journal for the month of May. References have been shown showing where you can find the detailed transactions for both sales and cash receipts. The closing balance of £150,000 Dr is included in the Trial Balance for the period ended May.

Answers to Exercises on Checking Your Books

1 The following accounts are normally reconciled:

- ✔ Bank Current account
- ✔ Bank deposit account
- ✔ Petty Cash account
- ✔ Credit card accounts

2 Usually small cash needs are handled using a Petty Cash fund. Usually an office manager handles this fund. You may wish to send a memo to your staff to advise them of the typical items of expenditure that are expected to be paid through petty cash.

- ✔ Typical petty cash items include:
- ✔ Tea, coffee, milk
- ✔ Postage
- ✔ Keys cut
- ✔ Small stationery items
- ✔ Office window cleaner

This list just offers a sample of the kinds of expenditure that might be posted through the petty cash account.

3 Not all companies will take payment via credit card from their customers. If yours does, take the time now to reflect on the procedures surrounding the credit card recipts. Can they be imporoved?

4 The entry for the Cash Payments Journal would be:

	Debit	Credit
Credit Card Fees	£225	
Cash		£225

The entry for the Cash Receipts Journal would be:

	Debit	Credit
Sales	£165	
Cash		£165

5 The entry for the Cash Payments Journal would be:

	Debit	Credit
Credit Card Fees	£320	
Cash		£320

The entry for the Cash Receipts Journal would be:

	Debit	Credit
Sales	£275	
Cash		£275

6 You would need to enter the invoice before closing the books for the June, so the expenses would be recorded against Junes receipts. The journal entry would be:

	Debit	Credit
Advertising Expense	£2,500	
Trade Creditors		£2,500

7 You would need to enter the invoice before closing the books for May, so the expenses would be recorded against May's receipts. The journal entry would be:

	Debit	Credit
Office Supplies Expense	£375	
Trade Creditors		£375

8 The bank statement does reconcile to the chequebook. Here is the proof:

Transactions	Beginning Balance	Deposits	Payments	Ending Balance
Balance per bank statement	£1,500	£6,000	(£6,500)	£1,000
Deposits in transit (those not shown on statement)		£2,000		£2,000
Outstanding cheques (cheques that haven't shown up yet)			(£1,700)	(£1,700)
Total	£1,500	£8,000	(£8,200)	£1,300
Balance per bank account or Cash book (which should be the same)				£1,300

9 The bank statement does not reconcile to the bank account There is a difference of £400. You must review the bank account for possible errors. Here is the solution:

Transactions	Beginning Balance	Deposits	Payments	Ending Balance
Balance per bank statement	£1,800	£7,000	(£6,500)	£2,300
Deposits in transit (those not shown on statement)		£1,000		£1,000
Outstanding cheques (cheques that haven't shown up yet)			(£2,500)	(£2,500)
Total	£1,800	£8,000	(£9,000)	£800
Balance per bank account or Cash book (which should be the same)				£1,200

10 You need to record the office supplies expense and you need to reflect the use of cash. Here is what the journal entry would look like:

	Debit	Credit
Office Supplies Expenses	£2,500	
Cash		£2,500

11 You need to record the sales and you need to record the receipt of cash. This is what the journal entry would look like:

	Debit	Credit
Cash	£5,300	
Sales		£5,300

12 Your entry into the Nominal Ledger accounts would be:

	Debit	Credit
Cash	£245,000	
Debtors		£45,000
Sales		£150,000
Owner's Capital		£50,000

Cash account

Date	Description	Ref. No.	Debit	Credit	Balance
	Opening Balance				£190,000 DR
30/6	Cash receipts journal	Page 10	£245,000		
	Closing balance				£435,000 DR

Debtors account

Date	Description	Ref. No.	Debit	Credit	Balance
	Opening Balance				£60,000 DR
30/6	Cash receipts journal	Page 10	£45,000		
	Closing balance				£15,000 DR

Sales account

Date	Description	Ref. No.	Debit	Credit	Balance
	Opening Balance				£200,000 CR
30/6	Cash receipts journa	Page 10		£150,000	
Closing balance					£350,000 CR

Capital account

Date	Description	Ref. No.	Debit	Credit	Balance
	Opening Balance				£50,000 CR
30/6	Cash receipts journal	Page 10		£50,000	
	Closing balance				£100,000 CR

13 Your entry into the Nominal Ledger accounts would be:

	Debit	Credit
Rent	£1,500	
Trade Creditors	£150,000	
Salaries Expenses	£35,000	
Credit Card Payable	£5,000	
Cash		£191,500

Rent account

Date	Description	Ref. No.	Debit	Credit	Balance
	Opening Balance				£9,000 DR
31/7	Cash payments journal	Page 15	£1,500		
	Closing balance				£10,500 DR

Trade Creditors account

Date	Description	Ref. No.	Debit	Credit	Balance
	Opening Balance				£210,000 CR
31/7	Cash payments journal	Page 15	£150,000		
	Closing balance				£60,000 CR

Salaries account

Date	Description	Ref. No.	Debit	Credit	Balance
	Opening Balance				£210,000 DR
31/7	Cash payments journal	Page 15	£35,000		
Closing balance					£245,000 DR

Credit card account

Date	Description	Ref. No.	Debit	Credit	Balance
	Opening Balance				£10,000 CR
31/7	Cash payments journal	Page 15	£5,000		
	Closing balance				£5,000 CR

Cash account

Date	Description	Ref. No.	Debit	Credit	Balance
	Opening Balance				£250,000 DR
31/7	Cash payments journal	Page 15		£191,500	
	Closing balance				£58,500 DR

Chapter 13

Correcting Your Books

. . . .

In This Chapter

▶ Checking the books

▶ Adjusting accounts

▶ Recharting

. . . .

After you have closed all your journals and posted their information to the Nominal Ledger, the next step in the process of closing the books is to test to see if there are any errors. This is when the rubber meets the road in bookkeeping. If all double-entry transactions have been correctly entered in the books, the books balance and the trial is successful. Unfortunately few bookkeepers find that the books balance on the first try.

In this chapter, we show you how to do a trial balance and how to find any errors. Then we explore how you can correct and adjust the books if necessary.

Doing a Trial Balance Worksheet

You may think that double-entry accounting, where every transaction must include at least two entries in the books – a debit and a credit, is too much work. When you start checking the books at the end of an accounting period and try to do a trial balance, you'll see the value of this double-entry system. After putting in hundreds, or even thousands, of entries, the initial trial balance shows you how valuable the careful balancing of each transaction can be.

Basically a trial balance is a worksheet, prepared either manually or by your computer system, which lists all the accounts in your nominal ledger at the end of an accounting period. You need the closing balances on all your nominal ledger accounts to be able to do this.

There are four basic steps to developing a trial balance:

1. **Prepare a worksheet with three columns: one for the account titles, one for the debits, and one for the credits.**

2. **Fill in all account titles and record their balances in the appropriate debit or credit columns.**

3. **Total the debit and credit columns.**

4. **Compare the column totals.**

The primary purpose of the trial balance is to ensure that the sum of your debits and credits is equal.

Q. You have summarised all your journal entries and posted them to the Nominal Ledger. Using your totals for each of the accounts at the end of May in the following list, prepare a trial balance:

Cash Debit	£3,000
Debtors Debit	£1,000
Stock Debit	£1,200
Equipment Debit	£5,050
Vehicle Debit	£25,000
Furniture Debit	£5,600
Creditors Credit	£2,200
Loans Payable Credit	£29,150
Owner's Capital	£5,000
Sales Credit	£20,000
Purchases Debit	£7,500
Advertising Debit	£1,625
Interest Expenses Debit	£345
Office Expenses Debit	£550
Payroll Taxes Debit	£425
Rent Expense Debit	£800
Salaries and Wages Debit	£3,500
Telephone Expenses Debit	£500
Utilities Expenses Debit	£255

A. The trial balance for May is

Account	Debit	Credit
Cash	£3,000	
Debtors	£1,000	
Stock	£1,200	
Equipment	£5,050	
Vehicle	£25,000	
Furniture	£5,600	
Creditors		£2,200
Loans Payable		£29,150
Owner's Capital		£5,000
Sales		£20,000
Purchases	£7,500	
Advertising	£1,625	
Interest Expenses	£345	
Office Expenses	£550	
Payroll Taxes	£425	
Rent Expense	£800	
Salaries and Wages	£3,500	
Telephone Expenses	£500	
Utilities Expenses	£255	
TOTALS	£56,350	£56,350

The debits equal the credits, so the trial balance is successful.

Exercise 1

You have summarised all your journal entries and posted them to the Nominal Ledger. Prepare a trial balance. Your totals for each of the accounts at the end of June are:

Cash Debit	£2,500
Debtors Debit	£1,500
Stock Debit	£1,000
Equipment Debit	£5,050
Vehicle Debit	£25,000
Furniture Debit	£5,600
Creditors Credit	£2,000
Loans Payable Credit	£28,150

Owner's Capital	$5,000	
Sales Credit	$27,000	
Purchases Debit	$12,500	
Advertising Debit	$2,625	
Interest Expenses Debit	$345	
Office Expenses Debit	$550	
Payroll Taxes Debit	$425	
Rent Expense Debit	$800	
Salaries and Wages Debit	$3,500	
Telephone Expenses Debit	$500	
Utilities Expenses Debit	$255	

Account	*Debit*	*Credit*

If your debits equal your credits in the trial balance, that's a good sign, but it's not a guarantee that your books are totally free of errors. It does mean that you did successfully enter all your transactions with balanced entries. If errors have slipped through the cracks, your accountant will probably pick them up when he prepares the financial reports.

If your books don't balance when you finish the trial balance, then you need to find the errors. Always do your trial balance with a pencil, so you can easily erase and correct the account balances and recalculate the columns. There are four steps you can take to find the errors:

1. **Check your maths.** First add up your columns again and keep your fingers crossed that you only made an error in calculation. That's the simplest error to find and correct.

2. **Compare your balances.** Double-check to be sure you wrote down the correct balances for all the accounts and that you put them in the correct columns as debits or credits. If you do find an error, correct it and then retotal the columns. Hopefully that will be the answer.

3. **Check your journal summaries.** If Steps 1 and 2 don't solve the problem, your next step is to check your maths from when you summed the journal entries to be sure you don't have any errors there. If you do find an error, correct your entries, correct the posts to the Nominal Ledger, retotal the accounts involved, and put the new totals onto your trial balance worksheet. Hopefully then you will find the debits and credits in balance.

4. **Check your journal entries and Nominal Ledger entries.** If all else fails, you have to check your actual transaction entries. Your financial information is useless if you can't find out why your debits don't equal your credits. As you become more used to what you should expect each month, you will be able to scan your entries and pick out accounts with balances that look questionable. Review the entries in those accounts first. For example, if you see a total in the Office Supplies account that looks unusually high or low, then recheck the transactions you recorded to that account.

Making Adjustments

Even though you may know your accounts are in balance using the trial balance, you're not done yet. You still need to make some adjustments to the numbers to reflect use of assets that did not involve cash. You probably need to make five key adjustments:

✔ **Asset depreciation:** You need to recognise the use of your long-term assets. I talk more about depreciation in Chapter 10.

✔ **Prepaid expenses:** Some expenses, such as insurance, must be paid on an annual basis, even though you benefit from that payment monthly. When you close the books for the month, you adjust the monthly expenses to recognise that month's use of the asset.

✔ **Stock:** If you're not using a computerised stock system that automatically updates stock every day, you'll need to adjust your Stock account to reflect the amount of stock at the end of the accounting period.

✔ **Bad debts:** If some customers haven't paid their bills and you decide to write off their accounts as bad debts, you need to make that adjustment in the books during the closing of the accounting period.

✔ **Unpaid salaries and wages:** Often a pay period involves two different months. For example you may pay employees for the last week of May during the month of June. You need to prepare an adjusting entry to acknowledge those May expenses even if you haven't yet paid the cash.

Depreciation

Depreciation commonly involves a business's largest non-cash expense. Businesses depreciate most assets that they use for more than a 12-month period, such as cars, furniture, buildings and equipment. Most small businesses record their depreciation expenses once a year when then prepare their annual reports, but some do record them monthly or quarterly. We assume an annual depreciation expense calculation in the problems below, but if you work in a business that records monthly depreciation expenses, you need to divide the annual depreciation expense by 12. Also to keep the calculation simple for this chapter, we use the straight-line depreciation calculation. You can review the more complicated types of depreciation calculations in Chapter 10.

Q. You are preparing to close the books at the end of the year and your company owns a van with a cost price of £20,000. Assume a five-year useful life. How much should you record for depreciation expenses for the year? What is your adjusting entry?

A. £20,000 = amount that will be depreciated

£20,000/5 = £4,000 amount that will be depreciated each year

	Debit	Credit
Depreciation Expense	£4,000	
Accumulated Depreciation – Vehicles		£4,000

The depreciation expense is shown on the Profit and Loss Statement (see Chapter 15) and the Accumulated Depreciation is shown on the Balance Sheet (see Chapter 14).

Exercise 2

Your company owns a copier with a cost basis of £30,000 . Assume a useful life of five years. How much should you record for depreciation expenses for the year? What is your adjusting entry?

Exercise 3

Your offices have furniture with a cost basis of £200,000. Assume a useful life of five years. How much should you record for depreciation expenses for the year? What is your adjusting entry?

Prepaid expenses

Sometimes your company has to pay in advance for expenses on items from which it benefits throughout the year, such as insurance or rent. Most insurance businesses require you to pay the premium at the start of the year, even though you get the benefit for the whole of the following year. When this happens you initially enter the payment as an asset called Prepaid Expenses and then allocate the expense on a monthly basis using an adjusting entry.

Q. Suppose your company pays £12,000 annually for insurance on all its vehicles. You receive an invoice dated 01.05.09 for £12,000, which you pay in May. The period of insurance relates to 1st May 2009 – 30th April 2010.You are closing the books for the month of May 2009. What adjusting entry do you need to make?

A. The initial invoice should be coded to prepaid expenses. If you were to code the invoice to insurance expenses, the Profit and Loss statement would show twelve months of insurance costs in May.

The initial double entry is as follows (when you post the original invoice):

	Debit	Credit
Prepaid Expenses	£12,000	
Cash		£12,000

You then need to calculate the monthly expense: £12,000/12 months = £1,000 per month.

Each month you need to post the following journal:

	Debit	Credit
Insurance expenses	£1,000	
Prepaid expenses		£1,000

By doing the journal above, you have charged £1,000 to the Profit and Loss account and reduced the prepaid expenses in the Balance sheet by the same amount.

Note: If you inadvertently charge the original invoice to insurance expenses, you simply need to do the following journal to correct:

	Debit	*Credit*
Insurance expenses		£11,000
Prepaid Expenses	£11,000	

This correcting journal has the same effect as the original journals. The Profit and Loss account will still be charged with £1000 (£12,000 – £11,000) and the Balance sheet will show a prepaid expense of £11,000 ($^{11}/_{12}$ of the original invoice).

Exercise 4

Suppose your company pays £6,000 for an advertising campaign which covers the period 1 January to 31 December. You have already received an invoice dated 15 January which you have paid at the end of January. You are closing the books for the month of May. How much should you have charged to the Profit and Loss account for the period to 31 May and what balance should remain in prepayments?

Exercise 5

Suppose your company pays £12,000 quarterly for rent on its retail outlet. You are closing the books for the month of May. What adjusting entry do you need to make?

Stock

Most businesses adjust the balance of their asset account stock at the end of each month. Some that use a computerised stock system may do so daily. In Chapter 7, we talk more about how to manage and value your stock. When closing the books for the month you must take these three steps to adjust your asset account stock:

1. Determine the stock remaining on hand.

2. Set a value for that stock.

3. Prepare an adjusting entry for the Nominal Ledger that reflects the stock remaining.

If you do have stock remaining, you want to reflect that asset on the Balance Sheet and you want to reduce the cost of that remaining stock as an expense for that month. The remaining stock will be sold the next month. If you used stock that was purchased the previous month, you need to adjust the Purchases Expenses to reflect the additional expenses.

Q. At the end of the month you find that you have £10,000 worth of stock remaining. You started the month with £9,500. What adjusting entry should you make to the books?

A. You first need to calculate the difference and determine whether you ended up with additional stock, which means you purchased stock that was not used that month. If that is the case you then need to prepare an adjusting entry to increase the asset stock and you need to decrease your Purchases Expenses because those purchases will be sold in the next month.

In this case, you find that you have £500 more in stock, so this is the adjusting entry you need to make:

	Debit	Credit
Stock	£500	
Purchases Expense		£500

This entry increases the Stock account on the Balance Sheet and decreases the Purchases Expense account on the Profit and Loss Statement.

Exercise 6

At the end of the month you find that you have £9,000 in ending Stock. You started the month with £8,000 in Stock. What adjusting entry would you make to the books?

Exercise 7

At the end of the month you calculate your ending Stock and find that your ending Stock value is £250 more than your beginning Stock value, which means you purchased Stock during the month that was not used. What adjusting entry should you make to the books?

Bad debts

Sometimes you have customers that just don't pay their invoices. We talk more about how to keep track of your customer accounts in Chapter 8. When you close your books at the end of the month, you should always review your customer accounts. At some point you must accept the fact that some customers will never pay. Most companies will write off nonpaying customers after they are more than six months late on paying their invoices as a bad debt expense. You can record bad debts by identifying specific customers that you don't think will pay or you can establish a bad debt percentage based on historical experience. For example, if you have found over the years that 5 per cent of your Debtors account will not be paid, then you can write off that percentage of Debtors each month.

Q. You identify six customers that are more than six months late and the total amount due from those customers is £1,500. What adjusting entry should you make to the books?

A. You would make this adjusting entry to the books:

	Debit	Credit
Bad Debt Expense	£1,500	
Debtors		£1,500

With this entry the Bad Debt Expense would be shown on the Profit and Loss Statement and the Debtors account balance would be reduced by £1,500 thereby reducing the asset.

Exercise 8

You identify six customers that are more than six months late and the total amount due from those customers is £2,000. What adjusting entry would you make to the books?

Exercise 9

Your company has determined that historically 5 per cent of its Debtors never pay. What adjusting entry should you make to the books if your Debtors account at the end of the month is £10,000?

Unpaid salaries and wages

Not all pay periods fall at the end of the month. You may pay fortnightly, which could mean that the end of the month falls in the middle of the pay period. You need to ensure that you record the payroll expenses that have been incurred but not yet paid. The easiest way to do this is to accrue the expense of half your payroll. When you actually pay the wages, you will then need to reverse the accrued expense.

Q. Your payroll for the last week of May will not be paid until June. Your salary and wages for the fortnightly payroll total £6,000 on June 7. How much would you record in payroll expenses for the month of May?

A. Your first step is to calculate the portion of the payroll that reflects payroll expenses for the month of May. Since the payroll is on June 7 reflecting a seven-day week, you can assume that half the payroll is for May and half is for June. So £3,000 is a May expense. Here is the entry you should make:

	Debit	Credit
Payroll Expenses	£3,000	
Accrued Payroll Expenses		£3,000

When cash is used to pay the employees in June, you then reverse this entry:

	Debit	Credit
Accrued Payroll Expenses	£3,000	
Payroll Expenses	£3,000	
Cash		£6,000

When recording this use of cash, half of the cash is used to reverse the accrual and half is used as new payroll expenses in June.

Exercise 10

Your payroll for the last full week in May is £10,000, but it won't be paid until June. How do you initially enter this in the books? How do you enter it when the cash is actually paid out? Assume the first full week of June is the same amount.

Exercise 11

Your payroll for the last four days of May will not be paid until June 8. The fortnightly payroll totals £5,000 and each working week is five days. How much do you record in payroll expenses for May? What would the entry be when you initially enter it into the books? What would the entry be when the cash is actually paid out?

Exercise 12

Your payroll for the last full week of March won't be paid until April 7. The total payroll for the two weeks is $8,000. How much do you record in payroll expenses for March? What is the entry when you initially enter this transaction into the books? What is the entry when the cash is actually paid out?

Reworking Your Chart of Accounts

After you fully close the books for the year, you may want to make changes to your Chart of Accounts. You may find that you didn't use an account through most of the year and you want to delete it completely the next year. Or you may find that you put all Office Expenses into one account and you think you can get a better handle on managing certain expenses, such as paper or postage, by creating separate expense accounts for the next year.

As long as you are just adding an expense account and all expense accounts start with a zero at the beginning of the year, you can just add the account and notify staff of the new account and its coding numbers for the next year. You should explain to your staff what types of expenses should be charged to that expense number. If you want to delete an expense account after it has been closed for the year, you can just delete it from the Chart of Accounts, though you must be sure to notify staff that they can longer use that account. You use the same process for revenue accounts, which also start with zero balance each year.

Asset, liability and equity accounts are handled differently because their balances carry over from year to year. For example, most businesses carry a cash balance from one year to the next, as well as buildings, furniture, equipment, and other assets. The same is true for liabilities and equity. You can't just zero out the balance of a loan on which you still owe money or invoices that still need to be paid. Instead you carry over the liability balances to the next year. Company owners certainly don't appreciate losing records of their investment, so you carry over the balances in equity accounts as well.

You can always add an account during the year, but you should only delete an account at the end of a year, so you don't risk creating problems with developing your financial statements. If you do decide to add an account during the year, you'll need to transfer any transactions related to the new account from the account in which they were initially entered.

Q. You decide that you want to track paper expenses separately rather than lump them into the Office Supplies Expense account. You add a Paper Expense account in the middle of the year. You've already entered £5,000 in transactions related to the buying of paper. What do you need to do to start that account?

A. First you need to establish a new account called Paper Expense to your Chart of Accounts. Then you would need to transfer the amount of transactions involving the purchases of paper from your Office Supplies Expense account to your Paper Expenses account. Here is what the transaction would look like:

	Debit	Credit
Paper Expense	£5,000	
Office Supplies Expense		£5,000

Exercise 13

You decide you want to track the amount being spent on postage separately. Prior to this you were entering these transactions in the Office Expense account. You make this decision in May, five months into your accounting year. You've already entered £1,000 for postage expenses. What would you need to do to start the account in the middle of the accounting year?

Exercise 14

You decide you want to track telephone expenses separately from other utilities. Prior to this you were entering these transactions in the Utilities Expense account. You make this decision in July, but have already recorded transactions totalling £1,400 in your books. What do you need to do to start this new account in the middle of the accounting year?

Answers to Exercises on Checking and Correcting Your Books

1   Here is the completed trial balance worksheet:

Account	Debit	Credit
Cash	£2,500	
Debtors (Accounts Receivable)	£1,500	
Stock	£1,000	
Equipment	£5,050	
Vehicle	£25,000	
Furniture	£5,600	
Creditors (Accounts Payable)		£2,000
Loans Payable		£28,150
Owner's Capital		£5,000
Sales		£27,000
Purchases	£12,500	
Advertising	£2,625	
Interest Expenses	£345	
Office Expenses	£550	
Payroll Taxes	£425	
Rent Expense	£800	
Salaries and Wages	£3,500	
Telephone Expenses	£500	
Utilities Expenses	£255	
TOTALS	£62,150	£62,150

2   Annual depreciation expense = £30,000/5 = £6,000

	Debit	Credit
Depreciation expense	£6,000	
Accumulated depreciation – Office Machines		£6,000

3   Annual depreciation expense = (£200,000)/5 = £40,000

	Debit	Credit
Depreciation expense	£40,000	
Accumulated depreciation — Furniture & Fittings		£40,000

4 The original invoice should be coded to prepaid expenses. You need to calculate the monthly charge for advertising which would be £6,000/12 months = £500 per month. Each month you must do the following journal:

	Debit	Credit
Advertising costs	£500	
Prepaid Expenses		£500

This journal will have the effect of charging the Profit and Loss account with £500 each month and reducing the prepayment in the Balance Sheet.

Therefore in May the following balances will be:

Advertising expenses (in Profit & Loss)	£2,500 (£500 × 5 months)
Prepayment in Balance Sheet	£3,500 (£6,000 – £2,500)

5 Monthly rent expense = £12,000/3 = £4,000

	Debit	Credit
Rent Expenses	£4,000	
Prepaid Expenses		£4,000

6 You ended the month with £1,000 more Stock than you started the month. So you need to increase the Stock on hand by £1,000 and decrease the Purchases expense by £1,000 since some of the Stock purchased will not be used until the next month. The entry would be:

	Debit	Credit
Stock	£1,000	
Purchases		£1,000

7 Your entry would be:

	Debit	Credit
Stock	£250	
Purchases		£250

This entry decreases the amount of the Purchases expenses because you purchased some of the Stock which was not used.

8 Your entry would be:

	Debit	Credit
Bad Debt Expense	£2,000	
Debtors (Accounts Receivable)		£2,000

9 First you need to calculate the amount of the bad debt expense:

Bad debt expense = £10,000 ×.05 = £500

Your entry would be:

	Debit	Credit
Bad debt expense	£500	
Debtors		£500

10 Your entry initially for May's accounts would be:

	Debit	Credit
Payroll Expenses	$10,000	
Accrued Payroll Expenses		$10,000

Your entry when you actually pay out the cash for the fortnightly payroll would be:

	Debit	Credit
Payroll Expenses	$10,000	
Accrued Payroll Expenses	$10,000	
Cash		$20,000

11 First you would need to calculate the per day payroll amount:

$5,000/10 = $500 per day

Four days of payroll = $2,000 for May payroll expense

Six days of payroll = $3,000 for June payroll expense

Your entry initially for Mays accounts would be:

	Debit	Credit
Payroll Expenses	$2,000	
Accrued Payroll Expenses		$2,000

Your entry when you actually pay out the cash would be:

	Debit	Credit
Payroll Expenses	$3,000	
Accrued Payroll Expenses	$2,000	
Cash		$5,000

12 First you need to calculate the payroll per week:

$8000/2 = $4,000

Your entry initially for March accounts would be:

	Debit	Credit
Payroll Expenses	$4,000	
Accrued Payroll Expenses		$4,000

Your entry when you actually pay out the cash would be:

	Debit	Credit
Payroll Expenses	$4,000	
Accrued Payroll Expenses	$4,000	
Cash		$8,000

13 First you would need to establish a new account called Postage Expenses in your Chart of Accounts. Then you would need to transfer the amount of transactions involving the payment of postage from your Office Expenses account to your new Postage Expenses account. The transaction looks like this:

	Debit	Credit
Postage Expense	£1,000	
Office Expense		£1,000

14 First you would need to establish a new account called Telephone Expenses in your Chart of Accounts. Then you would need to transfer the amount of transactions involving the payment of telephone bills from your Utilities Expenses account to your Telephone Expenses account. The transaction looks like this:

	Debit	Credit
Telephone Expenses	£1,400	
Utilities Expenses		£1,400

Part V
Putting on Your Best Financial Face

'Good heavens – this tax investigation must be really serious – you're the third tax inspector to visit my little taxidermist business this month.'

In this part . . .

Now you're ready to show off all your hard work keeping the books and find out whether or not your business made a profit. You'll learn how you use all the information you collected throughout the accounting period to prepare financial reports that give investors, lenders, vendors, tax officials and your employees, an idea about how well your company did during the month, the quarter or the year.

We also explore business ownership structures and the reports you must file with Her Majesty's Customs and Excise. Finally we talk about how you close out the books at year-end and get ready for the next year.

Chapter 14

Showing Everything's in Balance

In This Chapter

▶ Keeping things in balance

▶ Finding the numbers

▶ Preparing the Balance Sheet

▶ Analysing the numbers

*A*fter all the books are closed, it's time to prepare the financial results for not only yourself but Her Majesty's Revenue and Customs (HMRC), financial institutions, suppliers, and investors. In this chapter you'll explore the key parts of a Balance Sheet, which shows what your business owns and what it owes as of a particular date, as well as how much the owners have invested in the company.

Exploring the Balance Sheet

You get a snapshot of what the business owns (its assets) and what the business owes (its liabilities or debts) when you read the Balance Sheet. You also find out how much equity owners of the business hold. It's called the Balance Sheet because it shows your accounts are in balance based on this key accounting equation:

Assets = Liabilities + Equity

One column of the Balance Sheet totals the assets and the second column totals the liabilities and then totals the equity separately. The total of the liabilities and the equity should equal the total of the asset column.

Gathering the Numbers

Your first step in preparing the Balance Sheet will be to find all the numbers. If you've set up your Chart of Accounts properly, you should find the key accounts are at the top of the list. These include:

✔ Cash

✔ Debtors (Accounts Receivable)

✔ Stock

✔ Equipment

✔ Vehicles

✔ Furniture

✔ Creditors (Accounts Payable)

✔ Loans Payable

✔ Owner's Capital

You'll probably have a lot more accounts. Make a list of all your asset, liability, and equity accounts with their balances. If you're not sure whether something is an asset, liability, or equity account, you can review the types of accounts in Chapters 2 and 3.

Q. In which section of the Balance Sheet might you find the Cash account?

A. Cash is an asset and would be found in the Current Asset section of the Balance Sheet.

Once you've identified all your accounts you will need to group them into five groups:

✔ **Fixed Assets accounts:** Assets that you expect to own for more than 12 months.

✔ **Current Assets accounts:** Assets that you expect to use in the next 12 months.

✔ **Current Liabilities accounts:** Liabilities that you expect to pay in the next 12 months.

✔ **Long-Term Liabilities accounts:** Liabilities that you will pay over more than 12 months.

✔ **Equity accounts:** Accounts that reflect the claims owners have against the company.

Quick Quiz

1. In which part of the Balance Sheet would you find the Furniture account?

2. In which part of the Balance sheet would you find the Trade Creditors (Accounts Payable) account?

3. Describe the Owner's Capital account.

4. Where would you find the Land and Buildings Account.

5. Whereabouts in the Balance Sheet would you find the Credit Cards Payable account?

6. Where would you find the Retained Earnings account?

Preparing the Balance Sheet

Once you've grouped your accounts, you're ready to prepare the Balance Sheet. There are two types of formats used by companies:

✔ **Horizontal format:** A two-column format with assets on one side and liabilities and equity on the other side.

✔ **Vertical format:** A one column layout with assets listed first, then liabilities and then equities.

This section takes you through the pros and cons of both.

Horizontal format

We show the horizontal format in the following example.

Q. To practise preparing a Balance Sheet in the Horizontal format, use this list of accounts to prepare a Balance Sheet for the ABC Company as of the end of May 2009:

Cash	£3,000
Debtors	£1,000
Stock	£1,200
Equipment	£5,050
Furniture	£5,600
Vehicles	£25,000
Creditors	£2,200
Loans Payable	£29,150
Owners Capital	£5,000
Retained Earnings	£4,500

A. This is what the account format would look like:

Company ABC Balance Sheet; as of May 31, 2009

Fixed Assets		Capital	
Vehicles	£25,000	Opening balance	£ 5,000
Equipment	£5,050	Retained Earnings	£4,500
Furniture	£5,600	Total Equity	£9,500
Total Fixed Assets	£35,650		
Current Assets		**Long Term Liabilities**	
Stock	£1,200	Loans Payable	£29,150
Debtors	£1,000		
Cash	£3,000	**Current Liabilities**	
	£5,200	Creditors (Accounts Payable)	£2,200
Total Assets	£40,850	Total Liabilities and Equity	£40,850

Exercise 1

To practise preparing a Balance Sheet in the Horizontal format, use this list of accounts to prepare a Balance Sheet for the Abba Company as of the end of May 2009:

Cash	£5,000
Debtors	£2,000
Stock	£10,500
Equipment	£12,000
Furniture	£7,800
Building	£300,000
Creditors	£5,200
Loans Payable	£250,000

Owners Capital	£52,000
Retained Earnings	£30,100

Vertical format

We show the Vertical Format in the following example.

Q. To practise preparing a Balance Sheet in the Vertical format, use this list of accounts to prepare a Balance Sheet for the ABC Company as of the end of May 2009:

Cash	£3,000
Debtors	£1,000
Stock	£1,200
Equipment	£5,050
Furniture	£5,600
Vehicles	£25,000
Creditors	£2,200
Loans Payable	£29,150
Owners Capital	£5,000
Retained Earnings	£4,500

A. This is what the report format would look like:

Company ABC Balance Sheet; as of May 31, 2009

Fixed Assets

Equipment	£5,050	
Furniture	£5,600	
Vehicles	£25,000	
Total Fixed Assets		£35,650

Current Assets

Stock	£1,200	
Debtors	£1,000	
Cash	£3,000	
Total Current Assets	£5,200	

Less: Current Liabilities

Creditors	£2,200	
Net Current Assets		£3000
Total Assets less Current Liabilities		£38,650

Long-Term Liabilities

Loans Payable		£29,150
		£9,500
Equity		
Owner's Capital		£5,000
Retained Earnings		£4,500
Total Equity		£9,500

Exercise 2

To practise preparing a Balance Sheet in the Vertical format, use this list of accounts to prepare a Balance Sheet for the Abba Company as of the end of May 2009:

Cash	£5,000
Debtors	£2,000
Stock	£10,500
Equipment	£12,000
Furniture	£7,800
Building	£300,000
Creditors	£5,200
Loans Payable	£250,000
Owners Capital	£52,000
Retained Earnings	£30,100

Working with Your Balance Sheet Numbers

Every business person wants to know how he looks to the outside world and whether his company will look good to the banks or lenders from whom he may want to borrow money. If he's looking to raise additional cash for the business, he also wants to know how the numbers look to potential investors. There are three key ratios that financial institutions and investors use to find out the financial stability of a company based on the Balance Sheet numbers – current ratio, acid test ratio and debt to equity ratio.

Current ratio

This ratio compares your current assets to your current liabilities. It provides a quick glimpse of your company's ablitity to pay its bills.

The formual for calculating this ratio is:

Current assets/Current liabilites = Current ratio

Q. Suppose your Balance Sheet shows that your current assets equalled £52,000 and your current liabilities equalled £22,000. What would your current ratio be?

 A. Here is how you would calculate the current ratio:

£52,000/£22,000 = 2.36

So is that number good or bad? Lenders usually look for a current ratio of 1.2 to 2, so a financial institution would consider a current ratio of 2.36 a good sign. A current ratio under 1 could be considered a sign of trouble because it indicates the company doesn't have enough cash to pay its current bills. A current ratio over 2 may indicate that you are not investing your assets as well as you could. For example, if your company is holding a lot of cash, you may want to consider investing that money in some fixed assets such as additional equipment that you need to help grow the business.

Exercise 3

Suppose your Balance Sheet shows that your current assets equalled £22,000 and your current liabilities equalled £52,000. What would your current ratio be? Is that a good or bad sign to lenders?

Exercise 4

Suppose your Balance Sheet shows that your current assets equalled £32,000 and your current liabilities equaled £34,000. What would your current ratio be? Is that a good or bad sign to lenders?

Exercise 5

Suppose your Balance Sheet shows that your current assets equalled £45,000 and your current liabilities equalled £37,000. What would your current ratio be? Is that a good or bad sign to lenders?

Acid test (quick) ratio

The *acid test ratio* is a stricter test of your company's ability to pay its bills. The acid test ratio only includes the financial figures such as Cash, Bank and Debtors. The value of your stock is not included in this calculation because stock may or may not be able to be converted to cash quickly (sold to customers in the matter of a few days). In an economic downturn it could take a while to sell your stock. Many lenders do prefer using the acid test ratio to determine whether or not to loan your money.

Calculating the acid test ratio is a two- step process:

1. Determine your quick assets:

   Cash + Debtors = Quick assets

2. Calculate your acid test ratio:

   Quick assets/Current liabilities = Acid test ratio

Q. Suppose your Balance Sheet shows that your Cash equalled £25,000, and your Debtors equalled £17,000 and your current liabilities equalled £22,000. What would your current ratio be?

A. Here is how you would calculate the current ratio:

First calculate your quick assets:

£25,000 + £17,000 = £42,000

Next calculate your quick ratio:

£42,000/£22,000 = 1.91

So is that number good or bad? Lenders usually look for a acid test ratio of around 1 for a company to be considerd in good condition. So an acid test ratio of 1.91 is a good sign. The current ratio should be above 1 so that the company can meet all of their current liabilities without having to sell any stock.

Exercise 6

Suppose your Balance Sheet shows that your Cash account equalled £10,000, your Debtors account equalled £25,000 . Your current liabilities equalled £52,000. What would your acid test ratio be? Is that a good or bad sign to lenders?

Exercise 7

Suppose your Balance Sheet shows that your Cash account equalled £15,000, your Debtors equalled £17,000 Your current liabilities equalled £34,000. What would your acid test ratio be? Is that a good or bad sign to lenders?

Exercise 8

Suppose your Balance Sheet shows that your Cash account equaled £19,000, your Debtors equalled £21,000 Your current liabilities equaled £37,000. What would your acid test ratio be? Is that a good or bad sign to lenders?

Debt-to-equity ratio

Before a business owner should even approach a lender for an additional loan, he should always check out his debt condition. One common ratio used for this purpose is the debt-to-equity ratio. This ratio compares what a business owes to what a business owns.

Calculating the debt to equity ratio is a two-step process:

1. Calculate your total debt:

   Current liabilities + Long-term liabilities = Total debt

2. Calculate your debt-to-equity ratio:

   Total debt/Equity = Debt-to-equity ratio

Q. Suppose a business's current liabilities were £22,000 and its long-term liabilities were £75,000. The owner's equity in the company totalled £67,000. What would the debt-to-equity ratio be? Is this a good or bad sign for investors?

A. First calculate the total debt:

£22,000 + £75,000 = £97,000

Next calculate the debt to equity ratio:

£97,000/£67,000 = 1.44

This debt-to-equity ratio over 1 would be a bad sign. Banks prefer the debt-to-equity ratio to be close to one. A company with a debt-to-equity ratio over 1 indicates that the owner's do not have enough invested in the company. A debt-to-equity ratio of less than 1 would not be a problem for a lender.

Exercise 9

Suppose a business's current liabilities were $2,200 and its long-term liabilities were $35,000. The owner's equity in the company totalled $12,500. What would the debt to equity ratio be? Is this a good or bad sign?

Exercise 10

Suppose a business's current liabilities were $5,700 and its long-term liabilities were $35,000. The owner's equity in the company totalled $42,000. What would the debt to equity ratio be? Is this a good or bad sign?

Exercise 11

Suppose a business's current liabilities were $6,500 and its long-term liabilities were $150,000. The owner's equity in the company totalled $175,000. What would the debt to equity ratio be? Is this a good or bad sign?

Answers to Exercises on Developing a Balance Sheet

1 The Horizontal format would look like this:

Abba Company Balance Sheet; as of May 31, 2009

Fixed Assets		**Capital**	
Building	£300,000	Opening balance	£52,000
Equipment	£12,000	Net Profit for the year	£30,100
Furniture	£7,800		£82,100
	£319,800		
Current Assets		**Long Term Liabilities**	
		Loans Payable	£250,000
		Current Liabilities	
Stock	£10,500	Creditors	£5,200
Debtors	£2,000		
Cash	£5,000		
Total Current Assets	£17,500		
Total Assets	£337,300	Total Liabilities and Equity	£337,300

2 Here is what the Vertical format would look like:

Abba Company Balance Sheet; as of May 31, 2009

Fixed Assets		
Building	£300,000	
Equipment	£12,000	
Furniture	£7,800	
		£319,800
Current Assets		
Stock	£10,500	
Debtors	£2,000	
Cash	£5,000	
	£17,500	
Less: Current Liabilities		
Creditors	£5,200	
Net Current Assets		£12,300
Total Assets Less Current Liabilities		£332,100
Long Term Liabilities		
Loans Payable		£250,000
		£82,100
Capital		
Opening Balance		£52,000
Retained Earnings		£30,100
Total Equity		£82,100

3 Calculate the current ratio:

$22,000/$52,000 = 0.42

This ratio is considerably below 1.2, so it would be considered a very bad sign. A ratio this low would indicate that a company may have trouble paying its bills because its current liabilities are considerably higher than the money the company has on hand in current assets.

4 Calculate the current ratio:

$32,000/$34,000 = 0.94

The current ratio is slightly below the preferred minimum of 1.2, which would be considered a bad sign. A financial institution may loan money to this company, but consider it a higher risk. A company with this current ratio would pay higher interest rates than one in the 1.2 to 2 current ratio preferred range.

5 Calculate the current ratio:

$45,000/$37,000 = 1.22

The current ratio is at 1.22, so it would be considerd a good sign and the company probably would not have difficulty borrowing money.

6 First you would calculate your quick assets:

$10,000 + $25,000 = $35,000

Then you would calculate your acid test ratio:

$35,000/$52,000 = 0.67

An acid test ratio of under 1 would be considered a bad sign. A company with this ratio would have a difficult time getting loans from a financial institution.

7 First you would calculate your quick assets:

$15,000 + $17,000 = $32,000

Then you would calculate your acid test ratio:

$32,000/$34,000 = 0.94

An acid test ratio of under 1 would be considered a bad sign. Since this company's acid test ratio is close to one it could probably get a loan, but would have to pay a higher interest rate because it would be considered a higher risk.

8 First you would calculate your quick assets:

$19,000 + $21,000 = $40,000

Then you would calculate your acid test ratio:

$40,000/$37,000 = 1.08

An acid test ratio of over 1 would be considered a good sign. A company with this ratio would probably be able to get loans from a financial institution without difficulty.

9 First you would calculate your total debt:

$2,200 + $35,000 = $37,200

Then you would calculate your debt-to-equity ratio:

$37,200/$12,500 = 2.98

A debt-to-equity ratio of over 1 would be considered a bad sign. A company with this ratio would probably be able not be able to get loans from a financial institution until the owners put more money into the business from other sources, such as family and friends or a private investor.

First you would calculate your total debt:

£5,700 + £35,000 = £40,700

Then you would calculate your debt-to-equity ratio:

£40,700/£42,000 = 0.97

A debt-to-equity ratio near 1 would be considered a good sign. A company with this ratio would probably be able to get loans from a financial institution, but the institution may require additional funds from the owner or investors as well if the company is applying for a large unsecured loan. A loan secured with assets, such as a mortgage, would not be a problem.

11 First you would calculate your total debt:

£6,500 + £150,000 = £156,500

Then you would calculate your debt to equity ratio:

£156,500/£175,000 = 0.89

A debt-to-equity ratio of under 1 would be considered a good sign. A company with this ratio would probably be able to get loans from a financial institution.

Answers to Quick Quiz

1 The furniture account would be regarded as a Fixed Asset as it is kept in the business for more than 12 months.

2 Trade Creditors (Accounts Payable) are suppliers that the business owes money to. This is classified as a Current Liability.

3 Owners Capital can be described as the money invested in the business by the owners. When owners put money into the business it is described as Capital Introduced, and when money is taken out, it can be taken as Drawings (if the business is a sole trader or partnership) or Dividends if it is a Limited Company.

4 Land and Buildings are Fixed Assets as they are kept in the business for a long period of time.

5 The Credit Cards payable account is money owed by the business to credit cards. It is therefore a liability. As the debt is due to be repaid within 12 months it is considered a Current Liability Account.

6 Retained earnings tracks the earnings that are reinvested in the business each year and are part of the owner's equity in the company.

Chapter 15

Producing a Profit and Loss Statement

. . . .

In This Chapter

▶ Discovering a Profit and Loss Statement

▶ Getting the numbers

▶ Finding your bottom line

▶ Evaluating your results

. . . .

*E*very business person wants to know whether or not they made a profit. The Profit and Loss Statement gives you the information you need to calculate a business's profit or loss for the accounting period.

In this chapter you get to review the parts of a Profit and Loss Statement and how to develop one. You then have the chance to practise developing a Profit and Loss statement and analysing its results.

Exploring the Profit and Loss Statement

A Profit and Loss Statement summarises all the sales activities, costs incurred to produce those sales, and the expenses incurred to run the business. After reviewing these numbers a business discovers its bottom line during the accounting period being reported in the Profit and Loss Statement. With this statement you can answer the crucial question — did we make a profit?

When preparing a Profit and Loss Statement, the normal practice is to show two accounting periods. For monthly accounts, you show the current period and the year to date. For example, if you are showing the results for May 2009, you have a column for the month of May and a second column for the year-to-date results, say January to May (if you have a December year end). For year-end accounts you would probably have this year's results compared to prior year.

There are five key parts of a Profit and Loss Statement:

▶ **Sales or Revenue:** The top line of any Profit and Loss Statement shows the total sales or revenues collected during the accounting period being reported.

▶ **Cost of Goods Sold:** This line item shows the amount you spent to purchase the products you sold or the costs you incurred to provide the services you offer.

▶ **Gross Profit:** This line shows how much profit a business makes from its sales before including the overall expenses of running the business. This is calculated by subtracting Cost of Goods Sold from Sales or Revenue.

✔ **Operating Expenses:** The line items in this section of the Profit and Loss Statement will show how much was spent when operating the business. Operating expenses include advertising, administrative expenses, rent, utilities and any other expenses you incurred to run the business.

✔ **Net Profit or Loss:** This is the bottom line of the Profit and Loss Statement. When you subtract your operating expenses from your Gross Profit you will know whether or not the business made a profit.

Quick Quiz

1. Your Purchases account shows you purchased £10,000 worth of paper goods to be sold during the accounting period. In which section of the Profit and Loss Statement would you include that account?

2. Your Telephone Expenses account shows you paid a total of £2,000 for your company's telephones during the accounting period. In which section of the Profit and Loss Statement would you show that account?

3. Your Sales Discounts account shows you offered customers a total of £1,500 in discounts during the accounting period. In which section of the Profit and Loss Statement would you put that information?

4. In the space below, describe how you would calculate Gross Profit. Show the calculation required if it helps explain.

5. In the space below, explain how you would calculate net profit. Show the calculation required if it helps explain.

Formatting the Profit and Loss Statement

Here we show you a simplified UK format for the Profit and Loss Account..

Turnover	X
Cost of Sales	(X)
Gross Profit	X
Distrbution costs	(X)
Administrative Expenses	(X)
Operating Profit	X
Interest payable	(X)

Investment Income	X
Profit on ordinary activities before tax	X
Taxation	(X)
Profit on ordinary activities after tax	X

This example is what you would probably expect to see in your year-end accounts, but it does not give you enough detail for management reports. You might want to follow this format (note we have included some figures to make it look more realistic):

The Profit and Loss Statement with a little more detail added might look like this:

Revenues

Sales	£10,000
Cost of Goods Sold	(£5,000)
Gross Profit	£5,000

Operating Expenses

Advertising	£700
Salaries	£1,200
Supplies	£1,500
Interest Expenses	£500
Depreciation	£500
Total Operating Expenses	£4,400
Operating Profit	£600
Other Income	
Interest income	£200
Net Profit	**£800**

Exercise 1

Using these figures, prepare a Profit and Loss Statement using the format shown in the previous example.

Net Sales	£50,000
Interest Profit and Loss	£1,200
Cost of Goods Sold	£20,000
Advertising	£3,000
Salaries	£5,000
Supplies	£2,500
Interest Expenses	£1,300
Depreciation	£1,500

Preparing the Numbers

You may be wondering how you find the numbers for your Profit and Loss Statement. They're in your Nominal Ledger (see Chapter 4 for the lowdown on this). If you're not sure which accounts belong on the Profit and Loss Statement, we summarise the Profit and Loss Statement accounts in Chapter 3 where we discuss setting up your Chart of Accounts.

Net Sales

Most Profit and Loss Statements only list Net Sales in their revenue section and don't include all the accounts used to calculate those Net Sales. The key accounts used in calculating Net Sales include:

- ✔ **Sales of Goods or Services:** Totals all the money the company earned selling its products, services, or both in this account.
- ✔ **Sales Discounts:** Totals any discounts you offered to customers that reduced the full price of merchandise.
- ✔ **Sales Returns:** Totals all returns from customers.

To calculate Net Sales you subtract any Sales Discounts or Sales Returns from your Total Sales (also known as Gross Sales).

Exercise 2

Looking at your accounts you find you have the following balances at the end of an accounting period:

Sales of Goods	£20,000
Sales Discounts	£2,000
Sales Returns	£1,500

Using these figures, calculate your Net Sales in the space below:

Exercise 3

Looking at your accounts you find you have the following balances at the end of an accounting period:

Sales of Goods	£30,000
Sales Discounts	£4,500
Sales Returns	£2,700

Using these figures, calculate your Net Sales in the space below:

Exercise 4

Looking at your accounts you find you have the following balances at the end of an accounting period:

Sales of Goods	£40,000
Sales Discounts	£6,000
Sales Returns	£2,500

Using these figures, calculate your Net Sales in the space below:

Cost of Goods Sold

You also must calculate your Cost of Goods Sold using several different accounts. While the primary account in which you track the costs incurred in buying the products you plan to sell is Purchases, not everything you purchased will be sold during the accounting period for which you are preparing the Profit and Loss Statement. The Cost of Goods Sold number will reflect only those products you actually sold.

Suppose you started the month of May with £100 of stock in hand. You purchased £1,000 of stock during May and you have £200 of stock left to sell at the end of May. You are preparing an Profit and Loss Statement for the month of May. What would your Cost of Goods Sold be for the month of May?

You calculate your Cost of Goods Sold for May as follows:

Opening Stock	£100
Add Purchases	£1,000
Goods Available for Sale	£1,100
Less Closing Stock	(£200)
Cost of Goods Sold	£900

Exercise 5

Suppose you started the month of June with £200 of stock in hand. You purchased £2,000 of stock during June and you have £500 of stock left to sell at the end of June. You are preparing an Profit and Loss Statement for the month of June. What would your Cost of Goods Sold be for the month of June?

Exercise 6

Suppose you started the month of July with £500 of stock in hand. You purchased £1,500 of stock during July and you have £100 of stock left to sell at the end of July. You are preparing an Profit and Loss Statement for the month of July. What would your Cost of Goods Sold be for the month of July?

Administrative and sales expenses

You don't need to do any calculations after you total your other expense accounts. You would just list the total balance in each account on the Profit and Loss Statement.

Generally you will find that your Revenue accounts carry a credit balance and your Expense accounts carry a debit balance. For more information about how debits and credits work, review Chapter 2.

Analysing Your Profit and Loss Results

Most business owners want to figure out how to improve the profits of their business. There are many different analytical tools available. In this section we introduce you to three key ratios — Return on Sales, Return on Assets, and Return on Equity. These ratios don't mean much unless you know what the common ratio is for your type of business. Check with your local chamber of commerce to find out ratios for similar local businesses.

Return on Sales

The Return on Sales (ROS) ratio gives you an idea of how efficiently your company runs its operations. Using this ratio you can measure how much profit your company produced per pound of sales. You calculate ROS by dividing your net profit before taxes by your net sales.

Suppose your company had a net profit of £4,500 and sales of £18,875 for the month of May, you would calculate the Return on Sales Ratio as follows:

£4,500/£18,875 = 23.8 per cent

So in this case the company made 23.8 per cent for each pound of sales.

In order to make this percentage meaningful, you would need to compare it to other businesses within your industry. We recommend contacting your local businesslink office as they might be able to help you with comparable business information. See www.businesslink.gov.uk.

Exercise 7

Suppose your company had a net profit and Loss of £10,595 and sales of £40,500 for the month of June. Calculate the Return on Sales Ratio.

Exercise 8

Suppose your company had a net profit and Loss of £13,565 and sales of £75,725 for the month of July, calculate the Return on Sales Ratio.

Return on Assets

The Return on Assets (ROA) ratio lets you test how well you are using the company's assets to generate profits. If your company's ROA is the same or higher than other similar companies you are doing well. To calculate the ROA you divide net profit by total assets. You find total assets on your balance sheet, which is discussed in Chapter 14.

Your company's net profit for the month of May is £4,500 and its total assets are £40,050. You can calculate the Return of Assets ratio as follows:

£4,500/£40,050 = 11.2 per cent

This means your company made 11.2 per cent profit for each pound of assets it held. The ROA ratio can vary greatly depending on industries. It can be as low as 5 per cent for manufacturing industries that must spend a lot on equipment and factories, or as high as 20 per cent or higher for service industries that don't need to spend as much on their assets.

Exercise 9

Your company's net profit for the month of May is £5,300 and its total assets are £75,040. What is the Return of Assets ratio?

Exercise 10

Your company's net profit for the month of May is £10,700 and its total assets are £49,650. What is the Return of Assets ratio?

Return on Equity

The Return on Equity (ROE) ratio measures how successful your company was in earning money for its owners or investors. You calculate ROE by dividing net profit by shareholder's or owner's equity. You find the shareholder's or owner's equity on the Balance Sheet (Chapter 14).

Your company earned a net profit of £4,500 and its owner's equity is £50,500. You can calculate the Return on Equity ratio as follows:

£4,500/£50,500 = 8.9 per cent

So the owner's return on his investment is 8.9 per cent.

Exercise 11

Your company earned a net profit of £75,750 and its owner's equity is £500,000. Calculate the Return on Equity ratio.

Exercise 12

Your company earned a net profit of £52,500 and its owner's equity is £375,000. Calculate the Return on Equity ratio.

Answers to Exercises on Producing a Profit and Loss Statement

1 Using the figures given in the example, the Profit and Loss Statement would appear as follows:

Revenues

Sales	£50,000
Cost of Goods Sold	(£20,000)
Gross Profit	£30,000

Operating Expenses

Advertising	£3,000
Salaries	£5,000
Supplies	£2,500
Interest Expenses	£1,300
Depreciation	£1,500
Total Operating Expenses	£13,300
Operating Profit	£16,700
Other Income	
Interest income	£1,200
Net Profit	£17,900

2 The net sales are calculated as follows:

Sales of Goods Sold	£20,000	
Sales Discounts	£2,000	
Sales Returns	£1,500	
Net Sales		£16,500

3 Net Sales would be:

Sales of Goods	£30,000	
Sales Discounts	£4,500	
Sales Returns	£2,700	
Net Sales		£22,800

4 Net Sales would be:

Sales of Goods	£40,000	
Sales Discounts	£6,000	
Sales Returns	£2,500	
Net Sales		£31,500

5 Your Cost of Goods Sold for the month of June would be

Opening Stock	£200
Add Purchases	£2,000
Goods Available for Sale	£2,200
Less Closing Stock	(£500)
Cost of Goods Sold	£1,700

6 Your Cost of Goods Sold for the month of July would be:

Opening Stock	£500
Add Purchases	£1,500
Goods Available for Sale	£2,000
Less Closing Stock	(£100)
Cost of Goods Sold	£1,900

7 The Return on Sales Ratio would be:

£10,595/£40,500 = 26.2 per cent

So in this case the company made 26.2 per cent for each pound of sales.

8 The Return on Sales Ratio would be:

£13,565/£75,725 = 17.9 per cent

So in this case the company made 17.9 per cent for each pound of sales.

9 The Return on Assets ratio is:

£5,300/£75,040 = 7.06 per cent

10 The Return on Assets ratio is:

£10,700/£49,650 = 21.55 per cent

11 The Return on Equity ratio would be:

£75,750/£500,000 = 15.15 per cent

So the owner's return on his investment is 15.15 per cent.

12 The Return on Equity ratio would be:

£52,500/£375,000 = 14 per cent

So the owner's return on his investment is 14 per cent.

Answers to Quick Quiz

1 Purchases are included as part of your calculation for Cost of Goods Sold.

2 Telephone expenses are part of Operating Expenses for a business.

3 Sales discounts are included as part of your calculation for Net Sales.

4 Gross profit is calculated as follows:

Sales Revenue	X
Less Cost of Goods Sold	(X)
Gross Profit	X

The actual gross profit figure is often expressed as a percentage of sales to provide you with a gross profit margin.

For example:

Sales Revenue	£100,000
Cost of Goods Sold	(£75,000)
Gross Profit	£25,000

Gross profit margin would be 25,000/100,000 = 0.25 (25 per cent expressed as a percentage)

5   Net profit is often described as the 'bottom line', as it is the profit after all operating expenses have been taken from your gross profit.

You can express the net profit as a percentage of sales to provide you with a net profit margin.

For example:

Sales Revenue	$100,000
Cost of Goods Sold	($75,000)
Gross Profit	$25,000
Operating expenses	($15,000)
Net Profit	$10,000

The net profit margin would be 10,000/100,000 = 0.10 (10 per cent expressed as a percentage)

Chapter 16

Reporting for Not-For-Profit Organisations

In This Chapter

▶ Discovering what is different about Not-for-profit organisations

▶ Recording receipts and payments

▶ Developing an Income and Expenditure statement

▶ Accumulating funds

The businesses that we have discussed in previous chapters of this book have been striving to make a profit. They are concerned about profitability, and attempt to maximise sales and minimise expenses wherever possible.

But not every organisation is motivated by profit. Many clubs and societies exist for the benefit of their members. All they are concerned about is good stewardship of club funds and the ability to report back to their members in an easily understood format. Preparing the conventional Profit and Loss statement is overloading the members with too much information.

In this chapter we look at other ways that a not-for-profit organisation may report to its members.

Keeping Simple Receipts and Payments Records

Most organisations will need only the simplest of record keeping. In essence, all you, the bookkeeper, need to do is summarise the cash book, assuming that the club concerned operates on a cash basis only. We are assuming that it doesn't take credit for anything it buys and it receives only cash for subscriptions and any other fundraising activities. All you need is a simple receipts and payments account.

A simple receipts and payments account for an imaginary dance club would be as follows:

Let's Dance Club: Receipts and Payments for the year ended 31 December 2009			
Receipts		**Payments**	
Bank Balance @ 1 January 2009	£236	Printing and Stationery	£150
Subscriptions received in year	£650	Coach to Blackpool Theatre	£300
Annual Fundraising	£116	Village hall rent	£500
Bank Interest received	£11	Bank balance @ 31st December 09	£63
	£1,013		£1,013

Exercise 1

Using the figures shown in the following list, prepare a Receipts and Payments account for the Ashwood Stamp Collectors Club.

The opening bank balance at 1 January is £500

Closing bank balance at 31 December is £752

Subscriptions received in the year are £1570

Annual fund raising raises £370

Bank interest received is £23

Meeting room costs are £850

Coach trips to stamp collecting fairs cost £750

Printing and stationery costs total £111

Developing Income and Expenditure Accounts

Some not-for-profit organisations are a litte bit more complex than the examples we have shown so far. They may have assets such as a club house, and may even have liabilities. They may have a club bar, and will have to deal with suppliers for buying food and drink and also will have staffing issues. The receipts and payments account is not a great way to deal with a club that has assets and liabilities, because it only shows the cash movements.

You really need to provide:

- A Balance Sheet which shows all assets and liabilities as discussed in Chapter 14.
- An income and expenditure statement that shows the changes in the club's capital.

Instead of having a capital account (as you would find in a sole trader or partnership's balance sheet,) instead you will have an accumulated fund.

The Income and Expenditure account for a not-for-profit organisation is the equivalent of a Profit and Loss Statement for a profit-making business.

As far as accounting rules are concerned the Income and Expenditure account follows the same principles as the Profit and Loss Statement, in so far as the books are kept on an accrual accounting basis.

Profit Making business	*Not-for-profit Organisation*
Profit and Loss Statement	Income and Expenditure Account
Net Profit	Surplus of Income over Expenditure
Net Loss	Excess of Expenditure over Income
Capital account	Accumulated Fund

Preparing an Income and Expenditure account

This is very similar to preparing a Profit and Loss Statement – there is just different terminology involved.

The club reports directly back to its members, so it must keep accurate accounting records to be able to do this. The treasurer should consider keeping journals in much the same way as a profit-making business. Refer back to Chapter 15 for useful info on preparing financial statements.

We will show you using an example of how you can prepare an Income and Expenditure Account.

The treasurer of Shiregrove Cricket Club prepares an Income and Expenditure account and a Balance Sheet as well as a Profit and Loss Statement for the bar which is run to make a profit for the club.

In order to prepare the Income and Expenditure accounts, a Receipts and Payment account as shown in the previous section must first be completed. A sample Receipts and Payment account is shown in the following table.

Receipts		*Payments*	
Bank balance as at 1 January 2008	£380	Payment for bar supplies	£4000
Subscriptions received during year		*Wages*	
2007 Arrears	£190	Groundkeeper	£1,500
2008	£1,800	Barman	£1,000
2009 (In advance)	£250		
Other items			
Bar sales	£6,500	Bar expenses	£300
Donations received	£150	Club house repairs	£250
		Pitch maintenance	£200
		Treasurer's expenses	£200
		Club travel	£400
		Bank balance as at 31.12.08	£1,420
	£9, 270		£9.270

The members that read this statement agreed that it did not provide adequate information, as it did not give a clear indication of how well the bar had performed. In addition, it treated overdue and advance paid subscriptions as part of the current year's receipts. This was providing a misleading picture.

Other items which were not taken into account were as follows:

- No provision had been made for the depreciation of the clubhouse (£300 per annum) or depreciation of the club equipment (£150 per annum).
- At the year end there were bar stocks of £500 which had not been accounted for (in the previous year this had been £400).

- Unknown to the members, there were also some creditors as follows:

    - Bar supply creditor £200 (previous year had been £180)

    - Bar expenses owing £ 35 (previous year had been £28)

    - Travel costs owing £95 (previous year £233)

    - There were unpaid subscriptions in 2008 of £80

Using this information and with a little help from the club's accountant, the treasurer provided the following information:

- **A Statement of Affairs as at the 31 December 2007** which is a cash based equivalent of a Balance Sheet. See figure 16.3 below. (This shows the opening position at the start of the financial year for this example).

- **A Profit and Loss Statement for the bar, for the year ended 31 December 2008** as shown in the table. This is prepared in the same way as for a profit-making organisation.

- **The final accounts – Income and Expenditure for the year ended 31 December 2008 and Balance Sheet as at 31 December 2008** shown in figures 16.6 and 16.9 below.

Shiregrove Cricket Club: Statement of Affairs as at 31 December 2008

Fixed Assets		
Land		£10,000
Clubhouse		£5,000
Club equipment		£2,000
		£17,000
Current Assets		
Bar stock	£400	
Subscription Debtors	£190	
Cash at bank	£380	
	£970	
Less Current Liabilities		
Creditors	£180	
Bar expenses owing	£28	
Travel expenses owing	£233	
	£441	
Net current assets		***£529***
Financed by		£17,529
Accumulated fund (difference)		£17, 529

Statement of Affairs

A Statement of Affairs is a simplified Balance Sheet which is often used by organisations who do not have a formal book keeping system, and have very few transactions in each accounting year. The accountant preparing the statement, does so using incomplete records. That is, they often have inadequate records to work from.

The Profit and Loss statement for the bar is as follows:

Shiregrove Cricket Club:Bar Profit and Loss Statement
for the year ended 31 December 2008

Sales		£6,500
Less cost of goods sold:		
Opening stock	£400	
Add purchases	£4,020	
	£4,420	
Less closing stock	£500	
		£3,920
Gross Profit		£2,580
Less bar expenses	£307	
Bar wages	£1,000	
		£1,307
Net Profit (transferred to Income and Expenditure A/C)		£1,273

The workings for the Purchase and expense accounts for the bar are:

Purchases Account

Cash	£4,000	Balance brought forward	£180
Balance carried forward	£200	Profit and Loss Account	£4,020
	£4,200		£4,200

Bar Expenses Account

Cash	£300	Balance brought forward	£28
Balance carried forward	£35	Profit and Loss Account	£307
	£335		£335

Note: These calculations use the opening and closing creditors figures shown earlier in the example.

The Income and Expenditure Account reads like this

Shiregrove Cricket Club: Income and Expenditure Account
for the year ended 31 December 2008

Income		
Subscriptions for 2008		£1,880
Profit from the Bar		£1,273
Donations received		£150
		£3,303
Less Expenditure		
Wages – groundkeeper	£1,500	

(continued)

Shiregrove Cricket Club: Income and Expenditure Account for the year ended 31 December 2008 *(continued)*

Repairs		£250
Pitch Maintenance		£200
Treasurer's expenses		£200
Club travel		£262
Depreciation:		
Clubhouse	£300	
Club equipment	£150	
		£450
		£2862
Surplus of Income over expenditure		£441

The workings for Travel expenses are:

Travel Expenses Account

Cash	£400	Balance brought forward	£233
Balance carried forward	£95	Profit and Loss Account	£262
	£495		£495

The workings for subscriptions are:

Subscriptions for 2008	£1,800
Add Subcriptions unpaid	£80
	£1,880

The Balance Sheet is as follows:

Shiregrove Cricket Club: Balance Sheet as at 31 December 2008

Fixed Assets		
Land		£10,000
Clubhouse	£5,000	
Less depreciation	£300	
		£4,700
Club equipment	£2,000	
Less depreciation	£150	
		£1850
		£16,550
Current Assets		
Bar stocks	£500	
Debtors (subscriptions)	£80	
Cash at bank	£1,420	
	£2,000	

Current liabilities			
Creditors – Bar Supplies	£200		
Bar expenses owing	£35		
Travel costs owing	£95		
Prepaid subscriptions	£250		
		£580	
Net Current assets			***£1,420***
			£17,970
Financed by			
Accumulated fund			
Balance as at 1.1.08			£17,529
Add surplus of income over expenditure			£441
			£17,970

Exercise 2

You have been given the Receipts and Payments account for the year ended 31 December 2008 and the Statement of Affairs for the Year ended 31 December 2007 for Tall Trees Tennis Club. With the information given, please supply to the members of the club a Profit and Loss Statement for the Bar for the period to 31 December 2008, an Income and Expenditure Statement and a Balance Sheet as at the 31 December 2008. You should include all workings where necessary.

The information you have received is as follows:

Tall Trees Tennis Club Receipts and Payments Account for the Year ended 31 December 2008

Receipts		Payments	
Bank balance as at 1 January 2008	£732	Payment for bar supplies	£3,000
Subscriptions received during year:		**Wages:**	
2008	£3,200	Groundkeeper	£1,000
2009 (In advance)	£100	Barman	£700
Other income		**Other expenditure**	
Bar Sales	£4000	Bar expenses	£200
		Club house repairs	£150
		Pitch maintenance	£200
		Treasurers expenses	£100
		Club travel	£300
		Bank balance as at 31.12.08	£2,382
	£8,032		£8,032

No provision has been made for depreciation of the clubhouse at £200 per annum, or the club equipment at £150 per annum.

Bar stocks were £400 at 31 December 08 (previous year £300)

There were also several creditors:

	2007	2008
Bar supply creditor	£200	£300
Bar expenses owing	£42	£49
Club travel expenses	£12	£36

A Statement of Affairs has been produced which shows the opening position at 1 January 2008 as follows:

Tall Trees Tennis Club: Statement of Affairs as at 31 December 2008

Fixed Assets		
Land		£12,000
Clubhouse		£3,000
Club equipment		£1,500
		£16,500
Current Assets		
Bar stock	£300	
Cash at bank	£732	
	£1,032	
Less Current Liabilities		
Creditors – bar supply	£200	
Bar expenses owing	£42	
Travel expenses owing	£12	
	£254	
Net Current Assets		**£778**
		£17,278
Financed by		
Accumulated fund (difference)		£17,278

Tall Trees Tennis Club: Bar Profit and Loss Statement for the year ended 31 December 2008

Sales		£
Less cost of goods sold:		
Opening stock		£
Add purchases		£
		£
Less closing stock		£
Gross Profit		£
Less bar expenses	£	£
Bar wages	£	£
Net Profit (transferred to Income and Expenditure A/C)		£

Include your workings here for the Purchase and expense accounts for the bar

Purchases Account

Bar Expenses Account

Tall Trees Tennis Club: Income and Expenditure Account
for the year ended 31 December 2008

Income		
Subscriptions for 2008		£
Profit from the Bar		£
		£
Less Expenditure		
Wages – groundkeeper		£
Repairs		£
Pitch Maintenance		£
Treasurers expenses		£
Club travel		£
		£
Depreciation:		
Clubhouse	£	£
Club equipment	£	£
Surplus of Income over expenditure		£

Add your workings for Travel expenses

Travel Expenses Account

Tall Trees Tennis Club: Balance Sheet as at 31 December 2008

Fixed Assets			
Land			£
Clubhouse		£	
Less depreciation		£	£
Club equipment		£	
Less depreciation		£	£
			£
Current Assets			
Bar stocks		£	
Cash at bank		£	
		£	
Current Liabilities			
Creditors – Bar Supplies	£		
Bar expenses owing	£		
Travel costs owing	£		
Prepaid subscriptions		£	£
Net Current assets			*£*
			£
Financed by			
Accumulated fund			
Balance as at 1.1.08			
Add surplus of income over expenditure			£
			£

Quick Quiz

1. Not-for-proft organisations do not usually prepare Profit and Loss Statements. What do they prepare instead?

2. Instead of a capital account, what do clubs and societies tend to use?

Answers to Exercises on Reporting for Not-For-Profit Organisations

1

Ashwood Stamp Collectors Club : Receipts and Payments for the year ended 31 December 2009

Receipts		Payments	
Bank Balance @ 1st January 2009	£500	Printing and Stationery	£111
Subscriptions received in year	£1570	Coach to stamp collector fairs	£750
Annual Fundraising	£370	Village hall rent	£850
Bank Interest received	£23	Bank balance @ 31st December 09	£752
	£2,463		£2,463

2

Tall Trees Tennis Club: Bar Profit and Loss Statement for the year ended 31 December 2008

Sales		*£4,000*
Less cost of goods sold:		
Opening stock	£300	
Add purchases	£3,100	
	£3,400	
Less closing stock	£400	£3,000
Gross Profit		£1,000
Less bar expenses	£207	
Bar wages	£700	£907
Net Profit (transferred to Income and Expenditure A/C)		£93

Note: The above calculations use the opening and closing creditors figures shown earlier in the example.

Tall Trees Tennis Club: Income and Expenditure Account for the year ended 31 December 2008

Income		
Subscriptions for 2008		£3,200
Profit from the Bar		£93
		£3,293
Less Expenditure		
Wages – groundkeeper	£1000	
Repairs	£150	
Pitch Maintenance	£200	

(continued)

Tall Trees Tennis Club: Income and Expenditure Account for the year ended 31 December 2008 *(continued)*

Treasurers expenses		£100	
Club travel		£324	
		§	
Depreciation:			
Clubhouse	£200		
Club equipment	£150	£350	£2,124
Surplus of Income over expenditure			£1,169

The workings for travel expenses are:

Travel Expenses Account

Cash	£300	Balance brought forward	£12
Balance carried forward	£36	Profit and Loss Account	£324
	£336		£336

Tall Trees Tennis Club Balance Sheet as at 31 December 2008

Fixed Assets			
Land			£12,000
Clubhouse		£3,000	
Less depreciation		£200	£2,800
Club equipment		£1,500	
Less depreciation		£150	£1,350
			§
			£16,150
Current Assets			
Bar stocks		£400	
Cash at bank		£2,382	
		£2,782	
Current Liabilities			
Creditors – Bar Supplies	£300		
Bar expenses owing	£49		
Travel costs owing	£36		
Prepaid subscriptions	£100	£485	
Net Current assets			*£2,297*
			£18,447
Financed by			
Accumulated fund			
Balance as at 1.1.08			£17,278
Add surplus of income over expenditure			£1,169
			£18,447

Answers to Quick Quiz

1   Clubs and societies tend to prepare an Income and Expenditure account instead of a Profit and Loss Statement.

2   Not-for-profit organsiations will not have a capital account, instead they have an accumulated fund. Any surplus income will be posted to the accumulated fund at the end of each financial year.

Chapter 17

Doing Your Business Taxes

. . . .

In This Chapter

▶ Exploring business types

▶ Tax reporting

▶ Vexing about VAT

. . . .

*T*his is probably the chapter which everyone would probably prefer to skip, as tax is not the most riveting of subjects! However, it is probably one of the most important chapters, if you want to be financially ahead of the game. It pays to know what you can and cannot do when it comes to business taxes. A well-informed bookkeeper along with a knowledgeable accountant can provide sound advice to any business.

How a business pays taxes and reports its income to Her Majesty's Revenue and Customs (HMRC) depends upon how the business is structured. In this chapter, you can find a brief overview of business types and how taxes are handled for each type. You also get to review the key concepts you need to master in order to file business tax returns for a sole trader or a partnership. You can also find a very brief overview of some key tax issues involved in corporate tax preparation, but corporate taxation can be a textbook in itself so we won't be discussing the forms that all that involves.

Exploring Business Types

Not all businesses are the same. How a business is structured determines how that business is taxed. In this chapter, we discuss the following three types of business structures – sole traders, partnerships and limited companies.

> ✔ **Sole Traders** are businesses owned by one individual. These are the simplest form of business structure.
>
> ✔ **Partnerships** are businesses owned by two or more individuals. This structure is slightly more complicated than a sole proprietorship because partners must work out key issues of how to divide the profits, how a partner can sell his share if he or she decides to leave, what will happen to a partner's share if he dies, and how the partnership willbe dissolved if a partner wants to leave. Some partnerships add lots of staff and want to protect themselves from lawsuits, so they become Limited Liability Partnerships (LLP's).
>
> ✔ **Limited Companies (Ltd)** provide the safest business structure, particularly if your business faces a risk of being sued. Company law states that a Limited Company is a separate legal entity. It's owner's personal assets are protected from claims against the company. Many small business owners choose this option because of the additional protection it offers. However there is a quite a bit of additional paperwork that needs to be filed on a regular basis to meet the legal obligations of running a limited company. The owner of the business must form a Board of Directors who are responsible for the compliance with company regulations. There are also Public Limited Companies (PLC) which is a type of limited company, but the shares are offered to the public.

Each Limited Company must be registered with Companies House and is given a unique company registration number. The Companies House website is a good source of further information about what forms need to be filed. Go to www. companieshouse.gov.uk for further help. Another source of business advice is www.businesslink.gov.uk. Click on Starting up. There are links to advice on business names and structures.

Quick Quiz

1. You decide to start your own home business, but want protection from being held personally liable for your business activity. What type of business structure would you be likely to pick?

2. You and two of your friends decide to start a band and you need to pick a business structure. What type of business structure would you pick if you want to keep things as simple as possible?

3. You decide to start your own home business. What type of business structure would be easiest for you to use in order to get started?

Tax Reporting

Each business type must file different forms with HMRC when reporting their business activities. This section covers each type of reporting requirement for the three different business structures as described earlier in this chapter.

Sole traders

Sole traders don't have to file tax forms separately to report their business earnings. HMRC not consider the sole traders to be a separate legal entity, and they are not taxed as such. Instead, the sole trader reports their business earnings on their annual tax returns. This is the only financial reporting that they must do.

Effectively, sole traders pay income tax on their business profits.

Completing a tax return

The tax return provides spaces for sole traders to report their trading income, as well as any other income that they might receive during the tax year. For example, the sole trader may also have some employment income on the PAYE scheme and this needs to be declared in addition to the business income. There may also be dividends, interest, pensions and possible capital gains which may have occurred during the tax year – all these things are taken into account, so that an individual's tax may be assessed correctly. Once you have informed HMRC that you are self employed, they automatically send you a paper tax return, but you also have an option to file your return online.

As a bookkeeper for a sole trader, you will probably be responsible for pulling together the trading income and expenses for the business. In many cases you then pass this information on to the Company accountant so that they can calculate the taxable profit and complete and file the necessary tax return.

Completing your tax return online

HMRC are keen for individuals to complete their tax returns online, (we think it's supposed to make them more efficient, but only time will tell . . .) As an incentive, they offer a slightly extended deadline. From April 2008 the deadline for paper tax returns is 31 October, but the online filing date is three months later on 31 January. Filing online gives you that extra bit of time, as well as working out your tax bill for you!

To register for online services, go to www.hmrc.gov.uk and click on the *self assessment* link in the Online services panel on the left side of the home page. It usually takes up to 7 working days to get activated for online services, so allow plenty of time and register well in advance of any submission deadlines.

Supplementary Pages

Because peoples' tax affairs can be very different, HMRC provide supplementary pages. You must select the ones that are appropriate to your circumstances and attach to the main body of your tax return. The supplements are as follows:

- ✔ **Employment:** For more complicated employment situations, where perhaps an individual has more than one job.

- ✔ **Share schemes:** For employees who receive shares under an employee share scheme.

- ✔ **Self Employment:** This is where as a sole trader you declare your income and expenses and thus calculate a taxable profit.

- ✔ **Partnerships:** You declare your share of any partnership profits.

- ✔ **Land and Property:** Any rental income and expenses associated with land and property transactions must must be declared here.

- ✔ **Foreign:** This covers any overseas sources of income.

- ✔ **Trusts:** This covers any income received by way of a distribution of a trust which has been set up for you.

- ✔ **Capital Gains:** This should be completed where any gains are made from the disposal of assets rather than from trading income.

- ✔ **Non-residence:** This covers any income received by non-residents in the UK and thus liable to income tax.

You must inform HMRC that you are becoming self-employed, by completing Form CWF1, this should be done by the end of the third month of self-employment. This ensures that you are sent a tax return as well as being issued with a UTR (Unique Tax Reference) – this is effectively a form of identification between you and the tax office. As an employee of a company you quote your tax reference which can be found on your payslip, when contacting HMRC, but if you are self employed, you are expected to use the UTR number in any form of communication.

The CWF1 form is available for download as part of a leaflet called "Are you thinking of working for yourself?" Go to www.hmrc.gov.uk and click on 'self employed' which is a menu option for ' 'Individuals and employees" section. Then click 'Register as self employed' followed by 'First steps to register as self employed'. The 2009–10 tax rates are:

Tax Rate	2009/2010 Taxable Profit
Basic Rate: 20 per cent	£0 – £37,400
Higher Rate: 40 per cent	Over £37,400

Note: There is a starting rate of 10 per cent for savings only for amounts between £0 – £2,440.

Tax allowances

In addition to providing you with the tax rates as shown above, each individual will also be allocated an Income tax allowance which can be offset against the taxable profits calculated above. The current personal allowance for an individual for the tax year 2009/2010 is £6,475. You can check these figures at www.hmrc.gov.uk click on the Income tax sections for individuals and employees for further help.

Florence runs a florist shop and for the tax year 2009/2010 has calculated that her taxable profits are £10,500. She has a personal allowance of £6,475. Calculate how much tax she is likely to pay. We are assuming that there are no other tax complications.

Taxable Profits	£10,500
Less personal allowance	£6,475
Total income on which tax is due	£4,025
Tax at 20%: (£4025 x 0.20)	= £805

Exercise 1

You are a sole trader and you have calculated that your taxable profits will be £12400 for the tax year 2009/2010. You have a personal allowance of £6,475. How much tax are you likely to pay? Assume no other tax complications.

Exercise 2

You are a sole proprietor and you have calculated that your taxable profits will be £57,000 for the tax year 2009/2010. You have a personal allowance of £6,475. How much tax are you likely to pay? Assume no other tax complications.

Partnerships

If your business is structured as a partnership – that is, made up of more than one person – and it is not a limited liability company, then the business does not pay taxes.

Instead, the profits made from the partnership are split amongst the partners, and each partner must pay the tax due on their portion as though they were a sole trader. Obviously they must complete a supplementary partnership page for their tax return.

The partnership itself needs to complete a partnership tax return, which shows how the partnership profits are split. This return must be sent to the nominated partner who agrees to complete the return and send it back to HMRC. The nominated partner states what profit share is attributable to each partner and that partner is responsible for showing that share on his individual tax return.

Don't be tempted to ignore the partnership income on your personal tax return, as the partnership tax return acts as a cross reference and HMRC will find out if something does not tally!

If you have recently formed a partnership, you should inform HMRC as soon as possible, usually within three months of starting. They will need to issue you with a partnership UTR (Unique Tax Reference) so that this may be used when filing your partnership tax return.

Exercise 3

Smith and Partners have completed their accounts and have calculated that the business has taxable profits of £240,000 for the tax year 2009/2010. There are four partners in the business each with equal shares. Describe how much profit each partner is liable to pay tax on, and how should they report it to HMRC.

Limited companies

The tax affairs of limited companies are more complex than for a sole trader or partnership. Company accounts are open to the scrutiny of the public, as accounts must be filed with Companies House and once filed, they are available for download (for a small fee) to any individual who wishes to read them.

Companies must file a tax return, known as the CT600, to HMRC. The limited company pays corporation tax on its profit as well as tax on any dividends paid to its shareholders.

There are two types of CT600: a short four-page version, which is suitable for companies with straightforward tax affairs and an eight-page return for those with more complicated tax affairs. For details of which CT600 form you should fill in go to www.hmrc.gov.uk and click on 'Corporation Tax' in the Businesses and Corporations section.

Corporation tax rates vary according to how much taxable profit the company makes. The rates are shown in the following table:

Small Companies rate:	21 per cent
Marginal Small Companies relief lower limit	£300,00
Marginal Small Companies relief upper limit	£1,500,00
Marginal Small Company relief fraction	7/400
Main rate of Corporation Tax	28 per cent
Special rate for unit trusts and open ended investment companies	20 per cent

Small companies rate can be claimed by qualifying companies with profits of less than £300,000.

If you are just starting out in business, check with your accountant whether it is more beneficial to become a sole trader, partnership or limited company. It is not just the tax benefits you should considered, but also the administrative differences between the different structures. You should be aware that a limited company places more of an administrative burden on the owner of that business. This increases accounting, admin and legal costs. Make sure you understand all the implications before committing to your chosen structure.

Exercise 4

Your business is formed as a sole trader. Imagine you are your accountant. What tax forms would you be advising yourself to complete at the end of each tax year? Which supplementary sections would you complete?

Vexing about VAT

There is a lot of angst surrounding VAT, and many people perceive a visit from the VAT man as being the step before being thrown in the clink! They automatically assume that they are going to be accused of some fraudulent activity. Often this cannot be further from the truth, a visit from HMRC can often just be a compliance visit, just to check you are doing things properly. It is up to you as the bookkeeper to ensure that all the records are kept neatly and you fully understand what is expected of you. You must make sure that you understand the complexities of the VAT system and any peculiarities that may be relevant to the line of business you are working in. If in doubt, contact the VAT office and/or your local friendly accountant, who will be happy to make sure you are calculating your VAT correctly.

Having a look at VAT

VAT is a tax charged on most business goods and services made in the UK or the Isle of Man. VAT is also charged on goods and some services imported from certain places outside the European Union and on some goods and services coming into the UK from other EU countries. VAT applies to all business structures – sole traders, partnerships, limited companies, charities and so on. Basically all VAT registered companies act as unpaid collectors of VAT for HMRC. There are three different rates of VAT.

- ✔ **Standard Rate** which at the time of writing is 17.5%.

- ✔ **Reduced Rate** which is currently 5% and includes domestic fuel, energy saving installations and renovation of your private dwelling, for example self build.

- ✔ **Zero Rate (0%).** Many products and services are given a zero rating and include items such as some foods, childrens clothing and books.

There are also items which are exempt from VAT in other words they are outside the scope of VAT, this is not the same as zero rated. Your accountant may help you more fully understand the implications of such transactions. Exempt items include, insurance, providing credit, education and training (as long as certain conditions are met), fundraising events by charities and subscriptions to membership organisations. More information can be found about exempt items in VAT Notice 701/30. There are also certain land transactions which benefit from VAT exemption, but the exemption can be waived if a 'company 'opts to tax' – you can find more details on this in VAT Notice 742A. Both these notices are available as download documents from www.hmrc.gov.uk.

Calculating VAT

In a nutshell, VAT can be split into two parts:

- ✔ **Output Tax:** VAT that you must charge on your goods and services when you make each sale (those considered a Vatable supply). You must collect all the VAT for each sale and pass it on to HM Revenue and Customs (HMRC).

- ✔ **Input Tax:** VAT that you pay to your suppliers for the goods and services that you purchase for your business. You can reclaim the VAT on these items.

You will be expected to produce a VAT return each quarter which shows the total amount of Output tax less the total amount of Input tax. The amount remaining should be paid across to HMRC. An example could be:

Output tax	£7000
Input tax	£3000
Total payable to HMRC	£4000

If Input tax is a greater amount than output tax, then your company will be subject to a refund from HMRC. (Yes, that does happen!)

You only need to register for VAT once your business turnover exceeds £68,000, but you can voluntarily register even if your sales are under the £68,000 threshold. Registration allows you to reclaim the VAT on your purchases, but you also need to charge VAT on your sales on those transactions which are subject to VAT. If you are not sure about the VAT implications for your business then you can contact HMRC and they will be more than happy to help. They are not the ogres that some might perceive!

VAT Notice 700 – The VAT Guide is a very useful publication offered by HMRC and can be downloaded from their website www.hmrc.gov.uk.

There is a National Advice Service Helpline for matters concerning VAT on the following telephone no: 0845 010 9000.

If you use a computerised accounting system such as Sage 50, then you will find that your VAT return can be processed at the touch of a button (although the results will still need to be checked – you can't get away with it that easily!) If you would like to find out more, this subject is covered in detail in *Sage 50 Accounts For Dummies* by Jane Kelly (published by Wiley).

Answers to the Quick Quiz

1 You would be likely to choose a Limited Company. You can be sued personally if you structure your business as a sole proprietorship but you have additional protection with a Limited Company, your personal assets are protected.

2 The most simple structure is likely to be a Partnership. However you would need to agree how profits would be shared and what would happen if a member decided he/she wanted to leave the band. A simple partnership agreement should be set up to avoid complications in the future.

3 A Sole Trader is the easiest way to start up in business. You can start trading immediately, using your own name or a trading name.

Answers to Exercises on Doing Your Business Taxes

1

Tax Year 2009/2010

Taxable Profits =	£12,400
Less Personal allowance =	£6,475
Total income on which tax is due =	£5,925
Tax at 20% (0.20 x £5,925) =	£1,185

2

Taxable Profits =	£57,000
Less personal allowance =	£6,475
Total income on which tax is due =	£50,525
First £37,400 @ 20% =	£7,480
Next £13,125 (£50,525 - £37,400) @ 40% =	£5,250
Total tax payable =	£12,730

3 The partners each have an equal share of the profits, so profits must be divided into four, the profit each partner is liable to tax on is £60,000. The partners must declare their share of the profits on their individual tax returns. This should be shown on the supplementary partnership pages of the tax return. They should also nominate a partner to complete a Partnership return, which shows the full taxable profit of the partnership and how it has been divided to the individual partners.

4 You will need to inform HM Revenues and Customs that you have become self employed. As a result, they will issue you with an UTR (Unique Tax Reference) and will send you a tax return. This can be completed using the paper format or online. See details in the chapter for how to set this up. You will need to determine which supplementary pages are applicable to you, and if you are filling in a paper return, you will need to ensure that HMRC send you the appropriate additional pages. For example, if you have some investment property that you rent out, you will need to complete the supplementary Land and Property pages. If you are filing online, you simply select the additional pages you require using the click of a mouse!

Chapter 18

Completing Year-End Payroll and Reports

In This Chapter

▶ Reporting on employees at the payroll year end
▶ Submission deadlines

Getting your year end payroll reports done can be quite time consuming, but if you plan ahead and prepare adequately, then the procedure is pretty painless. This chapter reviews the types of forms that you need to complete, along with the deadlines for submission.

If you have been following the payroll procedures as outlined in Chapter 9 you should be familiar with completing a P11 deduction sheet for each employee and updating the 'yellow book' (P30Bc Employer Payslip Booklet) with details of your PAYE and National Insurance contributions (NIC) which are then sent to Her Majesty's Revenue and Customs (HMRC).

At the payroll year end, you will be required to summarise all of the information obtained whilst processing your monthly payroll. This must be sent to HMRC by specific deadlines which we outline later in this chapter.

 'Employer Helpbook E10', which HMRC publishes each year, covers finishing the tax year. You can obtain this from www.hmrc.gov.uk.

Form P14

A P14 is essentially a summary of the information that you have been gathering each month for every employee shown on the P11 (covered in Chapter 9).

The information shown in the P11 provides HMRC with a record of how much tax and National Insurance and any other deductions have been made for each employee.

You must take great care when completing the P14s and ensure that the information is accurate. The P14 is a duplicate copy form and the last sheet is actually called the P60, which is probably more familiar to you. This provides a summary of an employee's earnings for that tax year, and includes pay, tax and National Insurance summaries. The P60 does not get sent to HMRC, but instead is given directly to the employee.

Your P14 summary sheets should be submitted in alphabetical order by employee name.

Detailing Benefits on Forms P9D, P11D and P11D (b)

These forms only need to be completed where benefits in kind have been received by an employee during the tax year. For examples of benefits in kind, see the next section.

- ✔ **P9D:** To be used if an employee earns £8,500 or less. Earnings include all bonuses, tips and benefits.

- ✔ **P11D:** For employees who earned more than £8,500 and for almost all Directors. Note: Use a form P9D for Directors who earn less than £8,500, has no material interest in the company (they control less than 5% of the company share capital) and is either a full time working director, or a director of a charity or non-profit organization.

- ✔ **P11D (b):** You must confirm by 6 July that all P11D forms have been completed and sent to HM Revenues and Customs. You should also declare the total amount of class 1A NIC's you are due to pay. These are the extra NIC's that may be due on taxable benefits that are provided to your employees.

Types of benefit in kind

It is important to be able to establish what a benefit in kind is, as it will determine how many P11D's and P9D's you have to submit.

Examples of benefits in kind include:

- ✔ Use of a company car
- ✔ Medical Insurance
- ✔ Personal bills paid by the employer on behalf of the employee
- ✔ School fees of employees' children paid by the employer (although if the employer is reimbursing the employee for school fees, then a P11D is not due, but tax and NI must be paid on the amount reimbursed).
- ✔ Gym membership to a public gym (if the gym was just for staff use it would not constitute a benefit in kind as it would be available to all employees).

As you can see, benefits in kind are a bit of a minefield! It is wise to take some advice when deciding whether something is a benefit in kind or not.

There is an A-Z of Expenses and Benefits in Kind on the HMRC website which gives you guidance as to whether there is a PAYE or National Insurance liability and where to report the expenses and benefits provided (such as P11D). Go to www.hmrc.gov. uk and type *Expenses and benefits in kind A-Z* into the search box. This is a great tool that gives you concise answers on whether something is a benefit in kind or not and whether it should be reported on a P11D or not.

In order to work out what kind of forms you will need to complete at the year end, we will look at the following example:

Pastiche Ltd have 5 employees as follows:

Jim Turner – (Director)	Earnings £70,000 with a company car
May Grattan (Sales Director)	Earnings £48,000 with a company car
Stacie Beckham (Book Keeper)	£25,000, the company pays medical insurance
Victoria Denham (Part time Admin Asistant) Salary	£7,950, the company pays medical insurance
Daniella Levi (cleaner)	£5,000

From the information given above, Stacie Beckham the bookkeeper must decide which forms she needs to complete at the payroll year end. So far, she has completed the P11 deduction working sheets for each employee, but now she must also complete the following:

- ✔ P14/P60 for each employee

- ✔ P35 Annual employer summary for the company

- ✔ P9D for Victoria Denham (she has medical expenses. which would be treated as a benefit in kind)

- ✔ P11D's for Jim Turner, May Grattan and Stacie Beckham. They all have benefits in kind, but because they all earn over £8,500 a P11D must be completed for all three.

Exercise 1

Misteeq Ltd have three employees. Their remuneration packages are as follows:

Jo Dunn (Director)	Earnings £45,000 with a company car.
Marie Stansfield (Bookkeeper)	Earnings £25,000 she receives medical insurance.
Lara Cribb (Part time Admin assistant)	Earnings £7,995 and she receives medical insurance.

You must decide which forms need to be completed to meet your payroll year end obligations.

Forms P38, P38A and P38 (S)

These are reports that must be completed where you have not deducted PAYE – usually from part time, casual staff. Form P38 (S) applies to students.

P38 (S) is used when students work for you solely during the holidays. You don't need to deduct tax from them provided they:

- ✔ Fill in the student declaration

- ✔ Do not earn more than £6475 during the tax year – If a student's pay exceeds this amount, then you must complete a P46 using the original start date and deduct tax using the guidance in *CWG2 Employer Further Guidance to PAYE & NIC*

P35

This is the employers annual return and must be completed if you have done a P11 worksheet for any employees.

This is a four-part form, which lists every employee including directors, national insurance amounts and tax amounts that you have deducted from their pay.

Deadline dates

As you can imagine, there are several deadline dates that you need to be aware of for submitting your year end payroll reports. They are as follows:

- **19 May:** Latest date for Employers Annual returns (P35) and P14's to reach HM Revenue and Customs.

- **31 May:** Last date for giving P60 to each employee working for you.

- **6 July:** Is the deadline for P11D submission for the tax year 2008/2009 (you should check on the HMRC website for each future tax year, as this may change).

- **19 July:** You must pay all outstanding Class 1A national insurance contributions, so that payment reaches HMRC by 19 July.

- **22 July:** This is the last date for outstanding Class 1A national insurance contributions for those paying by electronic transfer.

Plan your Payroll year end timetable. Ensure that you have a note in your diary for each HM Revenue and Customs deadline.

Make sure you order adequate forms from the HM Revenue and Customs Orderline.

Make a note here of the quantities of forms that you will need. There are different forms for manual completion and those that can be used in your printer, so please ensure you select the correct ones.

When completing P60s, you need one for each person that worked for you during the tax year – and for whom you have completed a form P11. HMRC states that you must destroy P60's for those employees who no longer work for you at the end of the tax year.

The P14 is the duplicate form which has the P60 attached behind it. You must submit the P14 to HMRC but destroy the P60 for those employees who no longer work for you at the year end.

Employee Orderline

The following telephone number can be used to pre order your year end payroll forms, such as P60's and P11D's. They are all free, but you need to know what quantity you require prior to your phonecall. Telephone this number for help: 08457 646 646.

Sending Your Returns Online

Why not help try and save the planet by sending your your employee returns online? HMRC have estimated that over 43 million PAYE forms were sent online during 2007/2008 and this equates to saving 6000 trees in a year!

If you have not filed online before, you need to register and activate your account before you can send and receive PAYE information online. To see an online demonstration for registering for online services go to www.hmrc.gov.uk/demo/organisation/register.

If you have 50 or more employees, you or your agent *must* file your annual return forms online, otherwise you may face a penalty or a surcharge. Companies with fewer than 50 employees at the moment are being given an incentive of £75 (in the tax year 2008/2009) for completing their returns online.

Quick Quiz

1. Don James is a student and begins work in your company to earn money during the summer holidays. Which form should you ask him to fill in?

2. Maria Aitkins earns £12,000 and receives gym membership at her local public leisure centre. Does she need to fill in a P11D?

3. Splash Ltd have 65 employees – do they need to file their payroll year end online?

4. When should you submit your P60's to HM Revenue and Customs and what is the deadine for making sure each employee has a copy?

5. What is a P35 and what is the submission deadline?

Answer to Exercise on Completing Year End Payroll and Reports

1   From the information given in the exercise, you need to complete the following forms:

- ✔ P14/P60 for each employee.

- ✔ P35 Annual employer's summary to include information for all employees.

- ✔ P9D for Lara Cribb as she receives medical insurance which is classed as a benefit in kind. As she earns <£8500 a P9d will be required.

- ✔ P11d's will be required for both Jo Dunn and Marie Stansfield as they both receive benefits in kind – but as they both earn over £8500 a P11d will be required for both.

Answers to Quick Quiz

1   A P38 (S) would need to be completed and this ensures that you do not deduct any tax.

2   A P11d should be completed for Maria Aitkins, as the gym membership was to a public gym and not for employees only. Section K would need to be completed on the P11D.

3   Yes, all companies with more than 50 employees now need to file their annual returns online, otherwise they face a penalty.

4   The deadline for submitting P11ds to HMRC is 19th May. The company should ensure that a P60 is given to every employee who was in the employers employment on the last day of the tax year, by 1st June following the end of the tax year.

5   A P35 is the employees annual return which must be completed if you have done a P11 deduction working sheet for any employee. The deadline for submission is 19th May following the end of the tax year.

Chapter 19

Getting Ready for a New Bookkeeping Year

In This Chapter
▶ Closing the books
▶ Looking at customer accounts
▶ Reviewing supplier accounts
▶ Cycling into the new year

*A*t the end of every accounting period certain accounts are closed and others remain open. In this chapter, we review the accounts that continue from one business cycle to the next, as well as the accounts that must be closed at the end of each cycle and started with a zero balance in the next cycle. You also get to explore key decisions that must be made about customer and supplier accounts.

Finalising the Ledger

Once you've processed all possible payments for the year and accounted for all possible income, reviewed all your accounts, balanced out your books, and prepared the financial statements for the accounting period, it's time to finalise your Nominal Ledger and get ready for a new year. Some accounts carry over their balances into the new year (Balance Sheet accounts) and others start with a zero balance (Profit and Loss accounts).

Closing Profit and Loss accounts

Once you're sure you've made any needed corrections or adjustments that were identified when preparing your trial balance (Chapter 13) and you've collected the information needed from those accounts for your financial statements, you can then zero out the balances of all the Profit and Loss accounts. This includes all revenue, cost of goods sold, and expense accounts.

You don't throw away the accounting information for the prior accounting period. You just start new pages in your journals and Nominal Ledger accounts with a zero balance for the new accounting period.

If you're using a computerised accounting system, follow the procedures for closing the accounting period. The accounting system will archive the data for the accounting period and zero out the accounts during the closing process.

Carrying over Balance Sheet accounts

Balance Sheet accounts never get zeroed out. All these accounts carry their balance into the next year. You still have the underlying assets, such as cash in your bank accounts, furniture in your business or the buildings you own, so you don't want to zero out their values. You still owe your creditors and need to pay any debts either during the next accounting period or during some future accounting period. For example, a mortgage is paid over many years and its balance would be carried over until paid off. The owners of the company certainly still own their share of the company and you must carry over details of that ownership.

Q. You are closing the books for the accounting period and have a £75,000 balance in your Sales account. What will happen to that balance?

A. The answer is that when you close out that period, you should zero the balance. All Profit and Loss accounts start with a zero balance in a new accounting period.

Reviewing Customer Accounts

You will probably close your books on a monthly basis, but do a more extensive closing process at the end of a 12-month accounting period. During this year-end close it's a good idea to take a more critical look at your customer accounts. In Chapter 8 we discuss writing off accounts for bad debts, but at year-end it's time to take a harder look. Bad debt can be used as an expense to reduce taxes, so if you believe certain customers will never pay, it's a good idea to just write them off at year-end and not pay taxes on what otherwise would be shown as a profit for your company. Even if you're a sole trader, reducing net income will reduce the amount of taxes you must pay on your profits.

Q. At the end of the year when closing the books, you find you have six customers who are more than 90 days past due. You don't expect any of the customers to pay. The customers owe a total of £1,500. What entry should you make in your books?

A. You should make the following entry:

	Debit	Credit
Bad Debt	£1,500	
Debtors		£1,500

You should also reflect the write-off in each of the customer's accounts.

Exercise 1

At the end of the year when closing the books, you find you have three customers who are more than 90 days past due. You don't expect any of the customers to pay. The customers owe a total of £750. What entry should you make in your books?

Assessing Supplier Accounts

During the closing process you should also review your supplier accounts to be sure all invoices related to the prior accounting period are entered into the books. If you find an unpaid invoice that does reflect expenses for the period you are about to close, you should record that invoice by crediting the Creditors (Accounts Payable) account and debiting the appropriate account.

In reviewing your supplier accounts, you find that the most recent telephone bill of £135 is not paid or recorded, but it does reflect expenses incurred during the accounting period that is being closed. How should you record that in the books?

Here's how you would record the entry:

	Debit	*Credit*
Telephone Expenses	£135	
Creditors		£135

If you already completed your trial balance, you will need to adjust the numbers to reflect this missing expense.

Exercise 2

In reviewing your supplier accounts, you find that your most recent electricity bill, totalling £235 for electricity used in the prior month, was not paid or recorded, but does reflect expenses incurred during the accounting period that is being closed. How should you record that in the books?

Deleting Accounts

At the end of an accounting year is a good time to review all your accounts and decide whether or not you still need them. If you decide you don't need an account any longer, the closing process is an ideal time to delete accounts. You should never delete an account in the middle of an accounting year. If you do find that you want to delete an account in the middle, then start a list of accounts you want to delete at the end of the year.

If an account you want to delete is a Profit and Loss account, then it's very easy to delete. Because you will be zeroing out all the accounts, you can just delete the account from your Chart of Accounts. If the account is a balance sheet account and it does carry a balance, you will need to move the value of the assets, liabilities or equities to an account that will still be open. You would move the assets by making an entry in your Nominal Ledger.

Q. Suppose you want to consolidate all your vehicle asset accounts into one account at the end of the accounting year. You have an asset account called Vehicles — Vans with a debit balance of £20,000 and an asset account called Vehicles — Cars with a debit balance of £15,000. What entry would you need to make in the nominal ledger to close the two vehicle accounts and start a new one just called Vehicles?

A. Your entry would be:

	Debit	Credit
Vehicles	£35,000	
Vehicles – Vans		£20,000
Vehicles – Cars		£15,000

Exercise 3

Suppose you decide to consolidate your Credit Card Payable liability accounts into one at the end of the accounting year. You have a liability account called Credit Cards Payable – Mutual Bank with a credit balance of £5,000 and a liability account called Credit Cards Payable – First Bank with a credit balance of £500. What entry would you make in the Nominal Ledger to consolidate these accounts into an account called Credit Cards Payable?

Preparing to Restart the Business Cycle

The monthly closing process for any business can take a week or more as you make the necessary adjustments and corrections. Closing at year-end can take several weeks. Most businesses send out notices to their employees telling them any revenues or expenses that they want entered for the current year must be in accounting by a certain cutoff date.

During the closing process, a bookkeeper will probably be working with two sets of books: one set that is being closed and a new set for the new account cycle. If you are closing the books at month-end, you may just start a new journal page for the new month. But, at year-end you would more likely have a new set of journals for the new year.

If you are using a computerised accounting system, this restart of the accounting cycle will be managed by the software program, but it is a good idea to print out a report of your year-end account data before starting the closing process in case something goes wrong. Also you should back up your data on a disc before starting the closing process.

At year-end you will also need to make up new files for all your suppliers, contractors, and customers. If you have room in your office, you will probably use one file cabinet for the current year and one for the previous year. To set up the files for the new year, you would likely box up the files from two years ago and use those drawers for the new year. For example, if you are getting ready for 2009 and have one filing cabinet with 2008 files and one with 2007 files, you would box up the 2007 files to make room for the 2009 files. In Chapter 6, I discuss record keeping and how long you must keep your files.

Quick Quiz

1. You are closing the books for the accounting period and have a £50,000 balance in your Purchases account. What should you do with that balance?

2. You are closing the books for the accounting period and have a £25,000 balance in your Cash account. Describe what will happen to that balance.

3. You are closing the books for the accounting period and have a £150,000 balance in your Loans Payable account. Describe what will happen to that balance.

4. You are closing the books for the accounting period and have a £125,000 balance in your Owner's Equity account. Describe what will happen to that balance.

5. You are closing the books for the accounting period and have a £35,000 balance in your Advertising account. Describe what will happen to that balance.

Answers to Exercises on Getting Ready for a New Bookkeeping Year

1 You would need to write off the balances of the three customers with balances older than 90 days old.

You should make this entry:

	Debit	Credit
Bad Debt	£750	
Debtors		£750

2 To ensure that you include the electricity invoice for the accounting period, you should make this entry:

	Debit	Credit
Electricity Expenses	£235	
Creditors		£235

3 In order to consolidate the credit cards payable, you should make this entry into the Nominal Ledger:

	Debit	Credit
Credit Cards Payable – Mutual Bank	£5,000	
Credit Cards Payable – First Bank	£500	
Credit Cards Payable		£5,500

Answers to Quick Quiz

1 You would zero out the Purchases account at the end of the accounting period, because it is part of the Profit and Loss account, and is shown in the calculation for cost of goods sold.

2 When closing the accounting period you would carry over the cash balance to the next accounting period. You certainly want to keep track of your cash, it doesn't disappear just because you enter a new accounting period. The Cash account is a Balance Sheet account, as are all asset accounts.

3 When closing the accounting period all liabilities will carry over to the next accounting period. While you might wish you could zero out a loan, unfortunately you can't, and it must be carried over. All liability accounts are Balance Sheet accounts.

4 Any owners' equity is carried over to the next accounting period. Owners certainly don't want to lose track of the amount they've invested in the company. All equity accounts (Balance Sheet accounts) are carried over to the next accounting period.

5 Advertising expenses will be zeroed out at the end of the accounting period. The Advertising account is an expense account and it is shown on the Profit and Loss. You don't carry over expenses from one accounting period to the next.

Part VI
The Part of Tens

'You say my bookkeeping predecessor
was incompetent. What happened to him?'

In this part . . .

We join in the For Dummies series tradition of showing you some lists of ten key factors to maintaining your books and using the information collected. We highlight the top ten accounts you should monitor and the top ten ways to manage your business's cash using your books.

Chapter 20

Top Ten Ways to Manage Your Cash

In This Chapter

▶ Charting the way

▶ Handling transactions

▶ Reviewing financial results

▶ Tracking costs and setting prices

Many business owners think of bookkeeping as a necessary evil, but in reality if you make effective use of the data you collect, bookkeeping can be your best friend for managing your cash. The key to taking advantage of what bookkeeping has to offer is understanding the value of basic bookkeeping principles and taking advantage of the information you collect. This chapter reviews the top ten ways to manage your business cash with your books.

Charting the Way

You may think that a list of accounts, called the Chart of Accounts, is not a big deal. Well that's far from the truth. The Chart of Accounts dictates how your financial data will be collected and where your transactions will be put. It's crucial to define each account carefully and determine exactly what types of transactions will go where in order to be able to use the information you have collected effectively. We talk more about the Chart of Accounts and how to set one up in Chapter 3.

Balancing Your Entries

Keeping your books balanced is the only way to know how your business is doing. You can never know whether your profit numbers are accurate, if your business's books don't balance. In bookkeeping, a process called double-entry bookkeeping is used to keep the books balanced. We talk more about this basic principle and how to keep the books balanced in Chapter 2.

Posting Your Transactions

In order to be able to use the information regarding your business transactions, they must be posted accurately to your accounts. If you forgot to post a transaction to your books, your reports will not reflect that financial activity. Or, if you post a transaction to your books that is not accurate, your reports using that information will be wrong. We talk more about the posting process in Chapters 4 and 5.

Keeping On Top Of Credit Control

If your business sells to customers on credit, you certainly want to be sure your customers pay for their purchases in the future. Customer account information is collected in the Debtors account (otherwise known as Accounts Receivable), as well as in individual records for each customer. You should review reports based on customer payment history, called aging reports, on a monthly basis to be sure customers are paying on time. You may want to cut off customers from future purchases if their accounts are past due for 90 days or more. You set the rules for credit. We talk more about how to manage customer accounts in Chapter 8.

Paying Bills Accurately and on Time

If you want to continue getting supplies, products, and services from your suppliers and contractors, you must be sure you pay them accurately and on time. You also want to be sure that you don't pay anyone twice. Payments are managed through the Trade Creditors account (otherwise known as Accounts Payable account). You should review your payment history and be sure your are making timely and accurate payments. We talk more about managing your payments in Chapter 7.

Planning Profits

Nothing is more important to a business owner than the profits he will ultimately make. Yet many business owners don't take the time to plan their profit expectations at the beginning of each year, so they have nothing to use to gauge how well they are doing throughout the year. Take the time to develop profit expectations and a budget that will help you meet the expectations before the year starts. Then develop a series of internal financial reports using the numbers you collect in your bookkeeping system that will help you determine whether or not you are meeting your sales targets and maintaining control over your product costs and operating expenses. We talk more about monitoring sales in Chapter 8, costs and expense tracking in Chapter 7, and how to determine your net profit in Chapter 15.

Comparing Budget to Actual Expenses

Keeping a careful watch on how well your budget planning reflects what is actually going on in your business can help you meet your profit goals. Take the time to develop a budget that sets your expectations for the year and then develop internal reports that give you the ability to track how closely your actual expenses match that budget. If you see any major problems, correct them as soon as possible to be sure you'll be able to meet your target profit at the end of the year. We talk about managing expenses in Chapter 7.

Comparing Sales Goals to Actual Sales

In addition to watching your expenses, you also need to be sure your actual sales match the sales goals you set at the beginning of the year. Designing an internal report that allows you to track sales goals versus actual sales gives you the ability to monitor how well your business is doing. If you find your actual sales are below expectations, the earlier in the year you correct that problem the better chance you'll have to meet those year-end goals. We talk about how to track sales in Chapter 8.

Monitoring Cost Trends

It's important to know what is happening to the costs involved in purchasing the products you sell or the raw materials you use to manufacture your products. These costs trends can have a major impact on whether or not your company will earn the net income you expect. If you find the costs are trending upward, you may need to adjust the prices of the products you sell in order to meet your profit goals. We talk more about tracking cost trends in Chapter 7.

Making Pricing Decisions

Many factors must be considered when determining what price to charge your customers. You need to consider not only how much you pay to buy the product (or to manufacture the product) you sell, but you also must factor in what you pay your employees as well as other advertising and administrative expenses you incur in order to set a price. You can't set that price too high though or you may not find any customers willing to buy the product. Properly pricing your product can be a critical factor in determining whether or not your product will sell. While the numbers in your books regarding product costs and operating expenses are not the only factor in making a pricing decision, the information is critical to help you make that decision. You'll also need market research about what customers will pay for a product in addition to the product cost and operating expense data to set a price. We cover tracking costs and expenses in Chapter 7 and calculating profit in Chapter 15.

Chapter 21

Top Ten Accounts You Should Monitor

In This Chapter

▶ Recognising assets

▶ Acknowledging liabilities

▶ Tracking sales, goods purchased, and expenses

▶ Tracking owner's equity

*W*hile each and every account has its purpose in bookkeeping, all accounts are not created equally. Some accounts are more critical than others. This chapter looks at the top ten accounts for bookkeepers.

Cash

All of a business' transactions pass through this account, which is so important that there are actually two journals used to track the transactions — the Cash Receipts Journal and the Cash Payments Journal. We discuss these journals in Chapter 5. As the bookkeeper it is your responsibility to be sure that all cash — whether it is coming into the business or being sent out — is handled and recorded properly.

Debtors (Accounts Receivable)

If your company sells its products or services to customers on credit, then this account becomes very critical. The Debtors account tracks all money due from customers. As the bookkeeper, it's critical to keep this account up-to-date. You want to be sure that timely and accurate bills are sent to customers and that customers are paying their bills on time. We talk more about the Debtors process in Chapter 8.

Stock

Every company must have products to sell. Those money-making products must be carefully accounted for and tracked. The bookkeeper helps with this process by keeping accurate stock records, which are periodically tested by doing physical counts of the inventory on hand. Many shops/factories will close their doors for a day to do a physical stock count. We cover how to manage stock in Chapter 7.

Trade Creditors (Accounts Payable)

While no one likes to send money out of the business, tracking and paying bills in Trade Creditors is critical. You certainly don't want to pay anyone twice, but you also want to be sure you do pay the bills on time or your company may no longer get the supplies, stock, or other things that are needed to operate the business. Late paying companies are often cut off by suppliers or put on cash-only accounts, which means you must pay cash to get any supplies. You also may be able to get discounts and save money if you pay the bills early. We talk more about Trade Creditors in Chapter 7.

Loans Payable

Every company needs to purchase major items, such as equipment, vehicles, and furniture, but may not have the money to pay for it. Instead companies take long-term loans that must be paid over more than a 12-month period. In order to get the best rates for these loans, it's critical that the bookkeeper make all loan payments on time and accurately. We talk more about paying loans and interest due in Chapter 11.

Sales

No business can operate without taking in cash and most cash is taken in through the sales of the company's products or services. The Sales account tracks all incoming revenue collected from these sales. It's critical that the bookkeeper record sales in a timely and accurate manner, so the business owner knows exactly how much revenue has been collected every day. We talk more about sales in Chapter 8.

Purchases

Companies either manufacture the goods they sell or they purchase finished goods from various suppliers. Even if the goods are manufactured in house, raw materials will have to be purchased to make those goods. The Purchases account is used to track the purchase of any finished goods or raw materials. The Purchases account is a key component to calculating Cost of Goods Sold, which is subtracted from Sales to find out a company's gross profit. We talk more about the Purchases account in Chapter 7.

Payroll Expenses

You must pay employees to get them to stay around. Few people want to work for nothing. You track all money paid to employees in the Payroll Expenses account. For many businesses this can be their biggest expense. It's important for the bookkeeper to track these expenses accurately, but it's also important that all HM Revenue and Customs reports are filed and payroll taxes are paid. We talk more about payroll obligations in Chapter 9 and Chapter 18.

Office Overheads

Another key expense that can drain a company's profits is office overheads. These include paper, pens, paperclips, and any other supplies needed to run the office. Expenses related to office machinery also fall under this account. These expenses tend to creep up if not carefully monitored. We talk more about internal controls and record keeping in Chapter 6, including controls that can be put in place involving office overheads.

Capital

Accounts related to the Capital (or money invested by the owner) will vary depending upon the type of business for which you keep the books. Many small businesses are owned by one person or a group of partners. They are not incorporated and therefore there are no shares of stock that apportion ownership. Instead money put into the business by each of the owners is tracked in Capital accounts. Any money taken out of the business will be shown in Drawing accounts. In order to be fair to all owners, it's critical that the bookkeeper carefully monitors the Capital accounts. We talk more about business structures and types of ownership in Chapter 17.

Retained Earnings

Any profit made by the company that is reinvested for growing the company is called retained earnings. These are earnings that are not paid out to company owners. This account is cumulative, which means it shows the total of earnings that have been retained since the company opened its doors. While it doesn't take a lot of time for the bookkeeper to manage this account, its ongoing accuracy is important to investors and lenders who want to track how well the company is doing. We talk more about retained earnings in Chapter 14.

Chapter 22

Top Ten Problems You Should Practise

In This Chapter

▶ Recognising accounts and paying bills

▶ Tracking incoming cash and stock

▶ Balancing the books and reporting results

Take the time to be certain you've mastered the key concepts of bookkeeping by practising the problems related to these key bookkeeping concepts. This chapter highlights the key bookkeeping functions you want to be sure you can understand and can do.

Identifying Accounts and Using Double-Entry Bookkeeping

You'll find as a bookkeeper it is essential to enter transactions into the correct accounts, so you need to practise identifying what types of transactions go into what types of accounts. Plus, if you want to keep your books in balance, you must understand the basics of double-entry bookkeeping. Spend some extra time on both of these concepts by working the problems in Chapter 2.

Keeping Journals

Every financial transaction for your business will need to be entered into journals. They are the key day-to-day tracking tools for your company's financial history. Review what journals are and practise making journal entries in Chapter 5.

Paying Bills and Managing Stock

If you don't pay your creditors, and anyone else to whom your company owes money, you won't be in business for long. You also need to keep track of what you sell, how many products you have on hand, and know how to value that stock. You can better manage your company's outgoing cash and stock by practising these concepts in Chapter 7.

Monitoring Sales

Keeping track of money coming into the company is the fun part. Everyone enjoys entering incoming cash. It's what keeps the company on a good financial footing. Make sure you know how to enter your company's Sales by reviewing Chapter 8 and the problems related to tracking revenues.

Testing Your Balance

After you've entered all your company's transactions you need to be sure the books are in balance (see Chapter 13). If they aren't, the financial statements you generate based on the data collected will be useless. And because any company's lenders, suppliers, and owners want to know if the company finances are in balance, you need to also know how to prepare a Balance Sheet (see Chapter 14).

Reporting Profits

Every business owner loves to see how much money he made. You make this possible by pulling together the Profit and Loss accounts and preparing a Profit and Loss Statement (see Chapter 15).

Closing the Books and Starting Over

At the end of every accounting cycle you need to close out the books and prepare financial statements (see Chapter 12). And after closing out the books, you then have to get ready for the next bookkeeping year. You can practise the key steps of preparing for the next year by working the problems in Chapter 19.

Index

• A •

Account Debited column, 57
accountancy pads, 43
accountant, 76
accounting
  accounts, 17–18, 25–26
  computerized, 235
  double-entry bookkeeping, 20–26, 173, 251
  formula, 20, 191
  lingo, 19
  storing paperwork, 74–75
accounting cycle, 19, 20
accounting methods
  accrual accounting, 12–15, 16, 216
  cash-based accounting, 12–15, 16
accounts. *See also* Balance Sheet accounts
  adding, 37, 50, 183–184
  bookkeeping, 17–18
  Chart of Accounts, 191–192
  defined, 21
  deleting, 37, 183, 245–246
  monitoring, 255–257
  Profit and Loss Statement, 18, 28, 33–36
Accounts Payable (Trade Creditors)
  defined, 7, 19
  function of, 29, 31
  importance of, 256
  miscellaneous transactions, 61
  sample page, 46
Accounts Receivable (Debtors)
  described, 19, 26
  miscellaneous transactions and, 61
  monitoring, 255
  posting cash receipts, 54
  tracking customer payments, 252
accrual accounting method, 12–15, 16, 216
accruing invoices, 162
Accumulated Depreciation account, 141
accumulated funds, 216, 227
acid test (quick) ratio, 196–198
adding accounts, 37, 50, 183–184
address verification service fee, 159
adjusting
  asset depreciation, 176, 177–178
  bad debts, 176, 180–181
  overview, 26, 37
  prepaid expenses, 176, 178–180
  stock, 176
  unpaid salaries and wages, 176

administrative and sales expenses, 208
advance cash, 148
advertisements, 162
Advertising account, 35
Aged Debtors Summary, 111, 112, 115
allowances, sales, 109–110
assets. *See also* fixed assets
  current, 8, 18, 27, 29–30
  defined, 7–9, 18
  depreciating
    adjustments, 176, 177–178
    calculating, 137
    cost basis, 137–138
    methods, 139–141
    overview, 135–137
    problem solutions, 143
    reducing balance, 140–141
    schedules, 141–142
    straight-line, 139–140
    taxes and, 142
    useful life of asset, 137
  intangible, 8
  net book value of, 140
  not-for-profit organisations, 216
  tangible, 8
Auditing and Accounting account, 35
averaging method, 82, 83–84, 85, 86, 90

• B •

backing up computer data, 74
bad debt
  adjustments, 176, 180–181
  writing off, 112, 244
Balance Sheet. *See also* Balance Sheet accounts;
    trial balance
  carrying over to next year, 244
  described, 11, 27, 191
  formats/layout, 11, 20, 191, 192–195
  gathering the numbers, 191–192
  not-for-profit organisations, 220–221, 224
  problem solutions, 200–202
  ratios
    acid test (quick) ratio, 196–198
    current ratio, 195–196
    debt-to-equity ratio, 198–199
Balance Sheet accounts
  capital, 27
  cost of goods sold, 34
  current assets, 27, 29–30

Balance Sheet accounts *(continued)*
  current liabilities, 27, 31
  expenses, 35–36
  fixed assets, 27, 30
  long-term liabilities, 27, 32
  revenue, 34
balancing the books. *See also* Balance Sheet
  formula for, 8
  importance of, 260
  trial balance
    described, 20, 26, 173
    preparing, 173–176
    problem solutions, 185
bank, choosing, 68
bank account, 21, 26
  cheques, 68–70, 77
  deposits, 69
  reconciling, 163–165
  service charges, 68
Bank charges account, 35
bank loan
  described, 25
  interest on, 150–152
bank overdraft, 7, 150
bank service charges, 68
benefits, employee, 238–239
bills, paying, 252
bookkeeper, qualifications, 17
bookkeeping
  accounts, 17–18, 25–26
  double-entry, 20–26, 173, 251
  key functions, 259–260
  lingo, 19
  problem solutions, 25–26
  process, 19, 20
books. *See* checking the books; journals;
      Nominal ledger
budget planning, 252
Buildings account, 30
business cycle
  customer accounts, 244
  deleting accounts, 245–246
  Nominal ledger, finalising
    Balance Sheet accounts, 244
    Profit and Loss accounts, 243
  problem solutions, 248
  restarting, 246–247, 260
  supplier accounts, assessing, 245
business expense, 142
business types
  limited companies (Ltd), 12, 229–230, 233–234
  partnerships, 12, 229, 232–233
  sole traders, 11–12, 229, 230–232
businesslink website, 209, 230

calculators
  Inland Revenue, 123
  National Insurance Contributions (NICs), 121
capital, 7, 18, 38
Capital accounts
  described, 18, 27
  monitoring, 257
  using, 33
Capital Allowances, 142
capital gains, 231
Carriage Charges account, 34
cash
  advance, 148
  counting
    accruing invoices, 162
    credit card fees, 159–160
    overview, 157–158
    reconciling credit card statements, 160–161
  current accounts
    bank account, 68
    bank deposits, 69
    cheques, 68–70
  future cash inflows, 58
  future cash purchases, 60
  managing
    bill payments, 252
    budgeting, 252
    cost trends, 253
    planning profit expectations, 252
    posting transactions, 251–252
    reviewing financial results, 251–253
    tracking costs and prices, 9, 251–253
  monitoring, 255
  payments, 56–58
  petty cash
    as asset, 25
    float, 70, 71
    managing, 157, 169
    procedure for, 77
    theft, 73
    vouchers, 70–71
  problem solutions, 77–78
  purchases, 60–61
  receipts, 54–56
  sales income, 93–97
  savings accounts, 70, 147
  theft and fraud prevention, 75
Cash account, 26, 54, 56
Cash at Bank account, 29
Cash Credit column, 57
Cash Debit column, 54
cash handlers, 75
Cash in Hand account, 29

cash out form, 114
Cash Payments Journal
  described, 41, 157, 159
  overview, 47–48
  posting to, 56–58, 63–64
  sample page, 44
Cash Receipts Journal
  cash transactions, 157, 159
  described, 41, 42
  posting to, 55–56, 63
  tracking receipts, 54–56
cash register
  balancing, 157
  cash out form, 114
  controls, 73, 78, 102–104
cash summary form, 102–104
cash-based accounting method, 12–15, 16
chargeback and retrieval fees, 160
Chart of Accounts
  accounts for, 191–192
  adding an account, 37, 183
  deleting an account, 37, 183
  described, 251
  overview, 27–29
  problem solutions, 38
  Profit and Loss accounts, 28
  reworking, 183–184
  setting up, 37
checking the books. *See also* correcting the books
  bank accounts, reconciling, 163–165
  cash transactions
    accruing invoices, 162
    closing journals, 165–168
    credit card fees, 159–160
    credit card statements, 160–161
  closing journals and posting to Nominal Ledger,
    165–168
  counting the cash, 157–158
  problem solutions, 169–172
cheques
  controls, 69–70, 77
  fraud prevention, 75
  manual, 68
  paying invoices, 68, 87
  printing, 69
  signing, 69, 87
  voided, 68
closing balances, 173
closing journals and posting to Nominal Ledger,
  165–168
clubs and societies, 227
commissioned employees, 127
common ratio, 208
Companies House, 230, 233
compound interest, 146–147

computer
  backups, 74
  depreciation, 137
  records, 74–75
computerized accounting, 235
controls
  banking transactions
    cheques, 68–70, 77
    choosing a bank, 68
    deposits, 69
  cash, handling, 67–73
  cash registers, 73, 78, 102–104
  fraud prevention, 75–76
  petty cash, 70–72, 77
  problem solutions, 77–78
  record keeping, 74–75
  sales returns, 107
  savings accounts, 70
  theft protection, 75–76
corporation tax rates, 233–234
correcting the books. *See also* checking the books
  adjustments
    asset depreciation, 177–178
    bad debts, 180–181
    overview, 176
    prepaid expenses, 178–180
    stock, 179–180
    unpaid salaries and wages, 181–183
  Chart of Accounts, reworking, 183–184
  problem solutions, 185–188
  trial balance, checking for errors, 173–176
cost basis, calculating, 137–138
cost of fixed asset, 137
cost of goods sold
  calculating, 83–84, 90, 207–208
  described, 18, 203
  stock valuation method and, 86
Cost of Goods Sold accounts, 28, 33, 34–35
cost trends, tracking, 253
costs and expenses
  direct costs, 25
  tracking, 9, 251–253
counting cash
  accruing invoices, 162
  credit card fees, 159–160
  overview, 157–158
  reconciling credit card statements, 160–161
credit
  buying on, 93
  selling on, 98–101, 110–111, 252, 260
credit card
  cash advance, 148
  fees, 159–160
  interest calculations, 147–148
  reconciling the statements, 160–161

credit card (continued)
  recording payments, 148–150
  sales, 93
Credit card account, 26
Credit Card Payable account, 31, 246
credit notes for sales returns, 107–108
Creditors (Accounts Payable)
  defined, 7, 19
  function of, 29, 31
  importance of, 256
  miscellaneous transactions, 61
  sample page, 46
Creditors credit column, 60
credits and debits
  errors and, 175
  problem solutions, 25–26
  rules for using, 21–24
CT600 tax return form, 233
current assets
  described, 8, 18, 27
  types of, 29–30
current liabilities. See short-term liabilities
current ratio, 195–196
Customer accounts
  reviewing, 244, 252
  selling on credit, 98–101
customer support fee, 159
customers
  bad accounts, writing off, 112, 244
  described, 10
  monitoring, 110–111
  returns and allowances, 107–110
  reviewing customer accounts, 244
CWF1 form, 231
CWG2 Employer Further Guidance to
      PAYE & NIC, 239

• D •

daily finances, tracking, 9
daily periodic interest rate, 147
daily records, keeping, 9
Date column, 54
deadline dates for year-end payroll reports, 240
debits and credits
  errors and, 175
  problem solutions, 25–26
  rules for using, 21–24
debt
  bad accounts, writing off, 112
  credit card interest, 147–148
  long-term, 147
Debtors (Accounts Receivable)
  described, 19, 26
  miscellaneous transactions and, 61

  monitoring, 255
  posting cash receipts, 54
  tracking customer payments, 252
Debtors Credit column, 54
debt-to-equity ratio, 198–199
deleting accounts, 37, 183, 245–246
Deposit Account, 29
deposits, bank, 69
depreciation
  adjusting entries for, 50
  bookkeeping entries for, 141
  calculating, 137–138
  cost basis, 137–138
  defined, 19, 50
  methods, 139–141
  overview, 135–137
  problem solutions, 143–144
  reducing balance method, 140–141
  schedules, 141–142
  straight-line, 139–140
  taxes and, 142
  useful life of asset, 137
Depreciation account, 141
direct costs, 25
disallowed VAT, 138
discount rate fee, 159
discounts
  invoices, 87–89
  sales, 104–107
Dividends account, 38
double-entry bookkeeping
  debits and credits, 21–24, 25–26, 175
  described, 20–21, 173, 251
Drawing account, 33, 38

• E •

embezzlement, 75
Employee Costs account, 36
employees. See also payroll; payroll taxes
  benefits, 238–239
  commissioned, 127
  deductions, 237
  earning tips, 127–128
  foreign workers, 119
  hourly, 125–126
  new, setting up, 117
  records, 74
  salaried, 126
Employer Helpbook E10, 237
Employers Annual return (P35), 240
Equipment account, 30
equipment and software fees, 160
Equipment Rental account, 35
Equity accounts, 183, 192

errors
  adjustments, 50
  checking for, 173–176
exemption from VAT, 235
expandable files, 74
Expense accounts
  adding or deleting, 183
  administrative and sales, 208
  described, 18, 28, 33
  types of, 35–36, 38
Expenses and Benefits in Kind A-Z, 238

• F •

fees
  credit card, 159–160
  school, 238
  software and equipment, 160
FIFO (First In, First Out), 82, 84–85, 90, 91
file folders, 74
files
  expandable, 74
  Lever Arch Files, 74
  for new year, 247
filing cabinets, 74, 247
finances, tracking daily, 9
financial fraud, 75
financial stability, 195
fire safe, 74
First In, First Out (FIFO), 82, 84–85, 90, 91
Fixed Asset register, 142
fixed assets
  depreciating, 135, 137
  described, 8, 18, 26
  types of accounts for, 30
Fixed Assets accounts, 27, 30
float for Petty cash, 70, 71
Folio column, 54
foreign income, 231
foreign workers, 119
format/layout
  credit notes, 197
  horizontal, 11, 192, 193–194
  Profit and Loss Statement, 204–205
  vertical, 11, 192, 194–195
forms
  cash out, 114
  cash summary, 102–104
  CT600 tax return form, 233
  CWF1, 231
  Employers Annual return (P35), 240
  New Starter Forms, 118–119, 130
  payroll, 237–240
  P11, 237, 240
  P45 (starter form), 118, 129

P46 (starter form), 118–119, 129
  P14, 237
  P9D, P11D and P11D(b), 238–239
  preordering, 240
  P60, 237, 240
  P32, 129
  P38, P38A and P38 (S), 239
  sales receipt, 94
formulas
  accounting, 20, 191
  acid test (quick) ratio, 197
  Balance Sheet, 11, 20
  for balancing the books, 8
  calculating simple interest, 145
  current ratio, 195
  debt-to-equity, 198
  double-entry bookkeeping, 20
  straight-line depreciation, 139
fortnightly payperiod, 120
fraud, 75–77
furniture, 26, 51
Furniture and Fixtures account, 30

• G •

General Credit column, 54
General Debt Column, 61
General Journal
  described, 41
  miscellaneous transactions posted to, 61–62
  posting to, 48–49, 51, 65
  sample page, 45
gift card, 109
goals, sales, 253
Gross Profit, 203
gym membership benefits, 238

• H •

helplines
  National Advice Service Helpline, 235
  New Employer Helpline, 117
Her Majesty's Revenue and Customs (HMRC)
  accrual method required by, 13
  Employer Helpbook E10, 237
  Expenses and Benefits in Kind A-Z, 238
  information on setting up new employees, 117
  online tax return service, 231
  payroll taxes sent to, 129
  website, 231
hire purchase agreement, 152
Home Office Work Permit, 119
horizontal format/layout, 11, 192, 193–194
hourly employees, 125–126

• I •

imprest system, 71–72
income
  accounts, 34
  cash sales, 93–97
  foreign, 231
  interest, 152–153
  non-cash sales, 58–59
  non-residence, 231
Income and Expenditure statement
  Balance Sheet, 220–221, 224
  overview, 216
  preparing, 217–224
  problem solutions, 225–227
  Profit and Loss statement, 219
  Purchase and expense accounts, 219, 223
  Receipts and Payment account,
      215–216, 217–218, 221–222
  Statement of Affairs, 218, 222
  Travel expenses, 220
Income tax allowance, 232
incorporated. See Limited Companies (Ltd)
Inland Revenue tax calculator, 123
Input tax, 235
installation charges, 138
Institute of Certified Book Keepers, 17
Insurance account, 35
intangible assets, 8
interest
  bank loan, 147, 150–152
  compound, 146–147
  credit card, 147–150
  daily periodic interest rate, 147–148
  defined, 19
  income, 152–153
  problem solutions, 154–155
  simple, 145–146, 147
Interest Income account, 152
internal theft, 75
Internet, selling products over, 159
internet banking, 68
invoice numbers, 61
invoices
  accruing, 162
  described, 10
  discounts on, 87–89
  paying, 68, 87–89
  purchase, 61
  sales, 98–99, 100–101, 105, 106

• J •

journal entries, 20
journals. See also General Journal; Sales Journal;
    specific journals
  adjusting entries, 20, 26, 37
  closing and posting to the Ledger, 165–168

  credits and debits, 21–24, 25–26, 175
  defining, 10, 53
  described, 20, 21, 26, 259
  miscellaneous transactions, 61–62
  problem solutions, 63–65
  Purchases Journal, 41, 43, 46, 60–61, 64–65
  using, 22

• K •

Kelly, Jane (Sage 50 Accounts For Dummies), 235
kickbacks, 75

• L •

land, 30, 135, 231
Last In, First Out (LIFO), 82, 85–86, 90
layout/format
  credit notes, 197
  horizontal, 11, 192, 193–194
  Profit and Loss Statement, 204–205
  vertical, 11, 192, 194–195
Leasehold Improvements account, 30
ledgers. See also checking the books;
      Nominal ledger
  defined, 10
  posting to, 166–167
Legal and Professional account, 35
Lever Arch Files, 74
liabilities
  defined, 7–9, 18
  long-term, 8, 27, 32, 150
  not-for-profit organisations, 216
  short-term, 7–8, 27, 31
Liability accounts, 183
LIFO (Last In, First Out), 82, 85–86, 90
Limited Companies (Ltd)
  described, 12, 229–230
  taxation, 233–234
Limited Liability Partnerships (LLP's), 12, 229
lingo, bookkeeping, 19
loans
  bank loan, 25, 150–152
  paying, 256
  simple interest for, 147
Loans Payable account, 32
long-term debt, 147
long-term liabilities, 8, 27, 32, 150
Lower or Cost or Net Realisable Value (NRV), 83

• M •

mail order catalogues, 159
manual bookkeeping system, 22–23, 43, 117
materials purchased for resale, 25
maternity pay, 124
medical insurance, 238

methods of accounting
  accrual, 12–15, 16, 216
  cash-based, 12–15, 16
minimum wage, 127
Miscellaneous Expenses account, 36
miscellaneous transactions, 61–62
monitoring
  accounts, 255–257
  cash flow, 255
  cash payments, 56–57
  cash receipts, 54–56
  cash registers, 102–104
  costs and expenses, 251–253
  daily finances, 9
  office supplies, 87
  PAYE (Pay As You Earn), 31
  payroll, 256
  purchases, 60–61
  sales, 110–111, 256, 260
  sales returns, 109–110
  stock, 255
monthly minimum fee, 159
monthly payperiod, 120
mortgages, 8, 31, 147, 244
Motor Vehicle account, 25, 30, 36, 246

• N •

National Advice Service Helpline, 235
National Insurance Contributions (NICs)
  calculating, 121–122
  calculators, 121
  deducting, 117
  described, 7, 8
  records of, 237
  tips and, 127–128
National Insurance Number, 117
net book value, 140
net pay, 125
Net Profit, 204, 213
Net Realisable Value (NRV), 83
Net Sales, 109, 206–207
new accounting period, 243
New Employer Helpline, 117
New Employers Guide, 117, 118
New Starter Forms, 118–119, 130
Nominal ledger
  adjusting errors, 50
  defined, 10, 19
  developing, 43–45
  finalising, 243–244
  overview, 41–42
  posting to, 46–49, 166–167
  problem solutions, 51–52
non-cash sales, 58–59
non-residence income, 231

no-return policy, 107
not-for-profit organisations
  accumulated funds, 216, 227
  cash-based accounting for, 13
  Income and Expenditure statement
    Balance Sheet, 220–221, 224
    overview, 216
    preparing, 217–224
    problem solutions, 225–227
    Profit and Loss statement, 219
    Purchase and expense accounts, 219, 223
    Receipts and Payment account,
      215–216, 217–218, 221–222
    Statement of Affairs, 218, 222
    Travel expenses, 220
NRV (Net Realisable Value), 83

• O •

obligate (commit) to future cash purchases, 60
Office Expense account, 36
office overheads, 257
office supplies, 87, 257
online banking, 68
online PAYE service, 119, 241
online tax returns, 119, 231, 241
Operating Expenses, 204
operational responsibilities, 75
ordinary share capital, 33, 38
Other Income accounts, 34
Other Liabilities account, 32
Other Sales Costs account, 34
Output tax, 235
overdraft, bank, 7, 150
overheads, office, 257

• P •

Page Reference (PR) column, 54
paper trail, 9–10, 74
paperwork storage, 74–75
partnerships
  described, 12, 229
  taxation, 232–233
paternity pay, 124
pay periods, 120
PAYE (Pay As You Earn)
  calculating, 122–124
  deducting, 117
  described, 7, 8
  not deducted, 239
  online service, 119, 241
  tracking, 31
  year-end reports, 239
PAYE tax reference, 117

paying
  bills, 252
  by cheque, 68
  invoices, 68, 87–89
  loans, 256
payoffs, 75
payroll. *See also* employees; payroll taxes
  calculating
    for commissioned employees, 127
    for employees earning tips, 127–128
    for hourly employees, 125–126
    for salaried employees, 126
  checklist, 130
  defined, 19
  minimum wage, 127
  monitoring, 256
  net pay, 125
  New Starter Forms, 118–119, 130
  outsourcing, 129
  pay periods, 120
  problem solutions, 130–131
  setting up, 117
  unpaid salaries and wages, 176, 181–183
  year-end reports
    deadline dates, 240
    employee annual return, 240
    Employers Annual return (P35), 240
    Form P14, 237
    Forms P38, P38A and P38 (S), 239
    P9D, P11D and P11D(b), 238–239
    preordering forms, 240
    problem solutions, 242
    when PAYE not deducted, 239
payroll bureau, 121
Payroll Expenses account, 256
payroll taxes. *See also* taxes
  filing online, 119, 231, 241
  National Insurance Contributions (NICs)
    calculating, 121–122
    deducting, 117
    described, 7, 8
    records of, 237
    tips and, 127–128
  overview, 121
  PAYE (Pay As You Earn)
    calculating, 122–124
    deducting, 117
    described, 7, 8
    not deducted, 239
    online service, 119, 241
    tax reference, 117
    tracking, 31
    year-end reports, 239
  paying to HMRC, 129
  statutory payments, 124–125
  tax code, 122–123
  year-end reports, 237–240

payslip voucher, 129
P11, 237, 240
periodic stock count, 81, 91
perpetual stock count, 81, 91
petty cash
  as asset, 25
  float, 70, 71
  managing, 157, 169
  procedure for, 77
  theft, 73
  vouchers, 70–71
Petty Cash accounts, 70–72, 157
P45 (starter form), 118, 129
P46 (starter form), 118–119, 129
P14 form, 237
plant and machinery, 142
PLC (Public Limited Companies), 229
P9D, P11D and P11D(b) forms, 238–239
Postage account, 36
posting, 20, 251
PR (Page Reference) column, 54
preordering year-end payroll forms, 240
prepaid expenses, 50
pricing your product, 253
printing cheques, 69
product pricing, 253
Profit and Loss Statement
  accounts for, 18, 28, 33–36
  analysing
    overview, 208
    Return on Assets (ROA) ratio, 209–210
    Return on Equity (ROE) ratio, 210
    Return on Sales (ROS) ratio, 209
  closing, 243
  Cost of Goods Sold, 203, 207–208
  described, 11, 27, 203–204
  formatting, 204–205
  Gross Profit, 203
  Net Profit or Loss, 204
  Net Sales, 109, 206–207
  not-for-profit organisations, 219
  Operating Expenses, 204
  preparing, 203–208
  problem solutions, 211–213
  Sales or Revenue, 25, 203
Profit and Loss Statement accounts
  Cost of Goods Sold, 34
  Expense accounts, 35–36
  overview, 33
  Revenue accounts, 34
projecting future cash inflows, 58
P60, 237, 240
P38, P38A and P38 forms, 239
P35 (Employers Annual return) form, 240
P32 form, 129
Public Limited Companies (PLC), 229

publications
  CWG2 Employer Further Guidance to PAYE & NIC, 239
  Employer Helpbook E10, 237
  Expenses and Benefits in Kind A-Z, 238
  New Employers Guide, 117, 118
  Sage 50 Accounts For Dummies, 235
  'yellow book' (Employer Payslip Booklet), 129
Purchase accounts, 219, 223, 256
Purchase Discount account, 34
purchase invoices, 61
Purchase ledger, 10
Purchase Ledger Clerk, 87
Purchase Returns account, 34, 51
Purchases account
  Cost of Goods Sold, 34
  described, 18, 81
  posting to, 82
  sample page, 46
Purchases Debit column, 60
Purchases Journal
  described, 41
  monitoring purchases, 60–61
  posting to, 60–61, 64–65
  sample page, 43, 46
purchasing
  discounts, 87–89
  monitoring, 60–61
  paying invoices, 87–89
  problem solutions, 90–91
  stock
    office supplies, 87
    valuing, 82–86, 90

• Q •

quick (acid test) ratio, 196–198

• R •

ratios
  acid test (quick), 196–198
  common, 208
  current, 195–196
  debt-to-equity, 198–199
  Return on Assets (ROA), 209–210
  Return on Equity (ROE), 210
  Return on Sales (ROS), 209
receipts
  cash, 54–56
  sales, 94, 106
Receipts and Payment account, 215–216, 217–218, 221–222
reconciling bank accounts, 163–165
reconciling credit card statements, 160–161

record keeping
  computer, 74–75
  daily records, 9
  employee, 74
reducing balance depreciation, 140–141
register, cash
  balancing, 157
  cash out form, 114
  controls, 73, 78, 102–104
Rent expense account, 26, 36
reports
  Aged Debtors Summary, 111, 112, 115
  year-end payroll reports, 237–240
resale materials, 25
restarting the business cycle, 246–247, 260
Retained Earnings account, 33, 257
retained profits, 38
Return on Assets (ROA) ratio, 209–210
Return on Equity (ROE) ratio, 210
Return on Sales (ROS) ratio, 209
returns, sales, 107–110
Revenue accounts, 18, 28, 33, 34

• S •

Sage 50 Accounts, 142, 235
Sage 50 Accounts For Dummies (Kelly), 235
salaried employees, 126
salaries, unpaid, 176, 181–183
Salaries Debit column, 57
sales. See also Sales Journal
  allowances, 109–110
  bad accounts, writing off, 112
  cash register, 102–104
  on credit, 98–101
  credit card, 93
  defined, 18
  discounts, 104–107
  goals, 253
  income
    cash sales, 93–97
    non-cash sales, 58–59
  invoices, 98–99, 100–101, 105, 106
  monitoring, 110–111, 256, 260
  problem solutions, 113–115
  returns
    credit notes for, 107–108
    monitoring, 109–110
    no-return policy, 107
  VAT (Value Added Tax)
    cash-based accounting for, 13
    as current liability, 31
    described, 7, 234
    disallowed, 138
    exemptions, 235

sales *(continued)*
  rate for, 94, 234–235
  registration, 235
  sales returns and, 109
  VAT Guide, 235
Sales account, 54, 256
Sales Allowances account, 109
Sales Credit column, 54
Sales Discounts account, 34, 206
Sales Journal. *See also* sales
  described, 41
  non-cash sales, 58–59
  posting to, 47, 53, 59, 64, 94–97
  recording in, 10, 99
  sample page, 44
Sales ledger, 10
Sales of Goods or Services account, 34, 206
Sales or Revenue, 25, 203
sales receipt, 94, 106
Sales Returns accounts, 34, 109, 206
sales summary, 102–104, 107
savings accounts, 70, 147
schedules, depreciation, 141–142
school fees, 238
secure gateway fee, 159
self employment. *See* sole traders
selling on credit, 98–101, 110–111, 252
service charges, 68
Settlement Discount, 89
share schemes, 231
shipping and delivery, 138
short-term liabilities
  described, 27
  types of, 7–8, 31
sick pay, 124, 125
signing cheques, 69, 87
simple interest, 145–146, 147
skimming, 75
SMP (Statutory Maternity Pay), 124
software and equipment fees, 160
sole traders
  described, 11–12, 229
  tax returns, 230–232
specific identification, 83, 91
starter forms, 118–119
Statement of Affairs, 218, 222
Stationary Sick Pay (SSP), 124, 125
Statutory Maternity Pay (SMP), 124
Statutory Paternity Pay (SPP), 124–125
stock
  adjusting, 176
  buying, 9
  counting, 81, 91
  defined, 19
  managing, 81–82
  monitoring, 255

office supplies, 87
  valuing, 82–86
Stock account, 26, 29, 81
storing paperwork, 74–75
straight-line depreciation, 139–140
Subscriptions account, 35
Supplier accounts, 60, 245
suppliers
  assessing supplier accounts, 245
  paying by cheque, 68
Supplies account, 36

● **T** ●

"T" account, 21, 22–23
tangible assets, 8
tax calculator, 123
tax code, 122–123
taxes. *See also* payroll taxes
  business
    limited companies (Ltd), 233–234
    partnerships, 232–233
    sole traders, 230–232
  Capital Allowances, 142
  depreciation and, 142
  online returns, 119, 231, 241
  problem solutions, 236
  storing tax returns, 74
  on tips, 127
  VAT (Value Added Tax)
    calculating, 235
    cash-based accounting for, 13
    as current liability, 31
    described, 7, 234
    disallowed, 138
    exemptions, 235
    rate for, 94, 234–235
    registration, 235
    sales returns and, 109
    VAT Guide, 235
telephone expenses, 25, 36
theft protection, 75–77
tips, employees earning, 127–128
Trade Creditors (Accounts Payable)
  defined, 7, 19
  function of, 29, 31
  importance of, 256
  miscellaneous transactions, 61
  sample page, 46
Trade Creditors column, 57
transaction fees for credit cards, 159
transactions
  described, 20
  miscellaneous, 61–62
Travel and Entertainment account, 36
Travel expenses, 220

trial balance. *See also* Balance Sheet
  described, 20, 26, 173
  preparing, 173–176
  problem solutions, 185
tronc (a pool of tips), 127–128
trusts, 231

• *U* •

Unique Tax Reference (UTR), 231, 233
useful life of assets, 137
Utilities account, 36

• *V* •

valuing stock, 82–86, 90
VAT (Value Added Tax)
  calculating, 235
  cash-based accounting for, 13
  as current liability, 31
  described, 7, 234
  disallowed, 138
  exemptions, 235
  rate for, 94, 234–235
  registration, 235
  sales returns and, 109
  VAT Guide, 235
VAT Notice 742A, 235
Vehicles account, 25, 30, 36, 246
vertical format, 11, 192, 194–195
vocabulary, accounting, 19
voided cheques, 68
vouchers
  payslip, 129
  petty cash, 70–71

• *W* •

wages
  minimum, 127
  unpaid, 176, 181–183
websites
  businesslink, 209, 230
  Companies House, 230
  Employer Helpbook E10, 237
  Her Majesty's Revenue and Customs
    (HMRC), 231
  Institute of Certified Book Keepers, 17
  VAT Guide, 235
weekly payperiod, 120, 123
work permit for home office, 119
worksheets, 20
writing off bad debt, 112, 244

• *Y* •

year-end payroll reports
  deadline dates, 240
  forms
    Employers Annual return (P35), 240
    Form P14, 237
    Forms P38, P38A and P38 (S), 239
    P9D, P11D and P11D(b), 238–239
  preordering forms, 240
'yellow book' (Employer Payslip Booklet), 129

• *Z* •

zero balance, 243

Notes

Notes

Notes

Notes

Notes

FOR DUMMIES

Do Anything. Just Add Dummies

UK editions

BUSINESS

978-0-470-51806-9

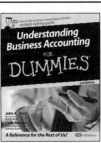
978-0-470-99245-6

978-0-470-75626-3

FINANCE

978-0-470-99280-7

978-0-470-99811-3

978-0-470-69515-9

PROPERTY

978-0-470-99448-1

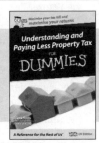
978-0-470-75872-4

978-0-7645-7054-4

Backgammon For Dummies
978-0-470-77085-6

Body Language For Dummies
978-0-470-51291-3

British Sign Language
For Dummies
978-0-470-69477-0

Business NLP For Dummies
978-0-470-69757-3

Children's Health For Dummies
978-0-470-02735-6

Cognitive Behavioural Coaching
For Dummies
978-0-470-71379-2

Counselling Skills For Dummies
978-0-470-51190-9

Digital Marketing For Dummies
978-0-470-05793-3

eBay.co.uk For Dummies,
2nd Edition
978-0-470-51807-6

English Grammar For Dummies
978-0-470-05752-0

Fertility & Infertility For Dummies
978-0-470-05750-6

Genealogy Online For Dummies
978-0-7645-7061-2

Golf For Dummies
978-0-470-01811-8

Green Living For Dummies
978-0-470-06038-4

Hypnotherapy For Dummies
978-0-470-01930-6

**Available wherever books are sold. For more information or to order direct go to
www.wiley.com or call +44 (0) 1243 843291**

13902_p1

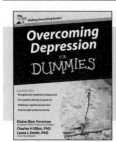

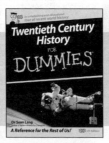
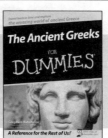

FOR DUMMIES®

The easy way to get more done and have more fun

LANGUAGES

978-0-7645-5194-9

978-0-7645-5193-2

978-0-471-77270-5

MUSIC

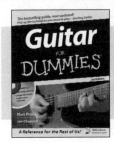

978-0-7645-9904-0

978-0-470-03275-6
UK Edition

978-0-7645-5105-5

SCIENCE & MATHS

978-0-7645-5326-4

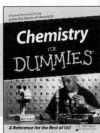

978-0-7645-5430-8

978-0-7645-5325-7

Art For Dummies
978-0-7645-5104-8

Baby & Toddler Sleep Solutions For
Dummies
978-0-470-11794-1

Bass Guitar For Dummies
978-0-7645-2487-5

Brain Games For Dummies
978-0-470-37378-1

Christianity For Dummies
978-0-7645-4482-8

Filmmaking For Dummies, 2nd
Edition
978-0-470-38694-1

Forensics For Dummies
978-0-7645-5580-0

German For Dummies
978-0-7645-5195-6

Hobby Farming For Dummies
978-0-470-28172-7

Jewelry Making & Beading For
Dummies
978-0-7645-2571-1

Knitting for Dummies, 2nd Edition
978-0-470-28747-7

Music Composition For Dummies
978-0-470-22421-2

Physics For Dummies
978-0-7645-5433-9

Sex For Dummies, 3rd Edition
978-0-470-04523-7

Solar Power Your Home For Dummies
978-0-470-17569-9

Tennis For Dummies
978-0-7645-5087-4

The Koran For Dummies
978-0-7645-5581-7

U.S. History For Dummies
978-0-7645-5249-6

Wine For Dummies, 4th Edition
978-0-470-04579-4

**Available wherever books are sold. For more information or to order direct go to
www.wiley.com or call +44 (0) 1243 843291**

13902_p3

FOR DUMMIES®

Helping you expand your horizons and achieve your potential

COMPUTER BASICS

978-0-470-27759-1

978-0-470-13728-4

978-0-471-75421-3

DIGITAL LIFESTYLE

978-0-470-25074-7

978-0-470-39062-7

978-0-470-17469-2

WEB & DESIGN

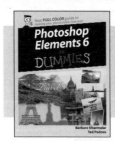

978-0-470-19238-2

978-0-470-32725-8

978-0-470-34502-3

Access 2007 For Dummies
978-0-470-04612-8

Adobe Creative Suite 3 Design Premium
All-in-One Desk Reference For Dummies
978-0-470-11724-8

AutoCAD 2009 For Dummies
978-0-470-22977-4

C++ For Dummies, 5th Edition
978-0-7645-6852-7

Computers For Seniors For Dummies
978-0-470-24055-7

Excel 2007 All-In-One Desk Reference F
or Dummies
978-0-470-03738-6

Flash CS3 For Dummies
978-0-470-12100-9

Mac OS X Leopard For Dummies
978-0-470-05433-8

Macs For Dummies, 10th Edition
978-0-470-27817-8

Networking All-in-One Desk Reference
For Dummies, 3rd Edition
978-0-470-17915-4

Office 2007 All-in-One Desk Reference
For Dummies
978-0-471-78279-7

Search Engine Optimization For
Dummies, 2nd Edition
978-0-471-97998-2

Second Life For Dummies
978-0-470-18025-9

The Internet For Dummies, 11th Edition
978-0-470-12174-0

Visual Studio 2008 All-In-One Desk
Reference For Dummies
978-0-470-19108-8

Web Analytics For Dummies
978-0-470-09824-0

Windows XP For Dummies, 2nd Edition
978-0-7645-7326-2

13902_p4